Straight Acting

Straight Acting

Popular Gay Drama from Wilde to Rattigan

Sean O'Connor

CASSELL

London and Washington

For a catalogue of related titles
in our Sexual Politics list
please write to us at an address below:

Cassell
Wellington House
125 Strand
London WC2R 0BB

PO Box 605
Herndon
VA 20172

© Sean O'Connor 1998

First published 1998

British Library Cataloguing-in-Publication Data
A catalogue record for this book is available from the British Library.

Library of Congress Cataloging-in-Publication Data
O'Connor, Sean, 1968–
    Straight acting: popular gay drama from Wilde to Rattigan/Sean
O'Connor.
        p.   cm.
    ISBN 0-304-32866-9 (hardcover).—ISBN 0-304-32864-2 (pbk.)
    1. English drama—Men authors—History and criticism.
2. Homosexuality and literature—Great Britain—History.   3. Popular
literature—Great Britain—History and criticism.   4. Gay men's
writings, English—History and criticism.   5. Maugham, W. Somerset
(William Somerset), 1874–1965—Dramatic works.   6. Coward, Noël.
1899–1973—Criticism and interpretation.   7. Rattigan, Terence—
Criticism and interpretation.   8. Wilde, Oscar, 1854–1900—
Influence.   9. Gay men in literature.   I. Title.
PR635.H65O28   1997
822'.91099206642—dc21
                                                                            97–13548
                                                                                 CIP

Typeset by BookEns Ltd, Royston, Herts.
Printed and bound in Great Britain by Biddles Ltd, Guildford and King's Lynn.

Contents

Foreword

Simon Watney

In *Straight Acting* Sean O'Connor writes brilliantly of the distinct, if over-lapping, theatrical worlds created in the first half of the twentieth century by the British playwrights Somerset Maugham, Noël Coward and Terence Rattigan, and of their complex, shared debts to Oscar Wilde. His chosen form – a chronology of essays – suits his purpose well. For this is happily not a book with a Big Idea. Rather, O'Connor invites us to reflect on the many shades and tones of sexual shame and secret love that flourished in a pre-1960s culture of suffocating respectability. Since he recognizes the continuities of popular culture as much as the disconti-nuities, he is admirably mindful and respectful of the subtleties of the writers whose work he analyses. Moreover, his discussions are framed with the confident commonsense of a thoughtful and experienced director, who never drifts off into waffle or jargon.

His response to the material has a thoroughly refreshing directness. Thus, for example, he notes at one point that

> as we move further away from *Brief Encounter* as a document of con-temporary life, and the film joins the mythology of 'Englishness', its conventions seem to me as foreign but its emotions as fresh and direct as a Restoration comedy or a Victorian sensational novel.

It is not the least of this book's achievements that it leaves the reader with a marked sense of early-twentieth-century British popular theatre as a period quite as distinct as that of the Jacobean tragedians or the Georgian stage. Nor have we moved on so far that we can no longer recognize the world of Coward's light comedies, or the various genres deployed by Rattigan, which O'Connor depicts with an acknowledged mixture of horror and respect as a particularly English territory where individuals struggle with the middle-class mores of the mid-twentieth century, [. . .] a world of seaside boarding houses, public schools and hotel lounges where individual freedom is checked by the pressures of gentility. It is a rich territory inhabited by those crippled with paranoia about sex, frustrated by the cruelties of age and isolated in their own painful, solitary English world.

Indeed, it is the sense of the emotional *richness* of the plays and films under discussion that so distinguishes O'Connor's readings. And how very welcome it is to find a critic who so convincingly and movingly depicts his own personal relation to the theatre of his grandparents' generation – 'grandparents', however, who were gay men earlier in the century, facing dilemmas which have hardly disappeared in the interim.

It is thus a particular pleasure to introduce a book which is delightfully well written and devoid of either pomposity or aggression. Sean O'Connor has done for modern theatre studies what Richard Dyer achieved in film studies. He demonstrates with great success that we may take popular West End theatre seriously, without resorting to the kinds of critical obfuscation that mars so much contemporary cultural study. O'Connor offers us an accessible, thoughtful introduction to early-twentieth-century English theatre, and in so doing he helps illuminate much about that era, both the pain and cruelty, and the creative courage and inspiration.

Simon Watney
London, February 1997

Acknowledgements

I'd like to thank Steve Cook and Roz Hopkins at Cassell for their support and their patience, the staff at the British Library, the Reading Room at the Theatre Museum and the BFI Library, Merlin Holland, Michael Imison, Joan Hirst, the late Derek Jarman, and Dr Keith Walker and Dr René Weis, both at University College London. I am much indebted to my family and several friends and colleagues who have provoked and cajoled me into getting this book finished (so I've done it just to stop them nagging), particularly Robert Kincaid, Joanna Sumner, Kirsty Dias, Jo O'Keefe, Joanna Butterworth, James Cary Parkes and David Kettle. Gareth Davis has kept me assuaged of guilt when I should have been writing by plying me with alcohol. My greatest debts are owed to Simon Watney, who provided the title and enormous support, and to Frith Banbury, who is fascinating, funny and a genuine inspiration.

I'm grateful to the following: International Music Publications Ltd for permission to quote *Cemetry Gates* (words and music by Steven Morrissey and Johnny Marr; © 1986 Morrissey and Marr Songs Ltd and Warner/ Chappell Music Ltd, London W1Y 3FA); Faber and Faber Ltd for permission to quote from *Collected Poems and Plays* by T. S. Eliot and from *The Whitsun Weddings* by Philip Larkin; Liveright Publishing Corporation for permission to quote from 'The Broken Tower' by Hart Crane, in *Complete Poems of Hart Crane*, edited by Marc Simon (copyright 1933, © 1958, 1966 by Liveright Publishing Corporation, copyright © 1986 by Marc Simon); Peters Fraser & Dunlop Group Ltd for permission to quote Nancy Mitford; William Heinemann, and A. P. Watt Ltd on behalf of the Royal Literary Fund, for permission to use extracts from Somerset Maugham. Extracts from Nöel Coward reprinted by kind permission of the Estate of Nöel Coward; extracts from Terence Rattigan reprinted by kind permission of the Trustees of the Terence Rattigan Trust; extract from the interview with Gilbert Harding reproduced from *Face to Face with John Freeman* with the permission of BBC Worldwide Ltd; extract from *Enemies of Promise* by Cyril Connolly reprinted by permission of the author c/o Rogers, Coleridge & White Ltd, 20 Powis Mews, London W11 1JN.

Sean O'Connor
August 1997

For Angelo Rossi

Introduction

Apologia

> *A dreaded sunny day*
> *So let's go where we're wanted*
> *And I meet you at the cemetry gates*
> *Keats and Yeats are on your side*
> But you lose
> *Because Wilde is on mine.*
>
> Morrissey[1]

> From birth we are relentlessly socialized into a heterosexual identity that we may later choose to reject but which remains an always familiar landscape – those on the margins of a culture know more about its centre than the centre can ever know about the margins.
> Andy Medhurst[2]

For much of the 1970s, every Saturday afternoon my parents and I would travel from our home in Bromborough to Birkenhead, the nearest large town, to visit my grandmother. They would dump me at Paterson Street and go off to shop at Birkenhead Market, a warren-like Victorian structure selling everything from paperback books at five pence each to sawdust-encrusted racks of lamb. The market reeked of a heady mix of butcher's off-cuts, day-old cakes and cheap cafés – 'Betty's best butties with best butter'. Rather than be dragged around the market, to be trampled and shoved by Birkonians keen to pick up their bargains and get home in time for the football results, I would stay with my grandmother, eat her scouse and watch the Saturday matinée on BBC2. My grandmother was widowed in the mid-1970s and, with hindsight, I feel she must have enjoyed the company that this Saturday shopping ritual gave her.

Though it's only recent history, we forget how enslaved we were to the tastes and timetables of television programmers before the general availability of video recorders. Then, the appearance of a favourite movie on TV was a special event. There was major excitement when *The Sound of Music* was shown on television for the first time, and a regular Bank Holiday thrill about the screening of the latest Bond movie. Saturday night film premières might even be in black and white, as this was that strange twilight period of afternoon close-downs and test-cards, the fag end of the transition from monochrome to colour on TV. Anything screened today in black and white on Channel 4 or BBC2 is automatically billed as a 'classic', regardless of whether it's *Citizen Kane* or *Murder at the Gallop*. In the 1970s, we in the audience had few choices. Our tastes were formulated differently then, because we had fewer dishes to choose from. The Saturday matinée, usually a double bill, was a wonderful lucky dip. Sometimes it was a florid Hollywood melodrama like *All That Heaven Allows*, sometimes a tepid British comedy like *Twice around the Daffodils*. I hungrily consumed these films and the more I saw, the more I began to develop likes and dislikes, a taste if you like. I collected celluloid images in my mind in the same way that my schoolmates collected those stupid football cards that came with a thin piece of chewing-gum. Particular scenes would stick in my mind and continued to resonate in my imagination: Kathleen Byron as the deranged nun seductively applying her lipstick in *Black Narcissus*, Bette Davis fumbling to plant bulbs near the end of *Dark Victory*. Particular lines would echo in my head and I'd even learn some of them by heart: 'That's not the Northern lights – that's Manderley!'; 'Oh Fred, I've been so foolish. I've fallen in love! I'm an ordinary woman – I didn't think such violent things could happen to ordinary people.'

I was particularly fond of films that starred Bette Davis, Celia Johnson, Cary Grant, Katharine Hepburn, Margaret Lockwood and Joan Fontaine. Some actors could move me in certain roles but not in others. I loved Jennifer Jones in *The Song of Bernadette* but was left cold by her in *A Farewell to Arms* ('I hate the rain; I sometimes see myself dead in it'). War films generally bored me. Except, of course, those with Greer Garson. I even began to distinguish the trademarks of particular directors and would watch anything by Alfred Hitchcock or George Cukor. At the time, I certainly wasn't aware what the attraction was. Nostalgia, possibly, for a recent past that seemed so much more attractive, stylish and romantic than my bland childish present. I think the plots intrigued me most immediately. Here were the stories of shy, bookish outsiders, usually women, that spoke directly to me. One Saturday evening when I was about seven, my father, who is a bit of a film buff himself, announced that he wanted to watch a particular film. It sounded to me like a chaps-in-the-jungle adventure thing, very Wilbur Smith, on which he's very keen. I asked him, 'Are there any women in it?' He looked surprised, 'I'm not sure, I should imagine so. Why?' I wasn't quite sure why I'd asked him either, but I knew that there was a difference between Saturday matinée-type films, which I liked, and Saturday evening-type films, which he liked. 'I don't know,' I said. 'I think films with women in are just more interesting.' But this wasn't a transvestite hankering of mine. I didn't think I was or even *wanted* to be Bette Davis in *Now Voyager* or Joan Fontaine in *Suspicion*. But their *dilemmas*, the triumph of the romantic loner and the metamorphosis of the ugly duckling, were plots with which I did identify, trapped as I felt in a never-ending childhood in a harsh, unlovely northwestern town without any prospect of escape, or even the relief that a small change might bring.

In the late 1970s, after months of research in *Which?* magazine, my Dad became the proud owner of the first video recorder in our street. It was, he told us, 'top of the range' and would 'last for years', being the 'most sophisticated model'. It was a Betamax, a whirring monster in teak, now, alas, consigned to that cemetery of twentieth-century good-ideas-at-the-time which includes the Sinclair C5 and the Sodastream. At that time most pre-recorded films were contemporary ones, as the studios had yet to transfer their huge backlogs of films to tape. But even these I couldn't swap with my friends at school, as their dads had been bitten by an altogether different and stronger strain of the video bug, courtesy of JVC. These were the halcyon days of the 'video nasty', when it was easier to buy copies of *The Texas Chainsaw Massacre* than to get hold of the June Allyson version of *Little Women*.

Disappointed by the choices offered by the early video age, I began to consume books from the library voraciously. At first, I was fairly promiscuous in my choice of material and would read anything that sounded intriguing or that had a good cover. Once I 'discovered' a writer I would plough through his or her work, regardless of its quality. I wasn't worried by the idea of a 'canon' or what I ought to read; my criterion for books was that they should make me want to read on. If they began to indulge in stylistic masturbation, I would lose patience and go on to something with a good story. Needless to say, Virginia Woolf didn't feature very strongly. (A little paddle in *The Waves* at the age of thirteen put me off watersports with Mrs Woolf for years.) Consequently, my brain is a mine of fairly useless information about the more obscure and idiosyncratic corners of the work of Agatha Christie, Nancy Mitford and Dennis Wheatley. I can't quite remember when I first began to read play-texts, but it was undoubtedly related to the films I had watched and enjoyed, such as *Witness for the Prosecution, Rebecca* or *The Monkey's Paw*. Once I discovered plays, I couldn't get enough of them. I wish I could say that I began to read them because of some theatrical instinct, the mighty call of Thespis. Sadly, it isn't true. I began to read plays because they were quicker to get through: no boring descriptions and plenty of conversation.

Initially I rarely saw plays actually performed on the stage and had to create productions of the plays I'd read in my imagination, usually cast with actors I'd admired in films. The Wirral doesn't really have a theatre, unless you count the Floral Pavilion in New Brighton. Optimistically named, New Brighton is the classic 'seaside town they forgot to pull down'. It is a (very) poor man's Blackpool, but without the tower, without the illuminations and without the Golden Mile; it does have its own rock, though. The Pavilion is a squat Victorian music-hall and continues to promote a varied theatrical diet from Frank Carson to the Birkenhead Operatic Society's umpteenth production of *Brigadoon*. The only drama here was the local Townswomen's Guild's annual one-act play festival. 'Proper' theatre happened across the water in Liverpool, at the Playhouse (traditional repertory), the Everyman (slightly avant-garde) and the Empire (touring shows and musicals). My first visit to a real theatre, like most people's I should imagine, was to see a Christmas production of *Peter Pan* at the Liverpool Empire, a cavernous theatre in a city bursting with cathedrals and architectural monuments to its prosperous but distant Victorian past. I was entranced when Peter asked us to resurrect Tinker-Bell. 'Did we believe in fairies?' I can never see a glitter-ball cast its own particular spell over an audience without a pleasant shiver going down the back of my neck. The hundreds of flickering mirrors shot magic all over the grandiose auditorium. At the time I had shouted to Peter at the top of my voice that, yes, I did believe in fairies! Now I know there are.

By the time I had graduated to secondary school, a Catholic boys' establishment run by an eccentric gallery of ageing Irish brothers and war-fractured masters creeping towards retirement, I had consumed Birkenhead Library's drama section, from Sophocles and Shaw to Ray Cooney and Enid Bagnold. At school, I was disappointed that our only forays into drama were not the Greek or Renaissance classics which Robert Donat had led me to expect from *Goodbye Mr Chips*, but Gilbert and Sullivan operettas in which small boys played the 'maidens' and the odd sixth-former would drag-up to play the ageing harridan, like Katisha in *The Mikado*. (I'm sure it will come as no surprise if I add that Lily Savage graduated from the same establishment.)

If I had realized in my teens that the hormonally charged ambience of the rugby team disguised such an undercurrent of strong but oh-so-casual homoeroticism, perhaps I would have been more enthusiastic about it at the time. As it happens, I disdained the very idea of measuring willies in the showers or the happily accidental fondlings of the communal bath. As a way of avoiding games afternoons which were cold, dirty and dull, I persuaded a small group of friends, all crap at rugby, to put on plays. Rehearsals were scheduled to clash with rugby practice on Wednesday afternoons. With the naive enthusiasm of Mickey Rooney and Judy Garland, we discussed what to produce. *Oedipus Rex* was a possibility, but seemed pretty thin in the chuckle department. We toyed with *Macbeth*, but couldn't agree which of us should play the wife. Eventually we decided on *The Importance of Being Earnest*. The production lasted for hours, and though it was endlessly amusing to play it must have been excruciating to watch. A video with a strange orange wash still exists for posterity. On Betamax, of course. Buoyed by our success, but having obviously cracked the classics, we next produced *Hands across the Sea*, a very funny short comedy of bad manners by Noël Coward. Why these plays, of all that I had read? What attracted me to them? I liked them because they were funny. I liked them because the characters were so outrageous. I liked the fact that the plots didn't seem to matter; the way the story was told was the important thing, the use of language. Here was a world where wit and humour triumphed and where the swaggering, mindless prowess of the sportsfield was ridiculed. With hindsight, I suppose that I had identified and was enjoying the sensibility of camp.

In the mid-1980s, I left the Northwest to study in London. I didn't think at the time that my decision to go to London was a particularly conscious one. Anywhere outside the Wirral would have suited me. On reflection I think that London was a magnet for me, as it is for so many other young gay men. It seemed fascinating and romantic because just about every book I'd read or film I'd seen seemed to involve it. *Nobody* of renown seemed to have hailed from the Wirral. The fact that Glenda Jackson had once worked in Boots in West Kirby and that Kenneth Halliwell had graduated from Wirral Grammar, only to achieve a rather dubious celebrity for hammering in Joe Orton's head, seemed pretty poor claims to fame. Years of watching *Blue Peter* had drummed into my head that they broadcast from LONDON W12 8QT and that we received their bounty huddled around our makeshift crystal sets in 'the regions', 'the provinces' or a whole list of euphemisms which stressed 'THIS IS WHERE IT'S AT AND YOU'RE NOWHERE NEAR IT!' And, yes, Morrissey had urged the pale and interesting youths of the 1980s to ditch our humdrum towns, like Lynn Redgrave and Rita Tushingham in *Smashing Time*, and head for the metropolis where Life would begin.

A decade ago, when I timorously stepped off the train at Euston with *Portrait of the Artist as a Young Man* (unread) weighing down my small brown suitcase, the gay scene was a very different creature from the one that exists today. Before the advent of the gay Euro-bar-cum-club-café, the scene was dominated in the West End by 'traditional' pubs. These were generally dark, usually tatty and often dirty, serving a strange collection of rent boys, media queens and raincoats. Somewhat fazed by the city, a college friend and I joined a youth group in King's Cross and ended up as regulars at a pub called The Bell. Near several colleges and next door to the independent Scala Cinema, the clientele of The Bell were quite particular: indie-types with pristine retro-haircuts and sharp politics. Here at least you stood a fair chance of meeting men of a similar age who also watched films, saw plays and read books; but I was shocked to discover that lots of these young gay men had shared my solitary experiences with books and films. I was gutted to find that Bette Davis was a 'gay icon', up there with Judy Garland and Barbara Stanwyck. I was even angry. I was hardly aware of Barbara Stanwyck! I hated Judy Garland! I thought *I* was the only one who identified with Bette *that* way. Now that so many other people shared her, I felt it was all cheap and silly and obvious. My friend Gareth had developed an obsession with Bette Davis whilst growing up in a mining community in South Wales. When asked by his mother on his eighteenth birthday which of all his presents he would treasure throughout his life, she was slightly worried that he chose an LP from a friend, *Miss Bette Davis Sings*, which included Bette's up-beat re-mix of the classic 'I've Written A Letter To Daddy'. Gareth, too, experienced the same surprise at finding that Bette Davis was an icon for gay men in London and that in the innocence of his youth he had been displaying, shall we say, telltale signs?

Unknowingly, I had been familiarizing myself with the vocabulary of a shared culture. Others had been attracted to the same books and films for the same reasons that I had, united by some subtle sense of difference. In the bookshops, theatres and cinemas of my adolescence, I had discovered a comforting sense of identity on the page, stage and screen, which could never have been voiced in a depressed, working-class town like Birkenhead in the 1970s and 1980s. I felt that in London at least I had access to a culture where I could share and develop this identity.

In the English department at university I met a mature student called Sally. She was a sharp-witted, no-nonsense woman in her sixties who had taken her first degree at Cambridge in the 1940s. Though studying Restoration literature, Sally had a lifetime's reading behind her and consequently seemed to have provocative opinions about everything. Once I rather naively took Sally on in one of those awful literary debates where you try to justify your own taste (SEAN *(tight-lipped)* I just like it, OK?). In passing, she happened to mention Noël Coward's *Private Lives*: 'Well, we all know what *that's* about, don't we?' Having decided at the time that only Shakespeare, or at a push Milton, was worthy of my fabulous critical skills, I hadn't given Coward any thought at all. 'What do you mean?' I asked. 'Boys buggering each other all over the carpet. Don't have to be a genius to see that.' When I thought about it, I saw that Sally might be right. But what surprised me was not the fact that Coward exhibited such a strong gay subtext, but that Sally (tweedy, pukka, straight) was aware of it too and had obviously been aware of its existence in Coward's work throughout her reading and theatregoing life. In her diaries, Frances Partridge recalls a visit to the first production of Britten's homo-opera, *Billy Budd*, in 1951 and recognizes it as 'a queer's heaven' where 'only homosexual emotions figure'.[3] She had also sussed Britten's none-too subtle hymn to boy-love, *Peter Grimes*, in 1945, believing that 'what Britten was consciously or unconsciously expressing in *Peter Grimes* was a plea for the freedom from persecution of homosexuals'.[4]

So is the subtext of Coward, or Britten, or Wilde or Maugham's work so very obvious? And has it always been? A recent production of Coward's *Design for Living* was hailed by critics as a radical exposure of the play's bisexual agenda. But the thesis of the play has always been pretty obvious; it's inherent throughout the dialogue. Leo tells Gilda that 'I love you. You love me. You love Otto. I love Otto. Otto loves me.'[5] Straightforward enough. But in this production Otto and Leo did actually kiss. Here the subtext was explicated for us, the implicit had been made explicit; there was no way the dumbest homophobe in the audience could miss the director's point.

Theatre is a collaborative process, a collusion between the playwright, the director, the designer, the performers and the audience. Each of these has an interpretive role. The diverse backgrounds and experiences of the individual audience members define their different perceptions of and attitudes to the work. Theatre is a process of interpretations, where Wilde believed that 'all interpretations are true' and 'no interpretation final'. Even 'realistic' drama is metaphorical and stage characters are ciphers or representations, for the arena of the stage is that of allegory. We are invited to read our lives in the action that takes place on stage. Prior to the blatancy of productions like Sean Mathias's *Design for Living*, there has been a tacit collusion between gay writer and gay audience. For gay people as audience members are practised at interpreting art, never taking anything at face value and locating themselves within texts that seem, superficially, to exclude them. We have had no choice but to read ourselves in works about heterosexual relationships and as, on the whole, we are born to and cultivated by straight parents, we understand the language of heterosexuality: we are 'culturally bi-lingual'. But perhaps the hints, suggestions and symbols that we feel are so obvious and exclusive to us in gay writing have not been as incomprehensible to heterosexuals as we like to think. In defending his early work, which had been condemned as 'decadent', Noël Coward had come to the conclusion that an 'unpleasant subject' such as drug addiction, adultery and, by extension, homosexuality was 'something that everyone knows about, but shrinks from the belief that other people know about it too'.[6] In the 1950s, Terence Rattigan tried to persuade the producer of the American production of *Separate Tables* to accept a rewrite which explicitly identified a central character as homosexual. Rattigan was very aware that English audiences had become accustomed to collaborating in his subterfuge:

an English audience knew my problem and accepted the fact that I had to skirt around it. They got the full impact of the play. ... An American audience, on the other hand, not conditioned to censorship and to the evasiveness to which British dramatists are now forced, may well take [the character's] stated offence not as a symbol at all, but as a literal fact.[7]

After my conversation with Sally at college, I began to wonder whether, if the emotions that inspired these works were specifically gay and were apparent, even obvious, to her, then perhaps my attraction to them as a young gay man back in Birkenhead had been something more substantial than 'just a feeling'. I began to realize that what had particularly appealed to me was that which was not said or stated but was suggested, implied or hinted at. The writers who excited me in my adolescence had offered me the freedom to site myself in their plays, films and stories, the freedom to explore the rich and dangerous territory of the subtext. Gay writers earlier this century, anticipating contemporary playwrights like Harold Pinter, had evolved a particular style which heightened the importance of subtext, for the subtext is the queens' realm.

In this book, I have concentrated on writers and plays which have interested or influenced me. It is very much an exploration of my own taste. I had originally intended to include the rather modish Joe Orton, but I have to confess that though the biography is fruity, the plays bore me rigid. John Lahr has almost single-handedly ensured Orton's literary canonization, but where would his reputation stand if his life had not come to such an untimely, romantic and marketable end? Would Orton too share the ill-frequented literary suburbs with those other iconoclasts of the 1960s, Arnold Wesker, Edward Bond, Ann Jellicoe and Shelagh Delaney? I have not attempted to write a history of twentieth-century 'gay' plays.[8] Both Michael Wilcox and Nicholas de Jongh have explored that ground more directly, focusing on plays that are more explicitly 'about' homosexuality, such as Mourdaint Shairp's *The Green Bay Tree* (1933), Philip King's *Serious Charge* (1955) and Keith Winter's *The Rats of Norway* (1933).[9] Nor have I attempted to write a chronology of twentieth-century dramatic writing by gay men, for such a study would run to many volumes. Ivor Novello, a major craftsman of British musical camp, surely deserves a study of his own, as does Rodney Ackland, whose work has only recently been recognized by the National Theatre.[10] The essays that follow do not presume to cover the whole broad and varied careers of the writers I have focused on, but the period that they inhabited, from the 1890s to the mid-1970s, does encompass the development, maturity and decline of a particular style of theatre, the 'well-made play'. New plays by Wilde, Maugham, Coward and Rattigan dominated the West End stage for almost a century and revivals of their work continue to be a mainstay of the repertoires of the West End as well as the touring circuit and repertory theatres. Without these writers there would be no West End theatre as we know it. Just how well would the 'well-made play' have been made without them? A major part of our theatrical culture has been dominated by gay writers like these and their sympathies have helped to shape our society by nurturing the imaginations and opinions of Joe Bloggs in the Dress Circle. Neil Bartlett observes the strange ironies of the theatre where actors dramatize heterosexuality and where gender itself is a kind of drag, as any four-year-old with the slightest acquaintance with Widow Twanky or Prince Charming could tell you:

Thousands of people go to see shows every night and have no idea that they are watching their fantasies acted out by gay people, while gay people still know what they have always known, that shows which 'say' nothing about us can still be some of the most powerful and exciting vehicles of our pleasures and our griefs.[11]

Though each of the writers I examine projects a distinctive voice in their work, Wilde, Maugham, Coward and Rattigan share a particular way of looking at the world, a strategy of discussing relationships and a similar agenda. Stylistically they have a great deal in common. They are certainly all traditionalists. As a rule, they do not experiment with form and language. But British drama was generally unshaken by the Modernist movement, avoiding the innovations of the poets and novelists of the 1920s.[12] In our present age when the division between the commercial theatre and the subsidized theatre appears more pronounced than ever, it seems appropriate to consider these avowedly commercial playwrights and how far their personal dilemmas as gay men affected their agendas as revealed in their work intended for a popular audience.

The period encompassed by this book also covers some of the most fascinating developments in British legislation that have directly affected gay men. Both the 1890s and the 1960s were periods of comparative liberalness. The Wilde scandal brought the concept of the 'naughty nineties' to an end and the years between the demise of Wilde and the rise of Orton were decades of legal control and social hostility towards homosexuality, which resulted in a culture of repression and concealment. It is the evolution and practice of a stage language of discretion, an ability to discuss and explore that which is unspeakable, that I attempt to explore in the work of these writers. The theme of transgressive behaviour, and particularly transgressive love, features heavily in the plays I examine, but it's always bound within the conventional, popular form of the 'well-made play'. This genre might even serve as an overriding image for the work of these writers: the exploration of transgression and alienation, but restrained within a tight, traditional three-act structure. Insecurity about age, the fading of beauty and the burden of secrecy are major themes in these plays, as are guilt, shame and embarrassment. Consequently, these works have spoken to me directly and eloquently of a sense of isolation and 'otherness' which I believe is an inherent part of their creators' art. To me, the anxieties of wartime are very apparent in *Blithe Spirit*, even though the war is never mentioned. Like the ghostly Elvira, Coward's sexuality haunts the play just as apparently, but just as discreetly, as the war does. Whether it's deliberately intended or subconsciously evolved, the subtext cannot help but be an expression of the author, whether he's aware of it or not: In Colin Dale's unlicensed and unproduced play of 1940, *Queer People*, the hero, a gay architect, is advised that unbeknown to him, his sexuality is apparent throughout his work, right down to the gradient of the floors or the arrangement of the rooms. His sometime lover quotes Samuel Butler's *The Way of All Flesh*,

> Every man's work, whether it be literature or music or pictures or architecture or anything else, is always a portrait of himself, and the more he tries to conceal himself the more clearly will his character appear in spite of him.[13]

The art of Wilde, Maugham, Coward and Rattigan is an art born of self-censorship, subterfuge and concealment, but it is also rich with oblique signals and references for those open to reading them. But this

11

art inspired by repression has also produced some of the most success-ful, important and life-enhancing plays of the twentieth-century; many of them, such as *Private Lives, The Deep Blue Sea* and *Blithe Spirit* are now regarded as classics which continue to inform our culture. Beginning with Oscar Wilde, I attempt to explore the resonances of his agenda for tolerance and his creed of individualism in the works of the popular gay writers who followed him. As a background, I have briefly charted the legal innovations which regulated the personal lives of gay writers throughout this period. The law policed the lives of gay men in private and the presentation of stage plays in public for much of this century. Such regulations necessitated the evolution of sophisticated strategies by gay dramatists to express their personal preoccupations on stage, albeit obliquely. At one particularly frenetic point in *Present Laughter*, between the slam of the bedroom/closet door, the doorbell rings and Essendine, Coward's alter ego sighs, 'With any luck it's the Lord Chamberlain'. As Alan Sinfield observes, for most of the twentieth century, the theatre, just like gay men, has been haunted by the 'ominous ring of the doorbell' that was the herald of the law.[14]

They shoot themselves, don't they?

Interviewer: What influence, if any, did Wilde have on you or others of your set, while you were growing up?

Cecil Beaton: A very negative influence, indeed, in terms of being hon-est about one's difference. The *name* was not spoken, and from time to time there were tidbits of news meant to intimidate anyone who might follow in his footsteps.[15]

Throughout history, writing by gay men as artists has been conditioned by the statutes which regulated their behaviour as individuals. Such reg-ulations in Britain during the past century inspired a culture of self-cen-sorship and subterfuge by gay writers. Oscar Wilde, surely the most famous homosexual of the nineteenth century, casts a long shadow across this short, turbulent twentieth century, both as a dramatist and as an individual. Wilde manipulated the dramatic forms which he had inherited from the mid-nineteenth century and created a new genre, a comic drama of morals. He distinguished himself from his contempor-aries by creating a stage language which eschewed naturalism in favour of a completely original style of artifice. The resonances of this artifice are felt in Coward's spare and witty dialogue and were later inherited in the 1960s by Joe Orton, 'the Oscar Wilde of Welfare State gentility'. But for much of this century Wilde's innovations as a writer were eclipsed by the infamous scandal associated with his crime 'not to be named amongst Christians'. Alan Sinfield observes that the Wilde trials helped to develop a recognizable image for homosexual men and from this the 'dominant twentieth-century queer identity' has evolved, 'mainly out of elements that came together at the Wilde trials: effeminacy, leisure, idleness, immorality, luxury, insouciance, decadence and aestheticism'.[16] Wilde's personal characteristics became the yardstick by which all homosexuals were measured and identified. His name became a convenient byword for 'evil men'. Just before the First World War, E. M. Forster's Maurice falteringly identifies himself as an 'unspeakable of the Oscar Wilde sort'. Wilde's crime seemed very mysterious to me in my early teens. Reading Nancy Mitford's *The Pursuit of Love*, I became fascinated and confused. The thinly disguised Mitford sisters debate the nature of Wilde's sin:

> But what did he *do*? I asked Fa once and he roared at me – goodness, it was terrifying. He said: 'If you mention that sewer's name again in this house I'll thrash you, do you hear, damn you?' So I asked Aunt Sadie and she looked awfully vague and said: 'O duck, I never really quite knew, but whatever it was it was worse than murder, fearfully bad. And, darling, don't talk about him at meals, will you?'[17]

Yes, but what *was* it exactly? I lived in ignorance until watching a TV trailer with my mother for *The Trials of Oscar Wilde*. 'But what did Oscar Wilde *do*?' I asked, all innocence. Mrs O'Connor replied quite candidly that 'He was a Homo Sexual' and left it at that. Suddenly I wasn't innocent any more and my face coloured. Not because I identified myself with *that word* but because I gathered it was not the sort of question I should ask and that my mother found it slightly embarrassing to answer. I'm sure she dismissed it as the natural questioning of a sexually curious adolescent, but I was glad that she had been honest and direct. After all she might have said, 'He was a pervert', which could well have made me feel very differently about how to broach the subject of my sexuality with my parents years later.

Inspired by a rather literal interpretation of Old Testament lore, hostility towards sexual relations between men has been integral to the preachings of the Christian tradition. Many cultures in history have equated homosexuality with sodomy and conveniently related it with other crimes against both God and the state, such as murder. In Britain, the death penalty for sodomy was initiated by Henry VIII, a man not exactly renowned for his tolerance of queens. By the early nineteenth century four out of five convicted sodomists were hanged, compared to only 63 out of 471 for other capital offences – a nasty little fact that must surely tarnish the Dairy Box image of Jane Austen's England that is currently so popular. This statute was tacitly abandoned after 1836 but was only finally abolished in England and Wales as late as 1861. It was replaced with a penalty of penal servitude that extended from ten years to life. In 1885, the Criminal Law Amendment Bill was initiated in order to regulate prostitution and to raise the age of consent for girls from thirteen to sixteen. The infamous Labouchère Amendment to the bill outlawed all male homosexual activities whether committed in public or in private:

> any male person, who, in public or private, commits, or is a party to the commission of, or procures or attempts to procure the commission by any male person of any act of gross indecency with another male person, shall be guilty of a misdemeanour, and being convicted thereof shall be liable at the discretion of the court to be imprisoned for any term not exceeding two years, with or without hard labour.[18]

All the major legislation affecting homosexuality from 1885 to the Wolfenden report of 1957 were attempts to deal with social problems relating to women and to regulate prostitution. No wonder, then, that the campaigns for the reform of statutes affecting women have been intertwined with those relating to gay men. The peripheral legal and social status of women throughout the nineteenth and early twentieth centuries has reflected the similar status of gay men. The tightening of the law concerning homosexuality at the end of the nineteenth century corresponded with a growing awareness and definition of the homosexual. The evolution and first use of the word 'homosexual' dates from this period. The term was introduced into the English language in Charles Gilbert Chaddock's 1892 translation of Krafft-Ebing's German textbook on sexual deviance, *Psychopathia Sexualis*. The *Oxford English Dictionary* failed to recognize 'homosexuality'as a word officially until 1976. A linguistic oversight – or wilful blindness?

The growing awareness and developing hostility towards homosexuality in the late nineteenth century was exacerbated by a series of racy and highly publicized homosexual scandals. Boulton and Park, the two outrageous transvestites who paraded the West End as Fanny and Stella, were arrested in 1870 leaving the Strand Theatre dressed as women.[19] A homosexual brothel was exposed at Cleveland Street between 1889 and 1890, a scandal which was rumoured to link an heir to the throne with several Post Office messenger boys. These events culminated in the three trials of Oscar Wilde in 1895. Wilde was particularly unfortunate to be the first major conviction under an Act barely a decade old. The vagueness of the Labouchère Amendment empowered it to encompass all male homosexual activities. Now that even private, consensual acts were policed under the Act, the door was open for blackmailers to exploit prominent and vulnerable men. Indeed, the Amendment became known as the 'blackmailer's charter' and its force was felt as strongly in the 1960s as it had been when first initiated nearly eighty years before. The story of Basil Dearden's *Victim* (1961), released on the threshold of reform, might have occurred at any time in the previous century. With its usual flair for eccentricity, Britain was the only country in Europe which penalized sexual acts between men in private. Both the Wilde case and the Cleveland Street scandal had involved newspaper boys, telegraph boys and labourers. These cases brought the aristocracy and the celebrities of the age into intimate association with the working classes. Such relationships, based on the transaction of sex and money or gifts, were thought to dangerously undermine social stability by eroding class barriers. Since Edward Gibbon's examination of the decline and fall of the Roman Empire, decadence, moral dissolution and imperial decay had been associated with the spread of homosexual behaviour. End-of-century apocalyptic panic intensified concerns about the decline of the nation and the disintegration of the Empire: 'Rome fell; other nations have fallen; and if England falls it will be this sin, and her unbelief in God, that will have been her ruin.'[20]

Such hostility towards gay men was both legally and socially condoned for the three-quarters of a century after Wilde's conviction, backed by the moral and legal support of church and state. In the 1920s lesbianism became a public issue for the first time since Queen Victoria had famously refused to give the very idea credence. There was an attempt in 1921 to criminalize lesbian behaviour along the lines of the Labouchère Amendment, but Parliament thought it better not to promote the idea by opening it up for public debate. Lord Desart claimed that it would be a 'very great mischief to tell the whole world that there is such an offence, to bring it to the notice of women who have never thought of it, never dreamt of it'.[21] But remember that this is the culture that at the very threshold of the permissive 1960s was still preoccupied with shielding its wives and servants from dirty books. Lesbianism continued to be a focus for public concern with the prosecution for obscenity of Radclyffe Hall's *The Well of Loneliness* in 1928.

The attitude towards male homosexuality between the wars seems to have been comparatively cool. In 1938 316 convictions were brought under the Wildean crime of gross indecency. But paranoia about homosexuality re-emerged with a vengeance after the Second World War. In an attempt to re-establish the moral standards of the 1930s that had been eroded by six years of war, a concerted 'drive against male vice' was initiated by the notoriously harsh Home Secretary, Sir David Maxwell Fyfe.[22] By 1955 convictions for gross indecency had increased to 2,322, seven times the prewar figure. Several infamous homosexual scandals characterized the mood of the early 1950s. The rich and famous became a particular target to hoist as examples to the general public. In 1951, Burgess and Maclean scandalized optimistic postwar Britain by defecting to the USSR. Gay men became the easy scapegoats of the cold war, filling the role of 'the enemy within'. In the same year, Alan Turing, who had cracked the Enigma code and thereby played a vital role in bringing Allied victory in the Second World War, was convicted under the Labouchère Amendment. He was bound over for a year on condition that he agree to submit to 'organotherapy' – a course of oestrogen injections; three years later he committed suicide by eating an apple dipped in cyanide. John Gielgud, one of the foremost classical actors of his day, was arrested for gross indecency in 1954 and his career was threatened by the brutal exposure of the case in the tabloids. As in the 1890s, scandal sheets cried that the fabric of deferential British society was under threat; for these homosexual scandals also involved the very people who were traditionally expected to set moral standards, the aristocracy. The trial of Lord Montagu and Peter Wildeblood in 1954 exposed a terrifying ignorance, prejudice and deceit on the part of the prosecution, who were ably supported by the tabloid press, willing dupes in reporting surmises, myths and outright lies which characterized Montagu and Wildeblood as homosexual monsters. Reflecting on the increasing hostility towards gay men in the postwar period, Noël Coward was saddened to have to record in his diary of 1955 that a proposed plan for altering 'the barbarous laws about homosexuality' was defeated by a huge majority. Even Coward, a lifelong conservative and royalist, despairs

> that a group of bigoted old gentlemen should have the power to make the administration of British justice a laughing-stock in the civilized world. . . . The police are empowered to frame private individuals, to extort terrified and probably inaccurate confessions and betrayals from scared young men.[23]

The ugly relationship between the law and the press throughout this period reaffirmed the stereotypical portrayal of the seduction of innocents by vicious homosexuals and characterized homosexuality as an infectious cancer which threatened wholesome heterosexual society. It is within this depressingly bleak period of British social history that Maugham, Coward and Rattigan attempted to continue to preach the Wildean creed of tolerance and individualism. No small feat, really.

William Somerset Maugham was twenty-six when Oscar Wilde died. The scandal affected him enormously at the time and Wilde's ostracism, the loss of his family and the destruction of his career was to haunt Maugham throughout his life. Even at his death in 1965, Maugham feared the public exposure of his sexuality and went to great lengths to carry on the concealment. Beginning in the 1930s, Maugham discouraged biographers and left instructions in his will that his executor should not co-operate with anyone wishing to write his life story. In the 1950s he held 'bonfire nights', destroying unpublished manuscripts and letters from such luminaries as H. G. Wells, T. S. Eliot, Rebecca West and Arnold Bennett. In November 1957 he addressed his friends and past acquaintances through the pages of the *Daily Mail*, requesting that they destroy any letters from him: 'Don't please think me ungracious but I hate having my letters published. I regard my letters as my personal affair and I cannot see that their publication after my death will be any useful contribution.'[24]

Noël Coward was born in 1899, just before Wilde's death; Terence Rattigan was born in 1911, just as Wilde's work began to be revived. Though both lived to see the decriminalization of homosexuality, their lives had been dominated as men and as artists by the demonization of their sexual preference. Coward was relieved to record the moment when the 'Homosexual Bill' was passed with a majority of fifty-five in 1966, but still appalled by the bigotry of some of the MPs who contributed to the debate:

> Really some of the opposition speeches were so bigoted, ignorant and silly that one can hardly believe that adult minds should be so basically idiotic. . . . Nothing will convince the bigots, but the blackmailers will be discouraged and fewer haunted, terrified young men will commit suicide.[25]

The law, the shadow of Wilde and the mores of conventional society have all contributed to make this a rather uncomfortable century for gay men. The burdens of guilt, shame and insecurity have shaped the lives of gay artists and conditioned the tenor of their work. The Sexual Offences Act of 1967 ultimately decriminalized homosexual behaviour in private between men over the age of twenty-one. When the Act was passed, Cecil Beaton wrote movingly of the sense of insecurity that the hostility towards homosexuality had had on him personally:

> Even now I can only vaguely realise that it was only comparatively late in life that I would go into a room full of people without a feeling of guilt. To go into a room full of men, or to go to a lavatory in The Savoy, needed quite an effort. . . . But when one realises what damage, what tragedy has been brought on by this lack of sympathy to a very delicate and difficult subject, this should be a great time of celebration. It is not that I would have wished to avail myself of further licence, but to feel that one was not a felon and an outcast could have helped enormously during the difficult young years.

Such feelings of social insecurity constituted one of the day-to-day consequences of the homophobic culture ushered in by the Wilde case which affected many ordinary men. But many of our greatest artists, writers and thinkers have also been casualties of the Wilde case, and their tragedies have been our irreparable, unforgivable loss. Witness the career of one of the century's most esteemed novelists and contributors to the Modernist movement, E. M. Forster. Between 1907 and 1910, Forster had published four novels. Fourteen years later, in 1924, he published *A Passage to India*. This was to be his last novel until *Maurice* was published posthumously in 1971. Forster's epigraph to *Howards End* (1910) had been 'Only connect . . .', a plea for tolerance, brotherhood and universal understanding. The tragic epigraph to *Maurice* reads:

Begun 1913
Finished 1914.
Dedicated to a happier year.

A happier year, nearly six decades later. How to account for this famous literary silence of more than half a century? After the publication of *Howards End*, Forster analysed the reasons for his artistic 'sterility' in his diary: 'Weariness of the only subject I both can and may treat – the love of men for women and vice versa.'[26] In the post-Wolfenden 1960s when the social and political climate was experiencing a definite sea change towards the liberal, Forster famously defended D. H. Lawrence's explicit paean to heterosexual love, *Lady Chatterley's Lover*, at the obscenity trial. But still he was reluctant to take a similar public stand in defence of homosexuality. On New Year's Eve 1964, Forster, one of the few survivors of early-twentieth-century letters, reflected on his career and considered his posthumous reputation in his diary: 'I should have been a much more famous writer if I had written or rather published more, but sex has prevented the latter.'[27] I find this simple admission tragic, not just for the man who recognizes that he has not fulfilled his own potential, but for us, for our culture to have been denied the mature fruits of one of the great civilized minds of the twentieth century. George V, that rather forgettable monarch who arrived after all the fuss was over and died before all the real fun began, famously observed that he had always assumed that homosexuals did the honourable thing, the English thing, and shot themselves. He is also attributed with exclaiming 'Bugger Bognor' on his deathbed; a rather obsessively anal imagination, surely, for a respectable husband and father of six? But many men in this period did do the honourable thing, the English thing, and exiled themselves or committed suicide. As a nation, as a culture, we should be ashamed.

Blue pencils, pink pens

Forster's dilemma reflects that of all homosexual writers working in the aftermath of the Wilde scandal and before the dawn of political reform in the late 1950s. But for writers working in the theatre, there was an additional challenge. The explicit expression of homosexual relationships and lifestyles on the British stage was bound by statutes established in law. Since 1737, the public production of plays was regulated by the Lord Chamberlain, a senior official of the Royal household. The Lord Chamberlain excised works that dealt with politics, religion and sexuality, effectively emasculating the theatre as an arena for the exploration of contemporary social issues. The discussion and examination of sexuality was severely policed. The very language used on the stage was edited, deleted and expunged. Clement Scott, the nineteenth-century drama critic, fervently defended the need for a censor and presented the 'logical' case, which was to support the Lord Chamberlain's powers until they were finally dissolved in 1968:

> the laws of decency and order must be administered by someone, and it is far better to check before than to correct after. The preliminary stroke of the kindly blue pencil in a tentative play or sketch is better than the spreading of objectionable matter. Hundreds of ears may be poisoned before the remedy is found.[28]

Hundreds of plays originally fell foul of this 'kindly blue pencil' and had to be revised by their authors in order to comply with the Lord Chamberlain's restrictions. Only then would they receive a public licence. Some plays were refused licences altogether and were not allowed to be performed in public. Consequently several writers and theatre managers resorted to presenting unlicensed plays in private club theatres, a strategy that continued even into the 1960s. Works now regarded as classics, such as *A View from the Bridge* (1955), *Cat on a Hot Tin Roof* (1955), *The Children's Hour* (1934) and John Osborne's *A Patriot for Me* (1965), were all first presented in this country in 'private' theatres. *The*

Children's Hour, Lillian Hellman's drama about the power of rumour, which happens to include a lesbian character ('a horribly unpleasant play'[29]), was submitted to the Lord Chamberlain in 1935, then again in 1936, 1939, 1942, 1945 and 1950. It had to wait until the 1990s to receive a full public production in London. This censorship even ran to a tacit regulation of literary classics. Marlowe's Renaissance work, *Edward II*, was not performed on the British stage for 286 years, until Harley Granville-Barker played the title role for the Elizabethan Stage Society in 1903, just eight years after Wilde's conviction. The explicit presentation of homosexuality in the theatre continued to be banned in Britain until Joan Littlewood's ground-breaking production of Shelagh Delaney's *A Taste of Honey* in 1958.

Unable to examine homosexuality directly, the opportunities for gay playwrights to express themselves in their art were limited. Forster, having tired of examining his own situation through the subterfuge of heterosexual relationships, chose a frustrating compromise: to write but not publish. Coward, Rattigan and Somerset Maugham made a virtue of necessity, each exploring heterosexual relationships with the keen, unsentimental eye of the outsider. In plays such as *Private Lives*, *The Deep Blue Sea* and *The Constant Wife*, marriage, the fundamental keystone of society, is dissected and challenged by the transgressive freedoms of adultery. Monogamy and the stability of 'family life' haunt these plays as ideal patterns which are seldom achieved. Respectability, decency and normality are held up as the touchstones of this culture. But these plays explore the lives of those attempting to emulate these ideals, failing, and then living the fictions of monogamy and cosy family life. The relationship between men and women is exposed as extraordinarily fragile. The ideal heterosexual love for which people die or kill, so relentlessly depicted in art and literature, is challenged. Romantic love is exposed as the stuff of fantasy or delusion.

Just as marriage is dissected, so is its extension, the family. In these plays, the twentieth-century family is in a state of crisis. In Coward's *Cavalcade*, often disparaged as little more than an epic spectacle of jingoistic propaganda, the worlds of the upper- and working-class families gradually move towards union, but the play's final song is 'Twentieth Century Blues' and the final image is one of chaos. *For Services Rendered*, one of Maugham's four late plays, ends with the complete breakdown of family and social relations. The Ardsley family struggle to apply their respectable Home Counties values to the challenges of blindness, sexual blackmail, cancer, suicide and madness. Just as the oblivious patriarch, Leonard Ardsley observes that 'This old England of ours isn't done for yet and I for one believe in it and all it stands for',[30] his daughter Eva, now retreating from the cruelties of the world into insanity, gives a cracked, heartbreaking rendering of 'God Save The King'. This is a culture going to the dogs. The observation of this decline by Maugham, Rattigan and Coward is viewed from the margins, as they examine the dilemmas of the disenfranchised and the politically voiceless. But these disenfranchised are both socially visible and common to all classes: like homosexuals, they pass unnoticed in the streets and do not wear their exclusion or oppression on their sleeves. These disenfranchised are women.

Shall we join the ladies?

As they presume to focus on the dilemmas of women, Maugham, Coward and Rattigan, like Tennessee Williams, have often been accused of literary transvestism. It's very easy, but not very helpful, to presume that Blanche Dubois is simply Williams in chiffon drag or that Hester in *The Deep Blue Sea* is 'really' a gay man just because Rattigan was himself. Such a superficial reading devalues Williams's and Rattigan's imaginative and artistic achievement and smacks of the ingrained misogyny and homophobia of literary studies. Blanche is certainly a cult figure in the gay pantheon of female icons.[31] But she is at once a complex, three-dimensional characterization of a woman as well as a figure who is able to articulate the dilemmas and obsessions which gay audiences share. This manipulation of central female characters who also 'represent' the tensions and ambiguities of homosexual desire is a strategy shared and developed by many of the most celebrated playwrights of the West End and Broadway; Tennessee Williams, William Inge, John Van Druten as well as Wilde, Maugham, Coward and Rattigan. Blanche is an apostle of Wilde, promoting a culture of artifice and deceit. Like the stage manager of her own life, she struggles to disguise the ugly truth of reality with paper lanterns. Her props are rhinestones and her costumes cheap summer furs. 'I don't want realism,' she cries. 'I want magic!'[32] She adopts the role of the demure schoolma'm, whilst harbouring a history of sexual excess and alcoholism. The persona Blanche projects at her sister's house in New Orleans is a self-conscious performance of respectability. Through Blanche, Williams shows that you don't have to be respectable or chaste to look as if you are; you just have to be a good actor. Of course Blanche is camp and certainly has many of the best lines, but on stage *A Streetcar Named Desire* (1947) is very much an even four-hander. Stella and Mitch's stories are just as emotionally demanding, if less melodramatic than Blanche and Stanley's. In an interview in the 1970s, Williams indicated that, though he identified with his female protagonist, he also identified with Stanley, recognizing that Stanley's butch drag is as much a camp performance of masculinity as Blanche's violets and chiffon are of femininity. As a gay man, Williams wants to *be* Stanley, who is young, virile and sexually attractive. At the same time, he wants to *have* Stanley, like Blanche does, for the same reasons. It is this struggle, this tension between Blanche and Stanley and Williams's complex, perhaps schizophrenic, involvement in it which redeems *A Streetcar Named Desire* from the melodrama of its plot and leaves us with such a compelling and satisfying piece of work:

Williams:	Flaubert was asked 'Who is Madame Bovary?' He said, 'Madame Bovary, c'est moi.'
Interviewer:	Well Blanche Dubois isn't you, is it?
Williams:	Mostly. I draw all my characters from myself. I can't draw a character unless I know it within myself.[33]

Williams and his British contemporaries tend to examine the situation of older women in love, rather than the sunny world of 'love's young dream'. Their most resonant creations are experienced women who share the awareness that love is fragile and beauty transient. Characters such as Mrs Goforth in Tennessee Williams's *The Milk Train Doesn't Stop Here Any More* (1962), and even Maugham's Lady Frederick, are exploited as self-consciously allegorical figures in the drama that surrounds them, the classic obsession with youth of declining age, an obsession shared by several of Wilde's characters, particularly in *The Picture of Dorian Gray*. The female protagonists of these dramas experience more of the cruelties of the world and fate because, unlike men, they have less power to shape and control the society they live in. This examination of the disparity between the worlds of men and women was popularly initiated by Wilde in the 1890s and continued to be explored by Shaw well into the twentieth century. Wilde's study of the 'oppressed majority' was heavily influenced by the works of the radical Norwegian dramatist, Henrik Ibsen. Ibsen explored the anxieties and hypocrisies of his age through the stories of a gallery of intelligent, suffocated women. These fictional creations influenced the debate about the position of women throughout the Western world as well as the portrayal of women on stage. Hedda Gabler, Nora Helmer, Rebecca West and Mrs Alving heralded a new age of comparative equality and social honesty. But whilst the focus of his plays was the home and family, Ibsen's target was society itself. He challenged establishment conventions such as the operation of justice, the sanctity of marriage and family life, and revealed contemporary society as unsettled, corrupt and hypocritical. The response to Ibsen's vision of society was vehemently hostile. Clement Scott famously denounced *Ghosts* as 'an open sewer; a loathsome sore unbandaged; a dirty act done publicly; a lazar-house with all its doors and windows open'.[34] Harold Hobson later compared Scott's denunciation of the play to the contemporary critical vitriol aimed at *A Streetcar Named Desire*; half a century on from Scott, the British were still shuddering at the notion of sex. Just as Williams places Maggie the Cat's bed centre stage, Ibsen drags the whispered discussions about venereal disease and sexual dysfunction into the drawing room. When the British première of *Cat on a Hot Tin Roof* coincided with a rare revival of Ibsen's *Little Eyolf* (1894), the agendas of the two men, seemingly so different, were revealed to be very much in sympathy. The frank discussion of sex allowed Ibsen, like Williams, to penetrate the heart of the tensions between men and women. Contemporary critics had been shocked, not only by Ibsen's depiction of women on the stage but also by the responses of women in the audience. At a performance of the first British production of *Ghosts*, one reviewer was clearly appalled: 'Many a man's face was expressive of disgust but I regret to say, that I did not mark such an expression upon any woman's countenance. Where is the Lord Chamberlain?'[35] In his preliminary notes for *Hedda Gabler*, Ibsen observed that 'Men and women don't belong to the same century', and when planning *A Doll's House* that 'A woman cannot be herself in modern society. It is an exclusively male society, with laws made by men and with persecutors and judges who assess female conduct from a male standpoint.'[36]

The arguments of *A Doll's House* (1879), *Ghosts* (1881) and *Hedda Gabler*

(1890) were to influence Wilde considerably in *Lady Windermere's Fan* (1892) and *A Woman of No Importance* (1893). The burdens of the past on the present, the freedom of the individual and a sexual hypocrisy which favours men over women are all themes which Wilde inherits from Ibsen. Ibsen's early comic romance *Love's Comedy* (1862) explores the contrast between the actual and the ideal which is to recur throughout Wilde's work and forms the basis of *An Ideal Husband* (1895). The lesser social and legal position of women which underpins the society explored by Wilde reverberates throughout the twentieth century. The crisis of Ibsen's Nora has its origin in social attitudes to her gender and is echoed in the lives of Wilde's Mrs Erlynne, Maugham's Lady Frederick and even Rattigan's Hester Collyer in the 1950s. Wilde's Lady Windermere could be Nora's sister when she describes how it is her husband who 'has broken the bond of marriage – not I. I only break its bondage'.

With the development of a feminist and suffrage movement, the late nineteenth century saw the evolution of the New Woman. As a consequence, women's rights within marriage, their right to hold property and their rights to certain grounds for divorce were all reassessed in this period. At the same time there was a corresponding attempt by doctors and lawyers to define and then regulate the homosexual. Women challenged the authority of their husbands, the lazy benefactors of patriarchy, and thus their agenda became associated with that of gay men in a movement for social change. Just as the positions of women and homosexuals were discussed in tandem in the late nineteenth century, nearly a century later the two causes were married again in the 1960s. The movement for homosexual equality in the 1960s and 1970s adopted many of the tactics and shared much of the vocabulary of the 1960s feminist movement. During these two periods attitudes to women and gay men were fundamentally reassessed and the legislation which affected them was radically altered. In the following chapters I will focus on the uneasy years between the definition of homosexuality in the 1890s and its liberation from criminality and medical surveillance in the 1960s.

1

Oscar and After

My works are dominated by myself.
    Oscar Wilde, *St James's Gazette*, 18 January 1895

For out of ourselves we can never pass, nor can there be in creation what in the creator was not.
    Oscar Wilde, *The Critic as Artist* (1891)

It is extraordinary that such a posing artificial old queen should have written one of the greatest comedies in the English language.
    Noël Coward on Oscar Wilde, *Diary*, 2 July 1962

The work of Oscar Wilde, like that of Joe Orton, has almost been suffocated by our insatiable desire to know more about the man. Both Wilde's and Orton's stories have all the elements which appeal to the clandestine *Hello!* reader in us all: tragedy, fame, sensation and sex. But are the man and his work symbiotically related? Can we objectively estimate Wilde's achievement solely on the basis of his writing? Should we? Does it really matter? In his introduction to the new edition of his grandfather's collected works, Merlin Holland attempts to evaluate Wilde's slippery status in English literature and the reasons why academic critics are reluctant to take Wilde seriously. Holland recalls a lecture given at a conference on Wilde, when a high-minded academic posed the question, 'Is Oscar Wilde really a great writer?' The lecturer was a specialist in Anglo-Irish literature and sneered at the critical and popular reference to Wilde as 'Oscar', 'as if', Holland comments, 'an author worthy of serious study should make himself less accessible and behave with somewhat more decorum'.[1] It is the ephemeral Kylies and Jasons of the world whom we generally refer to so intimately. The gravitas of the surname is reserved for 'great' canonical writers like Joyce, Lawrence and Eliot. In common parlance, the use of the surname traditionally identifies men; we refer to 'Oscar' as to a gossiping friend, an intimate or a woman. This intimacy with the reader and the public was initiated even when Wilde was alive: Wilde's wife Constance collected and published a volume of her husband's aphorisms called *Oscariana* in 1895.

Perhaps Wilde's intimacy with his public and ensuing popularity has contributed to the academic world's reluctance to take his work seriously. But despite the critics' ambivalence towards him, Holland records that there are 375 books alone dealing entirely with Wilde, as well as the thousands of references to him that exist in articles and dissertations. In a half-centenary assessment in 1950 *The Times Literary Supplement* had reflected that 'Apart from one perfect play, one memorable poem and *De Profundis*, Wilde left little with which, as literature, posterity need seriously concern itself.'[2] But posterity has proved kind to Wilde, and Holland has recently observed a sea change in Wilde's academic status. His popular reputation has never been in doubt, with revivals of his plays continuing to feed the West End and Broadway and editions of his writing available in translations all over the world. After his conviction, Wilde had become a point of reference for homosexuals in the early twentieth century as well as a conversational euphemism for discussing the popular crime that Christians were prohibited from mentioning. More recently, Wilde was adopted as a martyr by the developing gay movement. One of the last projects of the film-maker Derek Jarman was to shoot *The Picture of Dorian Gray*. At the same time, Jarman became a motivating force in the campaign to erect a memorial statue of Wilde outside Bow Street police station in time for the centenary of Wilde's death (a rather ordinary sculpture of a ballerina scratching her corns currently occupies the place opposite where the Wilde statue ought to stand). With the centenary of Wilde's death and the advent of the new millennium, attitudes to gender, sexuality and to the idea of sex itself have become complex and sophisticated. Wilde is no longer dismissed simply as a flawed queen by heterosexuals. On the contrary, he is lauded as a progressive, a champion of self-expression and advocate of tolerance for all. As Merlin Holland observes, 'The same public which crucified him for his lack of conformity and respect for Victorian values in 1895, today holds him up as a martyr for individuality.'[3]

Oscar Wilde's contemporary and fellow Irishman, W. B. Yeats, observed in his remembrances of the 1890s that the rarefied milieu of

Wilde's comedies was essentially foreign to their creator. Wilde's Irishness, like Yeats's and Shaw's, gave him a sense of difference from the outset. In the early 1890s, Wilde and Shaw only half-jokingly referred to their work as the beginnings of 'the great Celtic School' or the 'Hibernian School'. The story of the outsider was to become a characteristic theme of Wilde's work as well as a factual narrative that his life would tragically fulfil. Wilde began his infiltration of the dinner parties of fashionable London society, immortalizing it on the stage at the zenith of British imperial power. Like the dandies who languorously occupy the salons and ballrooms of his work, Wilde is the cynical observer and critic of British imperial culture rather than a part of its core. He focuses on a small corner of privileged English society and observes their foibles and hypocrisy with minute precision. Wildean society is an exclusive structure built of class, connections and wealth. It has evolved a complex code of behaviour and a conformity of manners which is practised and understood by its inhabitants. Wilde exposes the operation of this world, inviting us to peep through the keyhole at a series of functions which make up the 'season': balls, house parties and 'at homes'. These are the various public and private functions through which society operates and polices its members. The transgression of the strict social code results in ostracism, expulsion from the comforts of Eden. The walls of this social paradise are very difficult to scale. Algernon is advised by Lady Bracknell not to speak disrespectfully of society, as 'only people who can't get into it do that'.[4] Lord Illingworth in *A Woman of No Importance* warns that society is a 'necessary thing', for it is a way of formally controlling human behaviour and establishing shared values.

As well as advocating a singularly harsh morality, this society promotes a particular philosophy, a shared vision in the nineteenth century 'gospel of gold'. In *An Ideal Husband*, Sir Robert Chiltern has learned that wealth is power and that 'power over other men, power over the world, was the one thing worth having'.[5] Though he may not be an ideal husband, he is certainly the ideal Victorian. The leisure that Wilde's characters are blessed with is a sort of power too, the power to do nothing. The wealth that cossets these rarefied creatures is the reward of an aggressive, expansionist philosophy which aimed to control world trade at the same time as dominating world culture (at the expense, of course, of local traditional cultures). In Wilde's vision, the contemporary society of 1890s London becomes a symbol for the culture of patriarchy, the rule of straight white men from the leisured classes. Wilde's agenda is to expose the hypocrisies of this culture where marriage has become a sexual marketplace and morality a way of controlling the behaviour of 'other people'. Wilde's interest lies in the peripheral casualties of this culture.

As a dramatist, Wilde inherited the theatrical genres of the mid nineteenth century which had been developed and dominated by the likes of Arthur Wing Pinero, Henry Arthur Jones and Sydney Grundy. They had been particularly influential in popularizing melodrama and the drama of the 'woman with a past'. These hugely successful plays sated the audience's hunger for exposés of the lives of the rich and famous, with chorus girls infiltrating the salons of Belgravia and adulterous wives leaving the comforts of Little Puddleton for the casinos of Monte Carlo; they are the nineteenth-century ancestors of glossy sex-and-satin soaps like *Dynasty* and *Savannah*. Joan Crawford-types with past lives as bigamists, prostitutes and adulterers attempt surreptitiously to re-enter the society which has ostracized them. These transgressive women are always exposed and the status quo is usually re-established. The most popular and influential melodramas of the time end in retribution: the outsiders are caught, exposed and ultimately controlled by their betters, who are always, of course, men. The second Mrs Tanqueray famously commits suicide, Lady Audley is incarcerated in a lunatic asylum and Isabel Vane is reduced to acting as governess to the sickly child she has abandoned: 'Dead! Dead! And never called me mother!'[6]

Wilde's individuality, in contrast to his largely forgotten contemporaries, exhibits itself in his manipulation of these inherited genres. He retains the paraphernalia of melodrama such as overheard conversations, lost gloves, fans and handbags, as well as retaining the focal figure, the 'woman with a past'. Superficially, Wilde individualized the melodrama by marrying it with the language, paradoxes and speech rhythms of comedy. He later claimed that he had poeticized the drama, making of it 'as personal a mode of expression as the lyric or the sonnet',[7] but he underestimates his achievement: by centring on the dilemma of the sinner rather than the preacher and by choosing to leave his plays with uneasy endings which slyly undermine the status quo, Wilde had taken the Victorian melodrama and radicalized it. Like Chekhov, Wilde was interested in exploring the fate of individuals living with dilemmas, rather than happily resolving them. His plays end with uncomfortable conformity or self-imposed exile, never the security of 'happily ever after'.

Wilde had started writing for the stage as a rather excessive tragedian and ended his theatrical career as the author of one of the most original comedies in world literature. His development as a writer from tragedy to comedy is the ironic reverse of his own almost classical fall from celebrity to infamy. His earliest completed experiments with tragedy are all historical. *Salomé* is an extraordinary extravaganza of lust in the biblical dust, where obsession results in death: 'much lovely writing,' Max Beerbohm noted, 'I almost wonder that Oscar doesn't dramatize it.'[8] *Vera or The Nihilists* is a turgid tale of politics and passion in Imperial Russia, whilst *The Duchess of Padua* is a Browning-esque verse tragedy with some hefty thefts from Shakespeare and Webster. Stylistically, Wilde's next four plays completely depart from these early experiments; they are (broadly) society comedies and all have a modern setting. In *Lady Windermere's Fan*, *An Ideal Husband* and *A Woman of No Importance* Wilde developed his own particular genre, the contemporary comic melodrama of morals, which culminates in *The Importance of Being Earnest*. *The Importance* is both the greatest refinement of Wilde's developing style as well as a complete innovation. He radically departs from the plot structure of his earlier work and rejects the emotionalism of melodrama. The woman with a past is passed over in favour of the dandy. But Wilde consciously retains the crazy paraphernalia of melodrama, such as lost handbags and incriminating cigarette cases, thus exaggerating their absurdity as theatrical devices. *The Importance of Being Earnest* represents a genre all of its own; the first, and last, of its particular type.

Serious comedy, trivial people

In his comic melodramas, Wilde explores society through a series of antitheses. *Lady Windermere's Fan*, *An Ideal Husband* and *A Woman of No Importance* all revolve around the dilemma of a socially vulnerable individual attempting to conceal a sin that they have committed in the past. The protagonist is then challenged by a champion of puritanism. The mechanics of the plot now seal the protagonist's fate, whether he or she is to be exiled from society or reconciled to it. Throughout his work Wilde introduces us into a very exclusive and insular world. The incestuousness of this social clique is emphasized in several ways. Character names like Lady Stutfield, Lady Windermere or Mr Cardew turn up, or are mentioned, in different plays or stories. Even place-names recur in different texts: Selby is the country home of the Windermeres and also of Dorian Gray. And like a late nineteenth-century School for Scandal, Wilde convinces us of the reality of this society by constant reference to the reputations of characters who never actually appear. In the tradition of the Morality play or Restoration comedy, particular character types resurface in each of the plays: the woman with a past, the witty *femme fatale*, the dandy, the puritan and the draconian dowager. Mrs Arbuthnot and Mrs Erlynne have lived with the consequences of their past sins in very different ways, but ultimately both chose self-imposed exile. The *femme fatales* – Mrs Allonby and the blackmailing Mrs Cheveley – both look scandalous but behave just within society's bounds of tolerance. The wits and dandies – Lord Goring, Lord Illingworth and Algernon Moncrieff – could easily be imagined leaving the fictional boundaries of their respective plays and meeting up to dine at Willis's restaurant. The puritan wife in *An Ideal Husband* talks like the elder sister of the puritan Lady Windermere, and both seem close cousins of the American heiress in *A Woman of No Importance*. The morals and conventions of this society are defined and regulated by women. Society *grandes dames* such as the Duchess of Berwick (*Lady Windermere's Fan*) and Lady Hunstanton (*A Woman of No Importance*) betray the ingrained hypocrisy of their set in deploring the behaviour of 'bad' women yet continuing to dupe their own ignorant husbands. These women reach their apotheosis in Lady Bracknell, whose moral sense is arbitrary, fickle and opportunistic.

As well as sharing character traits true to type, the natives of this refined world share a specific language. This is a highly artificial, self-conscious style characterized by witty allusions, balanced sentences and sharp turns of phrase. The very rhythms of this language are alien to naturalistic speech. Everybody is practised at the sort of epigrammatic sallies which had established Wilde himself as one of the most sought-after guests in society. The *Daily Telegraph*, reviewing the première of *Lady Windermere's Fan*, noted that 'the author peoples his play with male and female editions of himself'.[9] Many critics referred to Wilde's characters as puppets, and to his art as little more than an extensive ventriloquism. But Wilde unashamedly harnessed multiple personalities to expound his philosophy: 'to arrive at what one really believes, one must speak through lips different from one's own'.[10] There is a sense of *déjà vu* about Wilde's works: we feel as if we have heard certain passages before. And indeed we have, for Wilde promiscuously lifts dialogue from earlier works and transposes it elsewhere. If Lord Illingworth in *A Woman of No Importance* sounds rather like Algy in *The Importance of Being Earnest* it is because they share many of the same speeches.* And if many of the characters sound alike, it's only because they all sound like Oscar. Yeats recalled his first, vivid impression of Wilde's mastery of conversation;

> the impression of artificiality that I think all Wilde's listeners have recorded came from the perfect rounding of the sentences and from the deliberation that made it possible. That very impression helped him, as the effect of metre, or of the antithetical prose of the seventeenth century, which is itself a true metre, helped its writers, for he could pass without incongruity from some unforeseen, swift stroke of wit to elaborate reverie.[11]

Dialogue is the core of Wilde's art. He himself observed that 'by its means [the artist] can both reveal and conceal himself'.[12] Significantly, some of Wilde's most important essays on art and aesthetics are also written as discussions; in the 1970s, *The Critic as Artist* was even staged by the experimental director/writer Charles Marowitz.[13]

The artist of conversation is the dandy. The dandies in his plays are often surrogate Wilde figures, waxing lyrical on art, beauty and leisure. Their stylized language has its origin in Wilde's own idiosyncratic voice. In examining Wilde's metamorphosis from the aesthete of the 1880s to the dandy of the 1890s, Alan Sinfield observes that the effeminacy of the dandy was not necessarily taken as an indication of their homosexuality. Rather their effeteness was associated with the leisure and wealth of the upper classes and was perceived to be carrying on an upper-class tradition. Though they seem extraordinarily camp to us, Wilde's dandies are, generally speaking, philanderers in pursuit of women. Sinfield notes how Wilde exploits the ambiguity of the dandy, the 'dissolute aristocrat [who] might indulge in any kind of debauchery; so while same-sex pas-

---

*LORD ILLINGWORTH All women become like their mothers. That is their tragedy.
MRS ALLONBY   No man does. That is his.
                            (*A Woman of No Importance*, Act II, *CW*, p. 487)
ALGERNON   All women become like their mothers. That is their tragedy.
                    No man does. That's his.
                           (*The Importance of Being Earnest*, Act I, *CW*, p. 371)

sion was not ruled in, neither was it ruled out'.[14] It's exactly the same sort of dangerous ambiguity that Coward exploits in his comedies of sexual licence. The plot of *The Importance of Being Earnest* clearly revolves around the attempts of the dandies Jack/Ernest and Algy to secure the hands of Gwendolen and Cecily, but it also explores their ambiguous double lives. Jack has invented for those in his country life a 'wicked' younger brother called Ernest and Algy has conjured up an invalid called Bunbury, creations who give them the excuses/freedom to live their double lives. Ironically, Jack/Ernest is Jack in the country where he has family responsibilities (earnest/sincere/straight) and Ernest in town where he is single (Jack-the-lad/duplicitous/?gay).

Wilde had adopted dandyism as a philosophy via the decadent French poet Baudelaire, who had already promoted it as a religion:

> Dandyism is not, as many unreflecting persons seem to think, an immoderate taste for dress and material elegance. These things are for the perfect dandy only a symbol of the aristocratic superiority of his spirit, the ardent need to produce something original ... it is a kind of religion of the self.[15]

Like our contemporary gay subculture, dandyism is not simply an affectation of styles and tastes, it is a 'sensibility', an attitude to life. The dandy is hostile towards the society he subversively inhabits. Like Wilde, the dandies of his plays are invited to society functions because of their wit, even though this wit can often be dangerous. The dandy formulates and lives by his own moral standards. His culture is the cult of the self and his creed is that of individualism. For the conventions of society, which are the mores of the herd, the dandy has nothing but contempt. Despite suffering at the hands of the herd for his attempt to live by his own moral code, Wilde remained unrepentant, even in the uncomfortable surroundings of Reading Gaol: 'I am far more of an individualist than I was. Nothing seems to me of the smallest value except what one gets out of oneself. My nature is seeking a fresh mode of realisation. That is all I am concerned with.'[16] The dandies in Wilde's plays generally play a choric role, commenting on the crises of the protagonists. When they are required to take an active role in the story, they become gelded as dandies. Lord Darlington starts off as the typical acerbic observer of Lady Windermere's marital problems, but when he becomes her potential lover, he is silenced and his objective role is fulfilled by Cecil Graham who takes no part in her ladyship's dilemma. The sexually ambiguous Lord Goring in *An Ideal Husband* significantly resists marital 'capture' by both Mrs Cheveley and Mabel Chiltern until the Chilterns' crisis is resolved and the curtain is about to fall. We never see him perform as a successful fiancé.

The quintessence of Wildism

Lady Windermere's Fan was premièred in 1892, the same year as Shaw's *Widowers' Houses*, Ibsen's *Ghosts* and *Hedda Gabler*. In *The Quintessence of Ibsenism* (1891) Shaw had used the phrase an 'ideal husband' several times. Wilde claimed he read Shaw's treatise often and eventually adopted the phrase as a title for his political drama four years later. All three dramatists explored the position of women as a way of exposing the wider hypocrisy of society. Wilde had been exposed to Victorian feminism from an early age through his mother, who wrote under the name 'Speranza'. Her work continued to be published in the 1880s and she vehemently espoused a romantic feminism heavily influenced by female images from Celtic mythology. Her writings idealize women as priestesses and queens, like H. Rider Haggard's *She-Who-Must-Be-Obeyed*. In 1887, Wilde had been offered the position of editor of a new women's magazine called *Lady's World*. He thought the title had 'a certain taint of vulgarity about it' and insisted to Cassell, the publishers, that it was not suitable for 'a magazine that aims at being the organ of women of intellect, culture and position'.[17] Cassell accepted Wilde's point and he accepted the editorship. The first issue with Wilde as editor was renamed *Woman's World*. Wilde's assistant editor emphasized that the keynote of the new-look magazine was 'the right of woman to equality of treatment with man' and the presentation of 'women who had gained high position by virtue of their skill as writers or workers in the world's great field of labour'.[18] Within a few short months Wilde had turned the magazine into a late nineteenth-century equivalent of *Cosmopolitan* or *Elle*.

Wilde's commitment to feminism reverberates not only in his journalistic writing, but throughout his plays and stories. Anticipating Terence Rattigan, Wilde distinguishes between two different types of love in his work. One is masculine love, objective and rational, the other is feminine love, steadfast, subjective and all-consuming.

> So I think
> That it is woman's mission by their love
> To save the souls of men.[19]
>
> Women are the best artists of the world,
> For they can take the common lives of men
> Soiled with the money-getting of our age,
> And with love make them beautiful.[20]

The love of Wilde's women is spiritual, almost mystic, their lives revolve 'in curves of emotions'. Wilde's men, on the other hand, love women in spite of their 'weaknesses, their follies, their imperfections'.[21] The plays attempt to reconcile these two types of love by examining the representatives of the mutation of this female/idealistic male/realistic dichotomy: the woman who expresses a male idea of love. This male love is 'wider, larger, more human than a woman's'[22] and embraces weakness. At its heart, this love is Christian: 'It is not the perfect', Sir Robert Chiltern warns his wife, 'but the imperfect who have need of love.'[23] This male sentiment is a reiteration of the Duchess of Padua's self-defence:

> Sure it is the guilty,
> Who, being very wretched, need love most.[24]

Though Wilde positions women at the centre of society – 'No man has any real success in this world unless he has got women to back him, and women rule society'[25] – he is very aware that women are also more vulnerable to the force of society's disapproval and more likely to be penalized, by other women, for falling foul of society's code of ethics.

The concern in the late nineteenth century with the position of women and the growth of feminism was given voice in the work of the iconoclastic Scandinavian playwright, Henrik Ibsen. Dilemmas surrounding paternity, maternity and the notion of inheritance are explored by Ibsen in *Ghosts* and *A Doll's House*, issues which are also central to *Lady Windermere's Fan* and *A Woman of No Importance*. Can we escape the 'sins of the fathers'? Will Osvald suffer from the sexual excesses of Captain Alving? Will Lady Windermere desert her child as her mother had abandoned her? The theme is explored in a comic vein in *The Importance of Being Earnest*, where Jack leads an invented double life – 'Ernest in town and Jack in the country' – but as an orphan, he actually has no real history to inherit. Wilde exploits the tradition of mistaken identity, a mainstay of Victorian farce and complicates it by introducing the tradition of the foundling popularized in Victorian melodrama. After a life of juggling his assumed identity with the one he has consciously invented, Jack eventually traces his genuine history via a misplaced handbag. The search for his genuine identity requires answers to a series of fundamental questions: What is my name? Where am I from? What is my class? How do I reconcile the diverse fragments of my character? Essentially, the play demands an answer to the question, Who am I?

As well as this examination of identity, the search for immediate ancestry involves a questioning of the ways in which we define our social and moral status. The notion of self-identity, of what makes an ideal spouse and a 'good' person, as well as a 'bad' one, is central to Wilde's three society comedies. The impossible demands of the ideal compared to the actual flaws of reality resonate throughout Wilde's work. Both Gwendolen and Cecily have adopted an absurd ideal of marrying a man called Ernest, which they adhere to quite irrationally: 'my ideal has always been to love someone of the name of Ernest. There is something in that name that inspires absolute confidence.'[26] Gwendolen and Cecily's ideal is a comic debunking of the ideal and the romantic. Love, money or duty, the solid Victorian reasons for marriage in Wildean society, are not a consideration in the world of *The Importance of Being Earnest*. Wilde had previously warned of the dangers of idealism in *An Ideal Husband*: 'Women think they are making ideals of men. What they are making of us are false idols merely.'[27] The notion of living with exclusive ideal standards is exposed as ridiculous in the comedy and dangerous in the melodrama.

Wilde undermines the image of the ideal Victorian wife, the 'angel in the house', in his exploration of the transgressive woman, the Magdalen figure. For Salomé, the Duchess of Padua, Mrs Erlynne and Mrs Arbuthnot, the force of sexual desire destabilizes the bonds of maternal, filial and marital love:

We are all animals at best, and love
Is merely passion with a holy name.[28]

These women risk security, their families and their social position for an attempt at sexual fulfilment. They take a trip on 'that rattle-trap streetcar' because, as Stella Kowalski observes, 'there are things that happen between a man and a woman in the dark that sort of make everything else – unimportant'.[29]

But the willingness to submit to desire felt by Wilde's women is complicated by his preoccupation with a sense of sin. Hester Collyer's sense of responsibility in Rattigan's *The Deep Blue Sea* is very Anglican; she doesn't feel the same sort of moral shame that Mrs Arbuthnot experiences in *A Woman of No Importance*. Sin, guilt, shame and the attendant burdens of Catholicism haunt Wilde's work just as they haunted his life. Wilde's mother had insisted that he and his brother be baptized as Catholic, much against his father's wishes, and though the Wildes were not actually brought up Catholic, the romance and traditions of the Catholic Church fascinated Wilde. He flirted with Catholicism throughout his life and finally underwent a 'proper' deathbed conversion, claiming that the Church of Rome was 'the only religion to die in'.[30] The characters in Wilde's plays who commit social misdemeanours or practise political deceptions insist on describing their folly in terms of sin or moral wrong, rather than as social crimes. For, as James Joyce observed, Wilde's creations are enthralled by a creed of beauty which 'at its very base is the truth inherent in the soul of Catholicism: that man cannot reach the divine except through the sense of separation and loss called sin'.[31] Wilde's living purgatory in Reading Gaol fuelled his own identification with the sufferings of Christ, which continued to the end of his life. Compared to the very English and specifically Anglican vision of Somerset Maugham and Rattigan, where sexual transgression is regarded as a social rather than a moral crime, Wilde's vision is Catholic, Irish and foreign. In his universe, sexual aberration burdens the sinner with guilt and shame, but such a universe also offers the possibility of mercy, forgiveness and absolution.

Lady Windermere's Fan: a play about a good woman

> Love is fed by the imagination, by which we become wiser than we know, better than we feel, nobler than we are: by which we can see Life as a whole: by which, and by which alone, we can understand others in their real as in their ideal relations.[32]

Wilde had originally entitled his first modern play *A Good Woman*, but blind to the irony of the title, his mother insisted that nobody would be interested in a creature as dull as that. Wilde might well have been influenced by the uproar that Thomas Hardy had provoked just a year before with his subtitle for *Tess of the D'Urbervilles*, 'A Pure Woman'. When it was finally published, the play was given the composite title, *Lady Windermere's Fan, A Play about a Good Woman*, for the application of conventional moral standards and the assessment of the moral status of others judged by their actions is the real focus of the play, rather than the erratic career of the heroine's ballroom accessory.

The play marks the beginning of Wilde's exploration of the relationship between the ideal and reality in contemporary life. The puritan Lady Windermere idealizes her 'model' husband as the epitome of virtue. She also idealizes the memory of her dead mother: '*She* allowed of no compromise. *I* allow of none.'[33] Whilst attempting to pursue her, Lord Darlington asks if Lady Windermere seriously thinks that 'women who have committed what the world calls a fault should never be forgiven?' Never, she replies. When her ideals are threatened, Lady Windermere's world collapses. Lord Windermere is rumoured to be having an affair with a Mrs Erlynne, whom he insists on inviting to Lady Windermere's coming-of-age party that evening. Lady Windermere is about to attain majority, to assume the responsibilities of maturity. Her crisis in the play represents her passage from ignorance to knowledge, from immaturity to maturity, from high-mindedness to generosity. Mrs Erlynne had committed a social fault years previously and is currently attempting to re-enter society. Windermere tries to persuade his wife to be generous to this fallen woman: 'Misfortunes one can endure – they come from outside, they are accidents. But to suffer for one's own faults – ah! There is the sting of life.'[34] Unable to prevent Mrs Erlynne from attending the party, Lady Windermere plans to strike her with her new fan, a birthday gift from Windermere, specially inscribed with his wife's name. Now Lady Windermere plans to soil this gift of love by using it in an act of public humiliation. From here on, the fan is to accumulate symbolic resonances whenever it appears. Fans are women's intimate possessions, behind which they gossip and protect (or hide) their faces. Since the Restoration the fan, like the mask, has been a symbol of sexual provocation.

At the party Lady Windermere merely drops the fan as she snubs Mrs

Erlynne. Humiliated by the presence of this apparently bad woman, Lady Windermere is persuaded to elope with Lord Darlington, who significantly picks up the fan and returns it to its owner. Darlington prevails with Lady Windermere by sketching a picture of her future, living as she would be with the charade of her husband's other life:

LORD DARLINGTON   What sort of life would you have with him? You would feel that he was lying to you every moment of the day. You would feel that the look in his eyes was false, his voice false, his touch false, his passion false. He would come to you when he was weary of others; you would have to comfort him. He would come to you when he was devoted to others; you would have to charm him. You would have to be to him the mask of his real life, the cloak to hide his secret.[35]

Like the painfully named Constance Wilde and Syrie Maugham, Lady Windermere is to become her husband's Bunbury. Windermere's other life is discussed in terms of Dorian Gray's mysterious, unnameable vices. But refusing to become the cloak to hide the secrets of a philandering husband, Lady Windermere prepares to abandon her child and elope with Lord Darlington. However, she has been too hasty in judging her husband's intentions and in condemning Mrs Erlynne by her reputation alone. It turns out that Mrs Erlynne is actually Lady Windermere's mother, who twenty years ago left her husband and child for another man. Just as Mrs Alving recognizes the ghosts of her husband and his mistress when she spies his children making love, Mrs Erlynne is haunted by her own mistakes. Determined that history will not repeat itself, she resolves to stop her daughter's elopement. She follows Lady Windermere to Darlington's rooms and pleads with her for her child's sake to return to Windermere, 'even if he had a thousand loves'. The women are interrupted by the arrival of a party of men including Windermere, Darlington and Mrs Erlynne's fiancé, Lord Augustus. When Lady Windermere's fan is discovered in Darlington's room and the men begin to speculate on the relationship between its owner and Darlington, it looks as if Lady Windermere is to be discovered, but Mrs Erlynne melodramatically reveals herself and claims the fan, thereby covering the unseen exit of her daughter. Mrs Erlynne uses the fan as a cloak to hide/protect her daughter's secret.

The next day, Mrs Erlynne visits Lady Windermere to return the fan. Having witnessed her presence in Darlington's rooms and deduced the worst, Lord Windermere now denounces Mrs Erlynne's apparent immorality, and is at a loss to understand his wife's change in attitude towards her. Mrs Erlynne asks for a photograph of Lady Windermere and her son as a memento, and whether she would be willing to give her the fan as a present. It is engraved with Lady Windermere's name, Margaret, which is also Mrs Erlynne's Christian name. The two women are much more alike than it had first appeared; the fan, a symbol of deception, now unites them as they deceive Windermere. Mrs Erlynne, once accused of adultery with Windermere, now inherits the fan which had been a gift of love to his wife. Windermere himself now regards the fan as 'soiled' by Mrs Erlynne's apparent dissoluteness. Concealing her true identity, Mrs Erlynne prefers to remain anonymous to her daughter rather than shatter the image of the ideal mother that Lady Windermere has in her heart:

MRS ERLYNNE Ideals are dangerous things. Realities are better. They wound, but they're better.[36]

Mrs Erlynne is Nora Helmer twenty years after slamming the door of the Doll's House, and her daughter threatens to follow the same pattern. Like Nora, Lady Windermere is prepared to ignore the 'sacred duty' of motherhood. But Mrs Erlynne is more conventional than Nora and having suffered the loss of her own child persuades Lady Windermere that whatever happens her place is with her offspring. Ibsen wrote of Nora: 'Weighted down and confused by her trust in authority, she loses her faith in her own morality, and in her fitness to bring up her children'.[37] This sense of moral confusion, instigated by the undermining of Nora's trust in her husband, is common to several of Wilde's heroines: 'We make gods of men and they leave us', Lady Windermere cries.[38] In *An Ideal Husband*, Lady Chiltern is mortified to discover that her husband is neither an ideal husband nor an ideal man: 'And how I worshipped you! You were to me something apart from common life, a thing pure, noble, honest, without stain. ... And now – oh, when I think that I made of a man like you my ideal!'[39] Wilde warns us not to canonize people as absolutely good or ideal, as human frailty will always disappoint us. Lady Chiltern's pragmatic sister-in-law Mabel decides to marry the unreliable, sexually ambiguous Lord Goring, but does so knowing all his faults. She rejects the myth of an ideal couple, preferring rather the chance to be a 'real wife'.

Both Lady Windermere and Lady Chiltern find themselves in compromising positions during their respective crises and experience the temptation and guilt of the transgressor. They learn not to be judgemental, but to tolerate the aberrations and idiosyncrasies of others. We are not necessarily the 'deed's creature'. Wilde's thesis is certainly liberal and basically Christian, but aimed at the hypocrisy of secular modern society: 'Let he who is without sin cast the first stone'. His advocation of tolerance is married to his creed of individualism:

> Those who have seen *Lady Windermere's Fan* will see that if there is one particular doctrine contained in it, it is that of sheer individualism. It is not for anyone to censure what anyone else does, and everyone should go his own way, to whatever place he chooses, in exactly the way he chooses.[40]

Wilde's creed of individualism invites us to question established mores and social conventions, particularly those that condition the treatment of women. Mrs Erlynne has transgressed society's rules, but in this social world men's infidelity is condoned: 'there is hardly a husband in London who does not waste his life over *some* shameful passion'.[41] Wilde had previously condemned the injustice of this double standard in his journalism and now proceeded to harness the argument for gender equality as part of his philosophy of absolute licence: 'It is indeed a burning shame that there should be one law for men and another law for women, I think there should be no law for anybody.'

Wilde advocates a society beyond the Utopian vision where each individual lives in harmonious equality; he promotes the surely impractical ideal of a society where individuals define the law for themselves. But a community of individuals who live by their own separate codes of behaviour is not a society. The values and regulations of society are an imposition and they restrain natural feeling. But society lives by self-imposed rules determined by common consent, and the majority are prepared to defend such regulations, fearing the chaos of a world without them. Nora's impulse is a Wildean struggle towards personal freedom: 'I must try to satisfy myself which is right, society or I.'[42] But Mrs Erlynne and Lady Windermere leave one doll's house only to replace it with a different type of restraint: another man. Once Lady Windermere's secure belief in her husband's standards is undermined, Lord Darlington is able to tempt her with the fulfilment of her natural impulses. Darlington advocates a precarious philosophy of risk, to succumb to passion: 'there are moments when one has to choose between living one's own ' fe, fully, entirely, completely – or dragging out some false, shallow, degrading existence that the world in its hypocrisy demands'.[43] This is the uncompromising belief of the true individualist. But Darlington is aware that for women, individualism may lead to the isolated life of the ostracized and the exiled. The reputation of Lord Illingworth in *A Woman of No Importance* is notorious, but he is still invited to society functions; Mrs Erlynne is not. Men like Darlington don't have to worry about social ostracism because their gender, wealth, birth and influence brand them with a sort of diplomatic immunity in a society where titles and money are premium currency. Mrs Erlynne has actually experienced such a life of alienation and is now desperate to return to the fold. She has attempted to live the full, entire and complete life outside society that Darlington advocates, but she paints a rather bleak picture of such an existence:

> You don't know what it is to fall into the pit, to be despised, mocked, abandoned, sneered at – to be an outcast! To find the door shut against one, to have to creep in by hideous byways, afraid every moment lest the mask should be stripped from one's face, and all the while to hear the laughter, the horrible laughter of the world, a thing more tragic than all the tears the world has ever shed. You don't know what it is. One pays for one's sin, and then one pays again, and all one's life one pays.[44]

Having succumbed to her own individualistic impulses twenty years before, Mrs Erlynne now convinces her daughter not to follow the same path. Despite claiming no maternal feelings herself, she persuades Lady Windermere to conform to hers by stressing her responsibility to her child. Mrs Erlynne has borne the loss of her daughter and has suppressed her maternal feelings: 'I have no ambition to play the part of a

mother'.[45] She regards motherhood as an assumed role rather than a natural impulse, and, like Ibsen's Nora, she has been able to divorce her
maternal responsibilities from her identity as a woman. She feels the
impulse of maternity only once, when she sacrifices her reputation in
order to protect her daughter's, but she finds that such an emotional role
doesn't suit her. She begs her daughter to conform to the role of demure
wife and mother, convinced as she is that Lady Windermere hasn't 'the
kind of brain that enables a woman to get back'.

The ending of the play is not the familiar one of disclosure and the
reaffirmation of the status quo usual in comedy. Rather, the conclusion
is one of half-truths and continued concealments, which Wilde implies
are necessary if 'civilized' life is to continue. Lady Windermere now
believes that her initial perception of Mrs Erlynne was wrong. By her
act of self-sacrifice in an effort to save Lady Windermere's reputation
and her marriage, Mrs Erlynne has proved herself to be a 'very good
woman'. But the security of her reputation and her marriage is maintained by an act of deception to which Mrs Erlynne is a willing accessory. Lady Windermere has undergone a moral metamorphosis. Having
been tempted by Darlington, she has realized her own frailty and gained
knowledge; her education is straight out of Genesis. She and Windermere will go to the Edenic garden of their country estate where the roses
are symbolically both white and red. Lady Windermere has certainly
become more tolerant and less judgemental than her previous puritanism would allow:

> There is the same world for all of us, and good and evil, sin and in-
> nocence, go through it hand in hand. To shut one's eyes to half of life
> that one may live securely is as though one blinded oneself that one
> might walk with more safety in a land of pit and precipice.[46]

But unbeknown to her, she is only permitted to see 'half of life'. Denied
the knowledge that Mrs Erlynne is her mother, she instead retains the
idealized image of her mother that has been the touchstone of her life,
but which Mrs Erlynne warns her is 'dangerous'. Her belief in her husband's fidelity is also reconfirmed: 'I will trust you absolutely'. The ideals
she held at the beginning of the play have almost entirely been re-established, despite the fact that the action of the play has undermined them.

Lord Windermere is likewise only partially aware at the end of the play, having no idea that his wife attempted to elope and abandon her child only the night before. His attitude towards Mrs Erlynne is now very priggish; God help Lady Windermere if she actually had run away or if she ever intends to do so: she would find no sympathy here, for Windermere's is only a qualified tolerance. He also claims to know Mrs Erlynne 'thoroughly', to which she enigmatically replies, 'I question that.' The dialogue echoes the exchange between the Windermeres in the first act, when Lady Windermere had threatened to strike Mrs Erlynne with the fan:

LADY WINDERMERE   If that woman crosses my threshold, I shall strike
                 her across the face with it.
LORD WINDERMERE   Margaret, you couldn't do such a thing.
LADY WINDERMERE   You don't know me![47]

Absolute knowledge is denied to the Windermeres. They know themselves and each other only slightly better at the end of the play than they did at the beginning. They will continue their married life in a state of partial ignorance: Windermere hiding the fact that Mrs Erlynne was found in a compromising position in Darlington's rooms, as well as her blood relationship to his wife, and Lady Windermere concealing her attempted elopement. Mrs Erlynne lies to Lord Augustus about her presence in Darlington's rooms, he appears to accept her story and proposes to her again. Her only condition for the marriage is that they exile themselves from England. Mrs Erlynne's initial ambition, to re-enter society, has now been thwarted by her own choice. Both Lady Windermere's and Mrs Erlynne's marriages and the society they inhabit will prosper on a foundation of carefully concealed secrets and half-truths. Though the play succeeds in privately subverting definitions of truth and goodness, the established public proprieties are preserved and the reigning values of society are upheld. Lady Windermere and Mrs Erlynne have tested the conventional social mores, but have not actually succeeded in changing them; they have only succeeded in cheating them.

A Woman of No Importance: a play about a good woman and a bad man:

We call a man a criminal, not because he violates the eternal code of morality – for there exists no such thing, but because he violates the ruling codes of the day.

Edward Carpenter [48]

The story has no plot and very few highlights, but it may show the bitter cruelty of self-righteous human beings who forget that Christ said 'Suffer the Children to come unto me' and base their religion on the Old Testament pronouncement that 'the sins of the fathers shall be visited upon the children, even unto the third and fourth generation'.

Vyvyan Holland[49]

Like *Lady Windermere's Fan*, *A Woman of No Importance* is an examination of the recriminations of a mother's past sexual 'sin' on the present, only this time the focus of the plot is a son rather than a daughter. Possibly because of its ill-defined genre, which veers from Shavian debate to full-blooded melodrama, *A Woman of No Importance* is the least frequently revived of Wilde's society comedies. Very little 'plot' is explored for most of the first three acts, which are given over to a series of discussions about the inequality of the positions of men and women in society. Wilde thought the first act perfect because it had no action at all.

Lady Hunstanton is hosting a select weekend party at her country house, Hunstanton Chase. As well as Lady Caroline Pontefract, the witty Mrs Allonby and the dim-witted Lady Stutfield, she has invited the ill-reputed Lord Illingworth and the American heiress Hester Worsley. Hester is an opinionated young puritan who insists on the punishment of 'sinful' women. Like the arch-bitch Madame de Merteuil in *Les Liaisons Dangereuses*, Mrs Allonby challenges Lord Illingworth to seduce Hester Worsley; the rakish Lord is only too keen to accept the challenge. Lord Illingworth is cultivating a young man called Gerald Arbuthnot, who is currently paying attentions to the puritanical Hester. Gerald's mother also lives in the neighbourhood but rarely takes part in society. Illingworth has asked Gerald to become his secretary, but when Mrs Arbuthnot arrives, she begs her son to refuse. It transpires that Mrs Arbuthnot had been Illingworth's lover twenty years before and that

45

Gerald is their illegitimate son. Illingworth is delighted when Mrs Arbuthnot reveals the truth to him. Intent on severing the relationship between Gerald and Illingworth, Mrs Arbuthnot tells her son the story of Illingworth's betrayal of a young woman, but is careful not to identify herself as the fallen woman of her tale, now realizing that she cannot persuade Gerald to give up the opportunity unless she reveals the truth.

As the second act reaches a climax, Illingworth is caught attempting to seduce Hester Worsley and Gerald threatens to kill him. Mrs Arbuthnot intervenes: 'Stop, Gerald, stop! He is your own father!'[50] Having been raised as a typical pillar of the establishment, Gerald now insists that his mother should marry Lord Illingworth to correct their fault. She is appalled and reminds him of the sacrifices she has already made on his behalf, ostracizing herself from society in order that she cause him no shame. She tells him that it is her dishonour that made him so precious to her. Hester is witness to Mrs Arbuthnot's confession and declares that 'God's law is only Love.' Hester, Gerald and Mrs Arbuthnot decide to leave England and find a world elsewhere in 'better, wiser, and less unjust lands. The world is very wide and very big.'[51]

Unlike Mrs Erlynne, who is keen to re-enter society, Mrs Arbuthnot has deliberately opted out of it and devoted herself to good causes and religion. Not out of piety but out of necessity: 'That was my mission, you imagined. It was not, but where else was I to go? . . . God's house is the only house where sinners are made welcome . . .'[52] Mrs Erlynne had discovered that she would rather remain 'childless' than suffer the burden of maternal feelings: 'I thought I had no heart. I find I have, and a heart doesn't suit me . . .'[53] Mrs Arbuthnot has taken the alternative option and filled her life with her maternal role. Keeping her son with her, she has voluntarily exiled herself from society before it has had the opportunity to ostracize her. She has never repented her sin because her much-beloved son Gerald was its fruit. Mrs Arbuthnot's devotion to Gerald is quite obsessive, with an unsettling Oedipal quality: 'you were always in my heart, Gerald, too much in my heart'.[54] Gerald is his 'mother's own boy', smothered with maternal affection. Yeats recalled that when Wilde had the opportunity to escape from England before his trial, his mother had said, 'If you stay, even if you go to prison, you will always be my son, it will make no difference to my affection, but if you go, I will never speak to you again.'[55] Lady Wilde's power over her son was such that he stayed. This ambiguous power of maternal affection is debated by Gerald and Lord Illingworth, the man who seeks to supersede Mrs Arbuthnot in Gerald's affections:

GERALD   No one ever had such a mother as I have had.
ILLINGWORTH   I am quite sure of that. Still I should imagine that most
                       mothers don't quite understand their sons. Don't rea-
                       lise, I mean, that a son has ambitions, a desire to see
                       life, to make himself a name. After all, Gerald, you
                       couldn't be expected to pass all your life in such a hole
                       as Wrockley, could you?
GERALD   Oh no! It would be dreadful!
ILLINGWORTH   A mother's love is very touching, of course, but it is
                       often curiously selfish. I mean, there is a good deal
                       of selfishness in it.
GERALD   *(slowly)* I suppose there is.[56]

Mrs Arbuthnot has raised Gerald to be a perfect gentleman, with manners and morals to match. In effect, she has brought him up to be the sort of moral pedant who will ultimately condemn her, and women like her, by his moral standards. One of the most moving scenes in the play is when Mrs Arbuthnot relates to Gerald the story of a young girl's betrayal by Illingworth, without revealing that she is actually discussing her own history: 'She suffered terribly – she suffers now. She will always suffer.'[57] If Illingworth could cause such pain to a woman, she asks, is he the sort of man Gerald should be with? Gerald replies that 'no nice girl' would have succumbed to Illingworth's desires. Winded by the simple severity of Gerald's condemnation of her, Mrs Arbuthnot immediately withdraws her objections to his employment by Lord Illingworth, recognizing for the first time that she has succeeded in raising a judgemental, puritanical prig.

The relationship between Gerald and Lord Illingworth is that 'between an elder and a younger man, when the elder has intellect and the younger man has all the joy, hope and glamour of life before him'.[58] It is the classic relationship that Wilde described in his defence of the 'love that dare not speak its name'. Illingworth tells Gerald that 'It is because I like you so much that I want you with me'. He instructs Gerald in how to dress and how to behave in society: 'you are going into a perfectly new life with me, and I want you to know how to live'.[59] Gerald is Illingworth's acolyte and many of the characters are obviously aware of the ambiguous tenor of the relationship, referring to Gerald as Illingworth's 'disciple'. Mrs Allonby observes, 'I believe he intends him to be an exact replica of himself', a very Narcissus. Ostensibly, Illingworth is keen for Gerald to become his 'private secretary', an ambiguous term then as now, and a possible euphemism for 'kept boy'. Lord Alfred Douglas's brother, Viscount Drumlanrig, had been assistant private secretary to Lord Rosebery, the Foreign Minister. In 1894, Drumlanrig died in a shooting accident. It was popularly rumoured at the time that he had killed himself because of his homosexual relationship with his employer. When discussing Gerald's future with Mrs Arbuthnot, Illingworth explains that 'The world will know him merely as my private secretary but to me he will be something very near, and very dear.'[60] The blood relationship which excuses Lord Illingworth's devotion to Gerald, on the one hand, makes it even more uneasy on the other, with its over-tones of incest. The homoeroticism of the relationship between Gerald and Lord Illingworth is very apparent and was noted (rather excessively) as early as 1907. In a letter to Duncan Grant about Beerbohm Tree's revival of the play, Lytton Strachey wrote:

> Mr Tree is a wicked lord, staying in a country house, who has made up his mind to bugger one of the guests -- a handsome young man of twenty. The handsome young man is delighted; when his mother enters, sees his Lordship and recognizes him as having copulated with her twenty years before, the result of which was – the handsome young man. She appeals to Lord Tree not to bugger his own son. He replies that that is an additional reason for doing so (oh he is a very wicked lord!). She then appeals to the handsome young man, who says, 'Dear me! What an abominable thing to do – to go and copulate without marrying! Oh no, I shall certainly pay no attention to anyone capable of doing that,'... [61]

Having discussed the virtues of women in the first act, the second is given over to a debate about the ideal man; the very notion of the ideal husband is summarily dismissed: 'There couldn't be such a thing. The institution is wrong.' Hester Worsley is shocked by the hypocrisy and corruption of English society as described and enjoyed by the other women at Hunstanton Chase. She attacks their lack of spiritual values and moral standards:

With all your pomp and wealth and art you don't know how to live . . .
you know nothing. You have lost life's secret. Oh, your English society seems to me shallow, selfish, foolish. It has blinded its eyes, and
stopped its ears. It lies like a leper in purple. It sits like a dead thing
smeared with gold. It is all wrong, all wrong.[62]

Hester's blistering condemnation of English society barely makes an
impression on her audience, but just as she continues to condemn
women who have sinned, Mrs Arbuthnot enters. Hester holds to a naive
and uncompromising puritanism, but at least she demands that if sinners are to be punished, men and women should be punished equally:

If a man and a woman have sinned, let them both go forth into the
desert to love or loathe each other there. Let them both be branded.
Set a mark, if you wish, on each, but don't punish the one and let the
other go free. Don't have one law for men and another for women.
You are unjust to women in England.[63]

But her words fall on deaf ears and Lady Caroline diffuses Hester's passionate speech with triviality: 'Might I, dear Miss Worsley, as you are
standing up, ask you for my cotton that is just behind you?'[64]

Mrs Arbuthnot has ostracized herself from society because of her
own sense of sinfulness, but paradoxically she is publicly believed to
be a 'good' woman: 'Mrs Arbuthnot doesn't know anything about the
wicked society in which we all live. She won't go into it. She is far too
good.'[65] As in *Lady Windermere's Fan*, Wilde subverts the conventional
meaning of the word 'good' in applying it to the fallen Mrs Arbuthnot.
Mrs Arbuthnot's sitting-room resembles that of a 'sweet saint' rather
than the sinner she is. Mrs Alving shocks Pastor Manders in *Ghosts* with
her reading of progressive books, but Mrs Arbuthnot has 'books that
don't shock one, pictures that one can look at without blushing.'[66] She
is not progressive; if anything, her past transgression has prompted her
to cling to conservatism. Mrs Erlynne is witty, vivacious and metropolitan. In comparison, Mrs Arbuthnot seems absurdly reclusive and provincial, even dull. It is the wicked Mrs Allonby, Wilde's female dandy,
rather than Mrs Arbuthnot who seems to share Mrs Erlynne's individualist philosophy of life. The Wildean notion of sin which haunts Mrs
Arbuthnot is a convenient method of self-policing. Sin breeds guilt,

which in turn breeds a feeling of personal shame, the badge of the outsider. Mrs Arbuthnot's assumption of society's creed of repression and guilt results in a renouncement of the values of the self.

Of all Wilde's society comedies, *A Woman of No Importance* is the most resonant with biblical references. The language of some of the speeches is nearer to the bejewelled excesses of *Salomé* than any of the other plays. Mrs Arbuthnot's fall parallels that of Eve, as she gains knowledge: 'The serpent [Illingworth?] deceived me and I did eat.' Mrs Arbuthnot gains a specifically sexual knowledge (at the annunciation the Virgin Mary claims, 'I have no knowledge of man'). Significantly, her first name is Rachel, the childless Old Testament wife of Jacob, who after many years was blessed with a single son: 'God hath taken away my reproach.' Her son Joseph turns out to be the archetypal nancy-boy and develops a give-away interest in colourful but well-cut overcoats. Like her biblical namesake, Rachel Arbuthnot's son means more to her 'than innocence'. In keeping with such biblical allusions, the action of the play begins in the Edenic garden at Hunstanton Chase, and it appears that Gerald had been conceived in Mrs Arbuthnot's father's garden. When Lord Illingworth points out to Mrs Allonby that 'The Book of Life begins with a man and a woman in a garden,' she replies that 'It ends with Revelations,' as will be the case at Lady Hunstanton's weekend party. Illingworth's seduction of Hester also takes place in the garden at Hunstanton Chase, threatening to repeat the fall of Mrs Arbuthnot twenty years before. At the end of the play, Gerald and Hester retire into the garden, which can be seen from Mrs Arbuthnot's sitting-room. So the garden can be paradisal, but also home to the serpent-like Lord Illingworth. Mrs Arbuthnot's own speeches are littered with biblical allusions and constructions, a clear indication of how she has accepted and absorbed the language of the culture that has condemned her:

MRS ARBUTHNOT We rank among the outcasts. Gerald is nameless. The sins of the parents should be visited on the children. It is God's law.[67]

But Mrs Arbuthnot has distinguished for herself between the word of God as interpreted by society and her own personal relationship to God. She has accepted that she must be judged by society's public interpretation of God's Law, rather than her own understanding of it. Consequently she is prepared for Gerald and Hester to condemn her. Gerald believes that his mother and Lord Illingworth must make public reparation for their past sin by getting married. Mrs Arbuthnot refuses to do so as it would jeopardize her personal relationship with God: 'marriage is a sacrament for those who love each other. . . . But not for my own sake will I lie to God, and in God's presence.'[68] Mrs Arbuthnot's plea is a revelation to Hester. She now recognizes that God's Law has been interpreted and mutated by society to support its own codes and regulations. Society has rejected the fundamental ethics that lie at the heart of Christianity: clemency, mercy and forgiveness:

HESTER   I was wrong. God's law is only Love.[69]

Hester invites Mrs Arbuthnot into the garden, a return to paradise. But the three must withdraw from society and exile themselves to a place that sounds not unlike the Israelites' 'land of milk and honey', a place of 'green valleys and fresh waters, and if we weep, well, we shall weep together.'[70]

Like Forster's Maurice and Scudder, the three will seek a distant, perhaps idealized greenwood beyond society. Together the three reinterpret biblical law and apply it to themselves, formulating a new kind of religion where Mrs Arbuthnot becomes a composite Magdalen/Mother/Eve. There is also the suggestion that Mrs Arbuthnot, like Christ, has assumed the sins of the world. In his apology to Mrs Arbuthnot – 'Mother, I am not worthy to receive either [Hester] or you' – Gerald echoes the words of the Catholic communion service: 'Father, I am not worthy to receive you, but only say the word and I shall be healed.' Mrs Arbuthnot, the Christ-like sinner, anticipates Wilde's interpretation of the Christ story in Reading Gaol, where he celebrates Christ both as an artist and as a criminal. For Wilde, Christ's life and philosophy revealed him as the 'most supreme of Individualists'.[71]

As in *Lady Windermere's Fan*, Wilde's ending is ambivalent. Mrs Arbuthnot is unrepentant and retains her integrity, but her sin is still condemned. She, Gerald and Hester realize that they cannot change society's mores, nor do they feel that they can live by them any more. Like Mrs Erlynne, Mrs Arbuthnot must go into exile, but in this case she is accompanied by her family, and we are left with the impression that the three will start a sort of colony with a new morality. Though she retires from a society she feels she cannot successfully fight, Mrs Arbuthnot's story doesn't end on a note of defeat. At the curtain of the first act, Lord Illingworth had recognized her handwriting as that of 'a woman of no importance'. At the end of the play, Gerald sees Lord Illingworth's glove and asks his mother to whom it belongs. To 'a man of no importance', is her reply. The cycle is complete: having been dismissed by Illingworth and the society that condones his behaviour towards her, she now dismisses them both.

An Ideal Husband: a play about a bad man

A Mask tells us more than a face.
　　Oscar Wilde, *Pen, Pencil and Poison* (1891)[72]

They thought it was a play about a bracelet. We must educate our critics – we really must educate them.
　　Oscar Wilde [73]

With the relentless exposure of contemporary sleaze scandals and increased concern about the moral example set by those in public life, *An Ideal Husband* has a very particular resonance in the 1990s. Peter Hall's hugely successful revival is currently running on Broadway and another cast performed the production simultaneously at the Old Vic in London until January 1997. The Old Vic production opened in January 1996 after an initial outing in the West End in 1992, and at the time of writing was the longest run of a Wilde play in theatre history. In Britain the play expresses the current preoccupation with declining standards and in America, the production apparently revealed a connection with the American classics which explode the 'American Dream'. Both *Cat on a Hot Tin Roof* and *All My Sons*, like Wilde's play, are exposures of success founded on bad money or dishonourable acts.

In *An Ideal Husband*, Wilde expands his examination of high society to encompass the world of politics. Sir Robert Chiltern is the successful and ambitious Under-Secretary for Foreign Affairs. He is visited, during a ball he is hosting, by the flirtatious Mrs Cheveley, recently arrived from Vienna. She attempts to blackmail him into speaking in favour of a corrupt Argentine development scheme in which she has heavily invested. During his time as secretary to the Foreign Minister, Sir Robert had written to a certain Baron Arnheim advising him to buy Suez Canal shares before the government announced their own purchase. Mrs Cheveley threatens to expose the scandal if he does not do as she asks. When the idealistic Lady Chiltern discovers her husband's plans, she insists that he must not speak in favour of the bill, for she had known Mrs Cheveley at school as a liar and a thief. Chiltern's confidant, Lord Goring, advises him to tell his wife the truth. But Chiltern is adamant that this would kill his wife's love for him. After an argument, Mrs Cheveley informs Lady Chiltern that her husband is 'fraudulent and dishonest'. Chiltern admits his past error but bitterly reproaches his wife for her idealization of him and fears that now his chances of negotiating with Mrs Cheveley will be ruined. Mrs Cheveley visits Lord Goring's house and offers to withdraw if Goring will marry her, but he refuses. Goring then reveals a lost brooch, apparently belonging to Mrs Cheveley, which he had picked up at the Chilterns' ball. It transpires that she had stolen it from his cousin ten years before.

The next day, Chiltern speaks against the Argentine scheme and is offered a Cabinet post. There is talk of his becoming Prime Minister 'some day'. But, encouraged by his wife, Chiltern intends to refuse the position and retire from public life. Lord Goring intervenes, arguing that Lady Chiltern should not be allowed to complete the destruction of her husband's career which Mrs Cheveley had initiated. She capitulates and persuades her husband to accept the post. Despite the deceitful foundations on which Chiltern's career is based, he and thousands like him will prosper. Such careers are the bedrock of the Empire.

Of all Wilde's society comedies, *An Ideal Husband* alone avoids an examination of the dilemmas of paternity or maternity, for the Chilterns are childless. They are surrounded by the trappings of wealth and opulence, yet their relationship seems tainted by a sense of loss or absence: 'God has given us a lonely house.'[74] The description of the couple develops Wilde's portrayal of the Windermeres, but is more mature and precisely etched. Wilde's focus is marriage, an intimate relationship between two people. His interest lies in how the flaws inherent in the relationship are exposed in a time of crisis. Chiltern and his wife are blind to their own imperfections and have no real knowledge of each other. Lady Chiltern has idolized Sir Robert as the model husband and the ideal man: 'I don't think you realise sufficiently, Robert, that you have brought into the political life of our time a nobler atmosphere, a finer attitude towards life, a freer air of purer aims and higher ideals – I know it, and for that I love you Robert.'[75] Lady Chiltern imagines herself married to some sort of saint. But her love for him isn't unconditional; it's dependent on his maintenance of an image of purity. Her strict moral principles cannot embrace the idea of his transgression, even if it were committed in the past, for she believes that 'One's past is what one is.' Wilde explores whether we can be defined and judged by our actions. Does the fact that Chiltern committed a bad act in the past brand him for ever as a bad man? Does it make him a lesser politician or unfit for public office? His wife certainly seems to think so:

LADY CHILTERN   You were to me something apart from common life, a thing pure, noble, honest, without stain. The world seemed to me finer because you were in it, and goodness more real because you lived. And now – oh, when I think that I made of a man like you my ideal![76]

Wilde's dilemma now is to reconcile a husband and wife who seem to be completely incompatible: the idealistic woman and the flawed man. Chiltern's political career can be easily resolved by negotiation with Mrs Cheveley. The focus of the play is the metamorphosis of Lady Chiltern's personal morality, which is the only way that the marriage can be resolved. Chiltern can't very well turn the clock back and say 'sorry'. Like Mme de Meurteuil's challenge to Valmont, the dilemma is to destroy the foundations of Lady Chiltern's deeply felt idealism and force her to restructure her personal moral beliefs so that they will embrace transgression. Instead of miraculously converting Sir Robert into a genuine ideal husband to suit Lady Chiltern's proscriptive values, Wilde alters the values of the wife to embrace the husband's sin.

Lady Chiltern, like Lady Windermere, is forced to experience the isolation of transgression during the crisis. Wanting to confide in Lord Goring, Lady Chiltern sends him a note: 'I want you. I trust you. I am coming to you.' When Mrs Cheveley lays her hands on the note, she believes it to be compromising and intends to expose Lady Chiltern to her husband. It is not the exposure of infidelity that Wilde threatens Lady Chiltern with, but the exposure of her hypocrisy: condemning her husband for a past misdemeanour whilst flouting her own moral rules. The compromising letter does reach Chiltern, but as it has not been addressed, he believes it to be a note of reconciliation from his estranged wife; the letter is open to innocent as well as compromising interpretation. Lady Chiltern realizes that all our actions are vulnerable to misinterpretation. The emergence of a compromising relationship with Lord Goring and her intention to lie about it has exposed her own frailty and forced her to accept her husband's flaws. At first, she has no intention of telling her husband the truth. Chiltern had discovered Mrs Cheveley secreted in Goring's drawing-room and assumed that they were lovers. Now Lady Chiltern must reveal that Mrs Cheveley was shown into the drawing-room by mistake, and that Goring had actually been expecting Lady Chiltern. It is only when she has to defend Goring's reputation that Lady Chiltern is forced to tell the truth. Chiltern wonders how she could believe that he would ever doubt her integrity, however compromising her note might have seemed. Lady Chiltern is prevailed upon by Lord Goring to persuade her husband to accept the Cabinet post offered to him. Her change of attitude enables the reconciliation to take place between the couple. But like a ventriloquist's dummy, Lady Chiltern repeats Lord Goring's words verbatim to her husband: 'A man's life is of more value than a woman's.' The subsequent 'new beginning' that the Chilterns foresee at the end of the play is imbued with an uncomfortable tone of insincerity.

Wilde's play was written at a time when the blackmailers were closing in on him. At the same time he was attempting to avoid involvement in the ugly family wranglings between Lord Alfred Douglas and the Marquis of Queensbury. It should be no surprise, then, that his play concentrated on a prominent man living under the threat of scandal. Though Chiltern's past crime is a political one, his life is haunted by an earlier relationship with an older man which might also have ignited a public scandal. Sir Robert once had an ambiguous relationship with Baron Arnheim. Chiltern's blackmailer, Mrs Cheveley, also had a relationship with Arnheim which had clearly been a sexual one. She implies that Chiltern's relationship with Arnheim was emotional or even sexual, for 'the same sin binds us':

SIR ROBERT	Did you know Baron Arnheim well?
MRS CHEVELEY	*(smiling)* Intimately. Did you?
SIR ROBERT	At one time.
MRS CHEVELEY	Wonderful man, wasn't he?
SIR ROBERT	*(after a pause)* He was very remarkable, in many ways.
MRS CHEVELEY	I often think it such a pity he never wrote his memoirs. They would have been most interesting.

SIR ROBERT	Yes: he knew men and cities well, like the old Greek.
MRS CHEVELEY	Without the dreadful disadvantage of having a Penelope waiting at home for him.[77]

This politely barbed scene reads like the gentle jousting of two former mistresses. Mrs Cheveley's introduction of the Baron's memoirs, and the revelations they might have contained, is intended to threaten Chiltern with the possibility of exposure. Arnheim is an unmarried Odysseus, who knew 'men and cities well', but being Greek, knew men the better. Sir Robert has laid the foundation of his fortune by selling a Cabinet secret, but his misdemeanour is discussed in terms of sin, particularly sexual sin. In his description of his relationship with Baron Arnheim, Chiltern describes him as 'a man of a most subtle and refined intellect. A man of culture, charm, and distinction' with a 'wonderfully fascinating quiet voice'. In the friendship between Arnheim and Chiltern, Wilde once again explores a relationship in which 'the elder man has intellect and the younger man has all the joy, hope and glamour of life before him'. Chiltern goes on to describe the home of his mentor, which echoes the decadent, luxurious world of Dorian Gray:

> with a strange smile on his pale, curved lips, he led me through his wonderful picture gallery, showed me his tapestries, his enamels, his jewels, his carved ivories, made me wonder at the strange loveliness of the luxury in which he lived;[78]

This is more than an attraction to home furnishings. Chiltern has been seduced by the sensuousness of Arnheim's world and possibly seduced by Arnheim himself. Wilde's stage directions for this play are unusually precise. Like Arnheim, Chiltern has decorated his house voluptuously with statues, paintings and tapestries. Wilde is particularly precise about the tapestry which dominates the first act, a copy of Boucher's *Triumph of Love*; but the play ends in the triumph not of love but of pragmatism.

When she first hears the revelations of her husband's relationship with Arnheim, Lady Chiltern believes that he has prostituted himself: 'What a mask you have been wearing all these years! A horrible painted mask! You sold yourself for money.'[79] The scandal of the homosexual brothel at Cleveland Street in 1889, which had involved aristocratic and parliamentary figures, would have been fresh in Lady Chiltern's mind. The language she uses about her husband's past crime implies that she believes that he could be vulnerable to blackmail for his part in a sex scandal:

> I know that there are men with horrible secrets in their lives – men who have done some shameful thing, and who in some critical moment have to pay for it, by doing some other act of shame – oh! Don't tell me you are such as they are![80]

Lady Chiltern fears that their marriage has merely been a cloak to hide her husband's secret life. Sir Robert confides to Lord Goring that he believes his wife would never have married him if she had been aware that his fortune and position were the fruits of his compromising relationship with Arnheim: 'I suppose most men would call [it] shameful and dishonourable?' Lord Goring agrees that society would be appalled, for though some may dare not speak its name, 'most men would call it ugly names'.[81]

All of Wilde's protagonists succeed in escaping the consequences of their actions, whether they stay put and prosper or leave for self-imposed exile. Sir Robert Chiltern is the most successful in getting away with it: his wife's idealism is tempered and he looks set to become Prime Minister at some point in the future. Significantly the women, Mrs Erlynne and Mrs Arbuthnot, both choose voluntary exile, whilst Lord Illingworth and Sir Robert Chiltern will both prosper despite their sins. Each of these protagonists challenges society's conventional mores, whilst preserving the impression that these values remain intact. In his essay, *The Decay of Lying*, Wilde had observed that 'What is interesting about people in good society. . . is the mask that each of them wears, not the reality that lies behind the mask. It is a humiliating confession, but we are all of us made of the same stuff'.[82] Lady Windermere retains her apparent innocence by deceit and Mrs Erlynne remains condemned as a 'bad' woman despite her good actions and repentance. Mrs Arbuthnot conceals her sin behind a mask of virtue. Sir Robert Chiltern continues to prosper and his wife's idealism is compromised (conveniently for him) as she becomes a knowing accessory and beneficiary of his deceit. In Wildean society, integrity, like normality, is all done with mirrors.

In their individual crises, Wilde's protagonists feel isolated from society because their desires are at odds with social behaviour. 'How alone I am in life,' exclaims Lady Windermere, 'How terribly alone!' In his work, Wilde harnessed the schizophrenic personality of the 1890s that had recently become embodied in the contemporary myth of *Dr Jekyll and Mr Hyde* (1886), a tale which seemed to express the dualities and hypocrisies of the late Victorian age. The hugely popular stage version of Stevenson's story was withdrawn by its own management in response to the Whitechapel murders of 1888, for art had uncomfortably anticipated life and now there were 'horrors enough on the streets'. But Wilde goes further than Stevenson, in that he examines the continual juggling of a double life and the lifelong assumption of the façade of virtue. A double life might serve to conceal something as trivial as a social indiscretion (as Bunbury does in *The Importance of Being Earnest*), but it can also disguise the aberrant and sinister behaviour of a Dorian Gray or a Mr Hyde.

On St Valentine's Day 1895, *The Importance of Being Earnest* joined *An Ideal Husband* in the West End. Wilde was the most celebrated playwright of his day, but his triumph was tragically short-lived. Even before his first trial, Wilde's name had been obscured by strips of paper on the hoardings outside the Haymarket and the St James's Theatre. What a curious and ignoble attempt to obliterate the man whilst continuing to benefit from his work. Obviously believing that any publicity was good publicity the management kept the plays running, naively assuming that the scandal concerning the man could be separated from his work in the minds of the public. *An Ideal Husband* was withdrawn on 27 April 1895, *The Importance* struggled on until it too closed on 8 May. At the same time Wilde's books were withdrawn from circulation. One wonders if the (presumably) predominantly straight audiences who still continue to flock to the current productions of *An Ideal Husband* in London and New York have divorced the notion of the man from his work. Or, a century late, have we finally learned the primary Wildean lesson of tolerance: 'Nobody is incapable of doing a foolish thing. Nobody is incapable of doing a wrong thing.'? Or perhaps Oscar is simply excused because he is a great, *dead* queer? After Wilde's conviction an attempt was made by the press to bury the whole sorry episode:

And so a most miserable case is ended. Lord Queensbury is triumphant and Mr Oscar Wilde is 'damned and done for'. The best thing for everyone now is to forget all about Oscar Wilde, his perpetual posings, his aesthetical teachings and his theatrical productions. Let him go into silence, and be heard no more.[83]

The press did remain silent about Wilde until the publication of *The Ballad of Reading Gaol* in 1898 and his tepid obituaries two years later. But the plays began to be revived after the turn of the century, when Victoria was dead and the scandals of the 1890s became the memories of another era. The first collected works appeared in 1908 and have since remained in print almost continually. So much for silence, Oscar.

2

Somerset Maugham, Warts and All

[His marriage to Constance Lloyd] was certainly the most immoral and perhaps the only really heartless act of Wilde's life. It can happen that a homosexual does not recognize his condition for a number of years and marries in good faith, but one cannot believe that Wilde was such an innocent . . . like normal men, many [homosexuals] long for the comfort and security of a home and the joys of having children, but to marry for such reasons is heartless. I have never seen a marriage of this kind – at least if the partners were under fifty – in which the wife, even when she knew all about her husband's tastes, did not suffer acutely.

W.H. Auden[1]

I had no illusions about you . . . I knew you were silly and frivolous and empty-headed. But I loved you. I knew that your aims and ideas were vulgar and commonplace. But I loved you. I knew that you were second-rate. But I loved you. It's comic to think how hard I tried to be amused by the things that amused you and how anxious I was to hide from you that I wasn't ignorant and vulgar and scandal-mongering and stupid. I know how frightened you were of intelligence and I did everything I could to make you think of me as big a fool as the rest of the men you know. I knew you'd only married me for convenience.

Somerset Maugham, *The Painted Veil*[2]

In June 1908, a *Punch* cartoon depicts a disgruntled William Shakespeare jealously observing the West End billboards for four of the season's new plays, *The Explorer*, *Mrs Dot*, *Jack Straw* and *Lady Frederick*. The Bard's ire is riled by neither the quality nor the originality of these plays, but by the fact that they were all written by the same hand. At the age of thirty-three W. Somerset Maugham's dramatic writings had made him rich and famous. A sometime medical student, Maugham had a handful of controversial, if not particularly successful, novels to his name by the time he began writing for the theatre in 1898. Almost a decade later in 1907 Maugham had had only one of his six full-length plays produced and theatrical success seemed to have eluded him. But fate intervened. In the autumn season of 1907 a play had unexpectedly failed at the Royal Court Theatre and the management needed something to take its place at the last minute. Maugham's agent suggested his client's 1903 comedy of manners and morals, *Lady Frederick*. The play was so successful that within a year four of Maugham's plays were running in the West End. Maugham's output continued to be prodigious throughout his life: plays, novels, travel books and the satirical short stories in which his tart talent particularly shone. But despite his popularity, Maugham very publicly gave up writing for the theatre in 1933 with his strange moral fable, *Sheppey*. The tenacious Maugham survived until the mid-1960s, uncomfortably breathing the air of a new culture completely alien to this most seasoned of Edwardian travellers. He never returned to the theatre writing which had provided him with his first great success.

E. M. Forster famously acknowledged in 'a droopy regretful voice' that 'Yes – oh dear yes – the novel tells a story'.[3] Maugham is often disparaged as 'merely' a storyteller and his achievements are little esteemed at present. His work is not regarded as equal to that of his contemporaries Forster, Lawrence, Joyce, Shaw and Virginia Woolf. Lytton Strachey patronizingly dismissed Maugham's work as 'Class Two, Division One'. He is not the subject of theses and other than *Of Human Bondage* few of his works form part of examination syllabuses. He is not 'serious' enough. He is not a 'stylistic innovator'. He is too 'populist'. Maugham occupies the literary doldrums from which Wilde has only recently emerged.

The resistance of academic institutions and literary critics to Maugham's work was established early on. Maugham observed in 1938 that when clever young men wrote essays on contemporary fiction they never even thought of considering him. He also claimed that he didn't resent the fact.

The cool regard of the critics has been balanced by a great popular enthusiasm for Maugham's work. George Orwell claimed to have been heavily influenced by Maugham's 'power of telling a story straight-forwardly and without frills', and almost alone amongst critics, Cyril Connolly esteemed Maugham alongside Lawrence and Joyce in *Enemies of Promise* (1938). Maugham's storytelling, his manipulation of what happens next is his greatest strength. Consequently, many of his novels, plays and stories have been successfully adapted for the stage and screen. From the 1920s to the 1950s, Maugham's work was a hugely fertile source of inspiration for the film industry from Hollywood to Pinewood. Studios and stars brought dozens of Maugham's stories to the screen, further increasing his popular status. The film version of *Rain* (1932), starring Joan Crawford, became the focus of a heated debate about censorship in the barely adolescent medium of film. Maugham's series of spy stories, *Ashenden*, were filmed by Hitchcock in 1936 as *The Secret Agent*, featuring John Gielgud and Madeleine Carroll. Greta Garbo starred as the adulterous Kitty Fane in *The Painted Veil* (1934) and Tyrone Power and Gene Tierney headed the bill of *The Razor's Edge* in 1946. William Wyler brilliantly brought *The Letter* to the screen with Bette Davis as the murderous heroine of fire and ice in 1940. In 1948, J. Arthur Rank filmed four of Maugham's short stories in the fashionable 'portmanteau' format under the title *Quartet*. The 74-year old Maugham appeared in person to introduce each story, a rare acknowledgement of literary stardom for a writer before the age of Booker or Whitbread celebrity.

The son of the solicitor to the British Ambassador in Paris, Somerset Maugham was born on British soil at the Parisian Embassy in 1874. His status from birth, an Englishman born abroad, informs the tone of objectivity which characterizes his work. Trained as a doctor at St Thomas's Hospital and set to cure the ills that bred in the depressed backstreets of south London during the 1890s, Maugham developed a clinical manner of detachment which informed his observation of the human species in print. He examines the English character under a magnifying microscope with neither sentimentality nor sympathy, which has earned him a reputation for coldness and misanthropy. His distinctive milieu encompasses the exotic, far-flung outposts of the British Empire from the paradisal South Sea Islands of *The Moon and Sixpence* to the suffocating jungle of *The Letter*. Like Forster, Maugham tests the emotions and moral convictions of his English characters by situating them abroad in an alien environment, where their inherited beliefs and manners are exposed as hollow, selfish and hypocritical. The huge number of specimens examined under Maugham's microscope create a gallery of grotesques: the greedy, selfish and manipulative who triumph over the weak, the shy and the trusting. Maugham inherits the mantle of Wilde in dissecting the character of empire-builders and of the parasites who prosper from British foreign policy. But whilst Wilde concentrated on the ballrooms and salons of fashionable society in London, Maugham depicts his characters at work colonizing the world. He later recalled the self-bolstering arrogance of the Victorian World Empire which was at its zenith when he was born:

A map showed in pink vast stretches of the earth's surface under the sovereignty of Queen Victoria. The mother country was immensely rich. The British were the world's bankers. British commerce sent its products to the uttermost parts of the earth, and their quality was generally acknowledged to be higher than those manufactured by any other nation. . . . The inhabitants of these islands of ours trusted in God, and God, they were assured, had taken the British Empire under his particular protection. . . . The British travelled a great deal on the Continent. . . . They felt that they were a race apart and no sooner had they landed in Calais than it was borne in upon them that they were now among nat-ives. . . . They alone washed, and the baths that they frequently travelled with were a tangible proof that they were not as others. They were healthy, athletic, sensible and in every way superior. Because they enjoyed their sojourn among the natives whose habits were so curiously un-English, because, though they thought them frivolous (the French), lazy (the Italians), stupid but funny (the Germans), with the kindness of their heart natural to them, they liked them. It never entered their heads that the courtesy which they received, the bows, the smiles, the desire to please were owing to their lavish spending, and that behind their backs the 'natives' mocked them for their uncouth dress, their gawkiness, their insolence, their silliness in letting themselves be consistently over-charged, their patronising tolerance; and it required disastrous wars for it to dawn on them how greatly they had been mistaken.[4]

Maugham's early life was characterized by tragedy and a crippling shyness which was to shade his life and establish the tone of his work. As a child, Maugham was extremely introverted, a condition aggravated by his development of a pronounced stammer.* His mother died of tuberculosis in 1882, to be followed by the death of his father only two

---

* Writing about his friend Arnold Bennett's stammer, Maugham observed, 'Few knew the humiliations it exposed him to . . . and the minor exasperation of thinking of a good, amusing or apt remark and not venturing to say it in case the stammer ruined it. Few knew the distressing sense it gave rise to of a bar to complete contact with other men. It may be that except for the stammer which forced him to introspection Arnold would never have become a writer.' Quoted by Robin Maugham in *Somerset and All the Maughams* (London: Penguin, 1975), p. 150.

years later. The death of his mother was a particularly devastating blow. Even in his eighties, he would say, 'I shall never get over her death', and retained a photograph of her at his own deathbed. The orphaned Maugham was shipped to England to live with his uncle in a cold and loveless rectory at Whitstable. He attended King's School, Canterbury, where the atmosphere was scarcely more welcoming. In *Of Human Bondage*, the protagonist's school is described by Maugham in terms of a prison, memories of his own school-days still smarting in his heart. Whilst resident in Paris, Maugham's first language had been French; now unexpectedly transported to England, the young Maugham struggled to acquire perfect English. At school he suffered on account of his stammer and was made extremely self-conscious because of his unfamiliarity with the English language. The young Maugham's Franco-English accent aggravated the xenophobia of his schoolmates and his speech impediment gave an extra excuse for their daily cruelties and humiliations, which he explores in the early, unhappy chapters of *Of Human Bondage*. In this semi-autobiographical novel, originally entitled *The Artistic Temperament of Philip Carey*, the Carey/Maugham figure has a club-foot which feeds his sense of insecurity and isolation. Carey's limp can be read both as a physical representation of Maugham's own stammer, which he found socially crippling, as well as a device to represent Philip's sense of difference. Philip's limp also expresses a psychological burden which Maugham found as difficult to reconcile himself to as his stammer — his homosexuality. Tennessee Williams uses the same device in *Cat on a Hot Tin Roof*, where Brick's broken leg becomes a symbol of his inability to consummate his relationship with his wife, Maggie. In his later years Maugham confided to his nephew Robin that one of his greatest mistakes was that 'I tried to persuade myself that I was three-quarters normal and that only a quarter of me was queer — whereas really it was the other way round'.[5]

In 1913 Maugham, then a celebrated playwright and novelist, began an affair with Syrie Barnardo, daughter of the philanthropist, Dr Thomas Barnardo, who set up the famous children's homes. She was then married to a man twenty-six years her senior, Henry Wellcome of the Burroughs Wellcome pharmaceutical company, who seemed at first to turn a blind eye to her extramarital indiscretions. It was only when Syrie became pregnant by Maugham in 1916 that Wellcome cited Maugham as co-respondent in a very ugly and very public divorce. Syrie ultimately lost the child, but like many co-respondents in similar cases at the time Maugham capitulated to the conventions of the day and married her out of a sense of duty. But by this time Maugham had become exclusively homosexual. Whilst working with an ambulance unit in France during the war, Maugham had met a young American, almost twenty years his junior, called Gerald Haxton. Haxton was athletic and masculine, 'as gay and irresponsible a companion as a careworn man could wish for'.[6] On leave in London in 1915 Haxton had been arrested and charged with the Wildean crime of gross indecency. Though he was acquitted, a few years later he was declared an undesirable alien and was never allowed to return to England again. Haxton's enforced exile must surely have been the deciding factor in Maugham's decision to live permanently abroad.

The unhappy triangular relationship between Maugham, Haxton and Syrie continued after the war and into the 1920s, with Maugham travelling to Tahiti, China and America in an unsuccessful attempt to avoid his tenacious wife. After many violent rows and public scenes, the Maughams finally divorced in 1927. But Maugham's bitterness about the marriage was to continue throughout his life. In an interview in the 1960s, his thoughts on marriage had become absolutely vitriolic:

A marriage, at best, is the most abnormal of relationships between man and woman. I refuse to believe that it was ever intended for man and woman to be bound together by a legal contract under one roof. It constitutes an invasion of privacy, an encroachment on individuality, the shattering of peace-of-mind, the interruption of independent thought and action, and the engulfment of an innocent human being in a bog of boredom.[7]

In 1962, at the age of eighty-eight, Maugham wrote his memoir *Looking Back*, in which he viciously attacked Syrie as 'a harlot, a thief, a vulgarian, a sponge and a fool'. He even questioned the paternity of his own daughter, Liza, and attempted to disinherit her whilst formally adopting Alan Searle, who had become his companion after Gerald Haxton's death in 1941. Syrie had been very popular in her day as a hostess as well as an interior designer. She had introduced the all-white drawing-rooms of the 1920s which so radically departed from the heavy chenille and mahogany taste of the Edwardians. *Looking Back* was deplored by many of Syrie's surviving society friends, including Noël Coward, who believed that Maugham must be going senile. Beverly Nichols, a sometime protégé of Maugham, thought *Looking Back* 'smeared with the patina of insanity' and attempted to defend Syrie's reputation in his equally mud-smeared memoir, *A Case of Human Bondage*. Maugham's experience of marriage with Syrie inevitably coloured the depiction of marriage in his work, which was to become his major theme.

Robert Calder argues that the most important value of Maugham's personal and professional life was freedom. His work is littered with characters who attempt to free themselves from restrictive spouses, parents, backgrounds, conventions: 'The main thing I've always asked from life is freedom. Outer and inner freedom, both in my way of living and my way of writing'.[8] The majority of Maugham's expansive *oeuvre* of novels, plays and short stories explore adultery or examine the destruction of some sort of romantic relationship. Marriage is regarded with enormous cynicism, many of the stories ending in vicious confrontation, sacrifice, death, suicide and murder. In Maugham's world love and sex are inevitably bound with death. Most of the marriages which he describes are dismantled from within and the destruction of the relationship is most usually initiated by the wife. It is the men who are most often the victims of female, or female-inspired, violence. Marriage, for Maugham, constitues the accessible symbol of the bondage he so deplored. The marriage contract is the basis of the Empire society whose inhabitants Maugham dissects, a legal and social contract evolved to regulate the passage of money and estates, and to maintain social stability by restricting sexual activity and promoting the myth of the family. For him, the individual's conflict with the imposed restrictions and huge expectations of the marriage contract becomes symbolic of a wider conflict between the individual and the restrictions of society itself.

Marriages made in hell

> Men marry because they are tired; women because they are curious; both are disappointed.
> Oscar Wilde, *The Picture of Dorian Gray*[9]

In the 1890s, Maugham had made a calculated decision to write comedies, as they stood a greater chance of commercial success than dramas.

In his preface to the *Collected Plays* in 1931, Maugham was unashamed about his hunger for success: 'I wanted money and I wanted fame.' This desire for success certainly shaped the tone, style and content of his early works. In his obituary of Maugham in 1965, Malcolm Muggeridge believed that financial success seemed to Maugham to be a sort of protection against the insecurity of the world and the unreliability of other people. Money, Maugham claimed, was like a 'sixth sense without which one cannot make a complete use of the other five. Without an adequate income half the possibilities of the world are cut off.'[10]

Maugham decided, like Coward after him, that his best chance of commercial success was to write a comedy with a great part for a middle-aged leading actress, who, if she liked the part well enough, might persuade a management to risk a production. This calculated strategy flattered the vanity of several leading actresses in Maugham's early career: *Smith* was written for Marie Lohr, *The Land of Promise* for Irene Vanbrugh and *Penelope* was penned as a vehicle for Marie Tempest, who was to be similarly seduced years later by another ambitious young writer, when she accepted the role of Judith Bliss in Noël Coward's *Hay Fever*. During his days as a medical student Maugham educated himself in the serious dramatic work of the contemporary theatre. Every week he took in performances by Henry Irving, Ellen Terry, Mrs Patrick Campbell and George Alexander. He saw the original productions of *An Ideal Husband* and *The Importance of Being Earnest* and also attended the first night of Henry James's disastrous *Guy Domville* in 1895. Maugham observed the humiliation of the great man's failure and determined not to repeat it. Though Maugham had certainly read and even translated Ibsen, he wasn't interested in drama either as an art form or as a vehicle for exploring social issues. He saw theatre as a transaction of pleasure and money between the audience and the playwright: 'The aim of the drama is not to instruct but to please.' But there is a huge gulf between Maugham's early comedies such as *Lady Frederick* and the dark bitterness of a late play like *For Services Rendered*. It's almost as if Maugham, like Wilde, retires from the theatre just as he finds his own original theatrical voice.

Lady Frederick

Maugham's dramatic work contains a gallery of great leading roles for women. Lady Frederick Berolles is a typical example of Maugham's heroines of the period before the Great War. She is the widow of a drunken Irish peer and on the verge of bankruptcy. She also carries a shady reputation. Whilst staying in Monte Carlo she attracts the attentions of a younger man, Charlie, Marquess of Mereston. Mereston's mother is determined to prevent the relationship as Lady Frederick ('designing female') has no fortune, has been implicated in an adulterous affair and (the horror, the horror!) dyes her hair. Like Wilde, Maugham examines the manners and morals of privileged society by exploring the negotiations and transactions of the marriage market. Maugham consciously invokes the comedies of Wilde by setting the play in the 1890s, rather than 1903 when the play was written. The play utilizes the familiar props of Wilde's social comedies: stolen letters, past love affairs and sexual blackmail. Lady Frederick is related to Wilde's heroines with secret pasts like Mrs Erlynne and Mrs Cheveley, who also share Lady Frederick's charm and worldliness. The tone of the play feels like an attempt to emulate Wilde's style as well as his milieu. But Maugham's epigrams seem forced and false compared to Wilde's: 'I have reached an age when love, ambition and wealth pale into insignificance beside a really well-grilled steak'.[11] Regardless of the tone or structure of the piece, Maugham was proud of the fact that he could conjure epigrams to order, if that's what the managements and audiences wanted. His style in *Lady Frederick* might even be a deliberate pastiche of Wilde's, if not homage: 'It's one of the injustices of fate that clothes only hang on a woman really well when she's lost every shred of reputation.'[12]

Lady Frederick is an outsider, her Irishness branding her difference from polite English society. Her sense of crisis in Monte Carlo is aggravated by an increasing anxiety about her age. She is beginning to feel the ravages of time and wishes she were eighteen again. Like her descendant Blanche Dubois, her only assurance of future security is marriage and her hopes of that are based on her physical attractiveness. She has nothing to offer in the vicious marriage market other than herself. It becomes clear that Lady Frederick must get married soon in order to pay off the debts which are rapidly closing in on her. Given the choice of marriage or bankruptcy, a match with the young, attractive and infatuated Charlie Mereston seems very tempting. Her relationship with Mereston, that between the relatively innocent youth and the experienced older partner, resounds with 'the love that dare not speak its name'. Like Wilde, Maugham sets youth and beauty at a premium in *Lady Frederick* and the play also advances the Wildean debate about the folly of establishing ideal criteria for human behaviour. In the play's most celebrated scene Lady Frederick invites Charlie to visit her in the morning before she has made herself up for the day. He has asked her to marry him the night before; she now dares him to ask her again once he has seen her first thing in the morning, warts and all. She voluntarily topples herself from the pedestal on which he has placed her. Like Sir Robert Chiltern in *An Ideal Husband*, she recognizes the dangers of idolizing people: 'Think of living up to the ideal Charlie has of me.'[13] She reveals that her cheeks are rouged, her hair is false, her eyebrows drawn and her pallor artificial, thus exposing the tricks by which she attempts to stay the signs of ageing: 'Now for the delicate soft bloom of youth. The great difficulty, you know, is to make both your cheeks the same colour.'[14]

The scene is very funny, but very cruel. Having established Lady Frederick's anxiety about her age and her insecurity about the future as her physical charms fade, Maugham puts her through her worst nightmare of humiliation. Like Blanche, Lady Frederick fears the unkind truth of the naked light-bulb: 'Never has daylight exposed so total a ruin.' Lady Frederick forces Charlie Mereston to witness her artifice and then asks him if he still wants to marry her. With commendable honesty in the face of her predicament, Lady Frederick makes Charlie realize that his love for her has been superficial infatuation. However much she needs the match to solve her current circumstances, she wants to be loved 'through and through':

> Just at present I can make a decent enough show by taking infinite pains; and my hand is not so heavy that the innocent eyes of your sex can discover how much of me is due to art. But in ten years you'll only be thirty-two, and then, if I married you, my whole life would be a mortal struggle to preserve some semblance of youth.[15]

The scene presents the truth behind Lady Frederick's social mask. Her youthful looks and beauty are an illusion, a trick. We see her adopt a social identity like a costume. Maugham shows Charlie Mereston as well as the audience the artifice that goes into the construction of femininity. Lady Frederick makes up like an actor preparing for the stage and her social persona is exposed as a performance, hiding her desperate anxieties about her dwindling finances and dwindling charms beneath a veneer of beauty and carefree behaviour. Looking at the scene now, I see echoes of it in the first act of Harvey Fierstein's *Torch Song Trilogy* (New York, 1982), where Arnold, a drag queen, makes up for a show at the same time as discussing his anxieties about men, the onset of age and the passing of beauty. Certainly, Lady Frederick's awareness of her own mask and the pressures of maintaining it seem to encapsulate the dilemma of gay men at the turn of the century, when the legacy of Wilde was an all-too-recent and uncomfortable memory.

The transactions of money, sex and marriage are closely related in *Lady Frederick*. She recognizes that her financial irresponsibility, her need to spend, has been a substitute for love. She had been married at seventeen because her mother thought it 'a good match', despite the fact that she was in love with another man. Ultimately her husband turned out to be dissolute and then, tragically, her child died. Having been disappointed in her first marriage, she is now very sceptical about romantic love: 'Then I didn't care any more. I did everything I could to stupefy myself. I squandered money as other women take morphia.'[16] Spending, shopping and acquisition are addictive drugs taken to counteract loneliness and the bruises of an unhappy marriage. When Charlie Mereston's mother tries to blackmail Lady Frederick with some incriminating letters from the past, Lady Frederick claims that she compromised herself in order to protect the reputation of her sister-in-law who 'had been foolish'. It becomes apparent that it is actually Lady Mereston's husband who had been conducting an affair without his wife's knowledge. The late Lord Mereston, Charlie's father, was a hypocrite, who loudly proclaimed 'I take my stand on the morality, the cleanliness and the purity of English Family life,'[17] whilst keeping a mistress from the *Folies Bergères*. As she possesses certain letters written by Lord Mereston and his mistress, Lady Frederick has the opportunity to expose him and shatter his widow's idealized memory of her husband: 'He preached at her steadily for twenty years, and she worshipped the very ground he trod on.'[18] However, despite Lady Mereston's attempt to sabotage Lady Frederick's chances of marrying Charlie, Lady Frederick refuses to lower herself to employing such tactics. Instead, she takes Lord Mereston's letters and burns them, thus allowing Lady Mereston to retain her illusions about her husband and at the same time sabotaging her own relationship with Charlie.

The odious Captain Montgomerie haunts the casinos and hotel lounges of Monte Carlo intent on marrying a title. He pursues Lady Frederick in an attempt to force her into an 'arrangement' by buying up her debts. Lady Frederick's future looks very bleak. An ageing single woman with bad debts and no fortune, her only option would appear to be to sell herself into marital slavery with a man she doesn't love. But Maugham never forgets that *Lady Frederick* is a comedy. As near as his heroine comes to ruin and despair, Maugham rewards her honesty. She is saved by her old flame, Paradine Fouldes, Lady Mereston's brother. Fouldes recognizes that despite her age and her lack of fortune, she is a woman of integrity: 'genuine to the bottom of her soul'. Paradine and Lady Frederick accept each other for what they are with no qualms about their flaws or past indiscretions. So all ends happily ever after. But despite the up-beat resolution of the play where virtue is seen to be rewarded, Maugham has raised uncomfortable issues about the dilemma of women in a society which sets a premium on beauty and wealth. For those without such golden passports, society can be a cruel and merciless creature.

Our Betters

The tone of Maugham's social comedies darkens considerably after the First World War as he exposes the broadening cracks in the land built for heroes to live in. The cynicism which is deflated at the end of *Lady Frederick* is allowed to linger in his much more virulent attacks on society, *Our Betters* and *Home and Beauty*. The conventions and concerns of Wildean society are still intact in *Lady Frederick*, but by the time of *Our Betters* (1915) and *Home and Beauty* (1919) society is hugely changed. These two plays chart the destabilization of Wilde's prewar society, which is challenged from without by the Americans in *Our Betters* and then dismantled from within by the wife in *Home and Beauty*. (The new freedoms of universal suffrage and the comparatively relaxed divorce laws inspire in her a sense of greed and selfishness. Rather than patch up some semblance of family life with one of her two husbands, she rejects it altogether.) In the 1920s and 1930s, Maugham begins to focus his satire on marital and family situations, as the 'society' he had known before the war no longer exists.

Maugham was forty when the First World War broke out and though he asked his friend Winston Churchill to look out a job for him, nothing came of it. His scathing satire of Anglo-American social relations, *Our Betters*, though written during the war in 1915, was not performed in

Britain until 1923. America didn't join the Allies until 1917 and Maugham's critical exploration of American adventuresses exploiting English society was thought by the Foreign Office to be politically insensitive. The shallowness of English society is established in *Our Betters* from the outset: 'if one wants to be a success in London one must either have looks, wit or a bank-balance'.[19] The hypocrisy of English society in this Jamesian tale is thrown into relief by its adoption by a circle of expatriate American snobs. Pearl, Lady Grayston, heads a salon of American adventuresses intent on securing titled matches. Like Lord Bracknell in *The Importance of Being Earnest*, Lord Grayston is *in absentia* and Pearl is able to continue her assault on the upper circles of society with the financial support of a vulgar American capitalist, Arthur Fenwick. Fenwick blindly adores Pearl: 'You're my guiding star, you're my ideal. You stand to me for all that's pure and noble and clean in womanhood'.[20] But Pearl proves to be ironically named: a seemingly pure, perfect jewel, she betrays her humble origins – 'the speck of dirt in the oyster'.

The new American society is contrasted with the traditional English milieu examined by Wilde. In *Lady Windermere's Fan*, the Duchess of Berwick is rude and ignorant about Australia – 'What a curious shape it is! Just like a large packing case. However, it is a very young country, isn't it?'[21] – but she is quite prepared to marry off her monosyllabic daughter to a wealthy colonial like Mr Hopper. Though she is happy to attach her daughter to the fortune that Hopper has made in Australia, she deplores the very idea that Agatha should actually go and live there: 'There are lots of vulgar people live in Grosvenor Square, but at any rate there are no horrid kangaroos crawling about.'[22] By 1917, the English aristocracy have become much less precious and are happy to go wherever the next dollar leads them. Where the English aristocracy is based on birthright, the bastardized Anglo-American strain of it is founded solely on wealth. Pearl's second-rate aristocracy represents the marriage of a magnified strain of Wildean individualism with cash and ambition:

PRINCESS   You've brought all the determination, insight, vigour, strength which have made our countrymen turn America into what it is to get what you wanted. In a way your life has been a work of art. And what makes it more complete is that what you've aimed at is trivial, transitory and worthless.[23]

The American expatriates have adopted the manners and preoccupations of English society and exaggerated them in the extreme. They attempt to become more English than the English by adopting typical traditional but superficial habits such as drinking tea:

CLAY   You Americans who live in America . . . despise the delectable habit of drinking tea because you are still partly barbarous. The hour we spend over it is the most delightful of the day. We do not make a business of eating as at luncheon or dinner. We are at ease with ourselves. We toy with pretty cakes as an excuse for conversation. We discuss the abstract, our souls, our morals; we play delicately with the concrete, our neighbour's new bonnet or her latest lover. We drink tea because we are a highly civilised nation.[24]

If the speech sounds familiar, it's because Thornton Clay attempts to emulate the sort of Wildean dandy he has seen in American repertory productions of *The Importance of Being Earnest*. But whereas Wilde's dandies are young and charming, Clay is a short, fat, bald American queen. This sort of leisured camperie was the tenor of the age in 1895, but after a major world war, his words sound hollow and ugly. But the Americans aren't content simply to ape English society, they want to *be* it; their major goal is to exchange their wealth for English titles by marrying impoverished aristocrats. Once securely entitled, the women begin to conduct adulterous affairs and keep young gigolos:

PRINCESS   It's the life they lead. They've got too much money and too few responsibilities. English women in our station have duties that are part of their birthright, but we, strangers in a strange land, have nothing to do but enjoy ourselves.[25]

The Euro-American aristocrats include the Principessa Della Cercola, originally just plain 'Flora' from Boston, and the Duchesse De Surennes, 'Minnie' from Chicago, who spends her father's millions on her worthless English lover, Tony Paxton. Pearl intends to marry her younger sister Bessie to the penniless Lord Bleane, despite Bessie's earlier betrothal to an upstanding young American, Fleming Harvey. Pearl invites a crowd of her friends to her country house for the weekend, ostensibly to clinch the match for Bessie, but Pearl also has her own dal-liances to occupy her. She is a monstrous man-eater and fancies Minnie's lover, Tony. Bored with the stuffy, demanding Minnie, Tony is also on the lookout for a brief sexual fling. At her weekend house party, Pearl's guests play a game of poker. The card game has an obvious sexual sig-nificance ('poke her'), which Williams was also to exploit in *A Streetcar Named Desire*, the original title of which was *The Poker Night*. To the out-rage of the weekend guests, Tony is discovered literally poking Pearl in the summer-house. Minnie is devastated, but Pearl's famous response is sassily unrepentant: 'You damned fool, I told you it was too risky'.[26] The British Lord Chamberlain insisted that the couple be caught *in flagrante* by Lord Bleane rather than the uncorrupted Bessie who discovered them in the American production and in the published text. Though caught red-handed in the summer-house, Pearl doesn't show the slight-est blush, she cannot understand why the guests are shocked by her behaviour. She has no sense of the strictures of conventional morality, for she has made up her own:

> People are so selfish. It just happens that I find no man so desirable as one that a friend of mine is in love with. I make allowances for the idiosyncrasies of my friends. Why shouldn't they make allowances for mine?[27]

However, Pearl does realize that the appearance of propriety is impor-tant to her status as a society hostess in London. This façade must be preserved at all costs. After the débâcle of the summer-house, Pearl exploits all her charm and wit to prevent the weekend party from split-ting up and the scandal reaching London. If she can keep her guests for the whole weekend, London society would not believe that anything was seriously amiss, despite any rumours of scandal that might be leaked. Pearl begins to manipulate her guests with great aplomb. Her first challenge is to patch up the relationship between Minnie and Tony. Her own relationship with Tony was strictly a one-off, as she wouldn't want to jeopardize her relationship with her husband, who provides her social position, or her lover Arthur Fenwick, who provides her with the cash to keep it up in great style.

Minnie is obsessive about her younger lover Tony, who is little more than a selfish gold-digger. To salve Minnie's despair Pearl arranges a meeting between Tony and Minnie. With characteristic arrogance, however, Tony twists the situation, blaming his infidelity on Minnie's obsessive behaviour:

> No man could stand being loved so much. D'you think it's jolly for me to feel that your eyes are glued on me whatever I'm doing? I can never put my hand out without finding yours there ready to press it.[28]

Minnie has become sexually dependent on Tony and in their reconciliation she must now humiliate herself in order to get him back. This involves a secure offer of marriage and a wedding settlement of £1,000 a year. Her dependence on this worthless man is pitiful. When their differences are resolved, and the financial arrangement has been agreed, she tells him, 'Oh Tony, I do love you so.' He responds with a cruelly non-committal expression of power: 'That's right'.[29]

Maugham contrasts these awful social vipers with Pearl's sister Bessie and her former fiancé, Fleming Harvey. Fleming has only recently arrived from America and is untainted by the opportunistic mores of the expatriates. Like the puritanical American heiress in *A Woman of No Importance*, Fleming rails against the vices of the vulgar, immoral Anglo-American society which Pearl has created around her:

> There's something in these surroundings that makes me feel terribly uncomfortable. Under the brilliant surface I suspect all kinds of ugly and shameful secrets that everyone knows and pretends not to. This is a strange house in which the husband is never seen and Arthur Fenwick, a vulgar sensualist, acts as host; and it's an attractive spectacle, this painted duchess devouring with her eyes a boy young enough to be her son. And the conversation – I don't want to seem a prude, I daresay people over here talk more freely than the people I've known; but surely there are women who don't have lovers, there are such things as honour and decency and self-restraint.[30]

Ironically, Fleming, an American, defends the values of honour, decency and self-restraint which come to represent the essentially 'English' character in works such as Coward's *Brief Encounter*. Like Fleming, Bessie eventually despises the world that Pearl holds so dear, where the appearance of propriety is valued higher than personal integrity. Bessie condemns Pearl as a 'slut' for keeping a lover like Arthur Fenwick whilst seducing her friend's younger lover. Pearl tries to defend her behaviour by explaining to Bessie that their position in English society is very precarious, as it is only because of their money that the Americans are tolerated: 'in their hearts they still look upon us as savages and Red Indians'.

PEARL   Very early in my career I discovered that the English can never resist getting something for nothing. If a dancer is the rage, they'll see her at my house. If a fiddler is in vogue, they'll hear him at my concert. I give them balls. I give them dinners. I've made myself the fashion, I've got power, I've got influence. But everything I've got – my success, my reputation, my noto-riety – I've bought it, bought it, bought it.

BESSIE   How humiliating!

PEARL   And, finally, I've bought you a husband.[31]

Pearl claims that the fashionable surroundings in which Bessie has been shown off have prompted Lord Bleane to ask for her hand. Appalled, Bessie breaks off the engagement and determines to return to God's own country with Fleming:

Don't you see that we're not strong enough for the life over here? It goes to our head; we lose our bearings; we put away our own code, and we can't adopt the code of the country we come to. We drift. There's nothing for us to do but amuse ourselves, and we fall to pieces. But in America we're safe. And perhaps America wants us.[32]

The English society portrayed in *Our Betters* is a weak, tawdry milieu rapidly falling to its knees. Forced to make alliances with anyone who has the money to buy it, society has sold itself into a market of mass cultural prostitution. The young and pure will return to their homeland, leaving Pearl and her like to further corrupt and dominate the English social scene. As in Wilde's comic melodramas, the appearance of propri-ety is upheld, although the action of the play reveals that society is rotten to its core.

Home and Beauty

If marriage is a mockery in *Our Betters*, it becomes an absurdity in *Home and Beauty*, a farce of postwar disillusionment. *Home and Beauty* was written and is set in 1918 and, like many narratives which deal with the domestic consequences of the end of a war, such as Rebecca West's *The Return of the Soldier* (1918) and *The Years Between* (1945) by Daphne du Maurier, this play examines a world which has changed and explores how individuals cope with the changes in their loved ones that the pressures of world conflict have brought about. Though sharing many of the narrative elements with these related works, *Home and Beauty* has a radically different tone, for it is the bitterest of black comedies. It's cynicism is not about war or politics but human nature, most specifically about the fidelity of women.

The acerbic tone of the play is set from the very first scene where Victoria Lowndes is having her nails manicured. Coal is rationed and the only room to have a proper fire is Victoria's bedroom, the first indication of her selfishness. Victoria, her mother and her manicurist, though separated by class, are all united by a deep cynicism about men and the institution of marriage:

MRS SHUTTLEWORTH   The difference between men and women is that men are not naturally addicted to matrimony. With patience, firmness, and occasional rewards you can train them to it just as you can train a dog to walk on its hind legs. But a dog would rather walk on all fours and a man would rather be free. Marriage is a habit.[33]

Victoria has made rather a habit of it herself, if not a hobby. She is currently married to Frederick Lowndes, the best friend and best man of her first husband William, who is thought to have died a hero's death early on in the war. Having comforted his friend's widow, Frederick ultimately married her. As in the opening scenes of Noël Coward's *Private Lives* and *Blithe Spirit*, Victoria spends an unhealthy amount of time talking disparagingly of her present marriage and idealizing her former one. When Victoria declares that 'I would give anything in the world to have my dear, dear Bill back again', Freddie informs her that 'dear, dear Bill' should be arriving in about three minutes' time. Bill has phoned from Harwich to say that he's alive and well and would Freddie break the news to Victoria? He is obviously expecting to take his place as Victoria's husband and head of the household. When Bill appears, Victoria's mother is convinced that he must be a ghost. His return is the flesh-and-blood embodiment of the dilemma that Elvira threatens when she materializes in *Blithe Spirit*. Suffering from amnesia, he is only recently recovered, and the truth of Victoria's remarriage to Freddie only becomes clear when he discovers that Freddie and Victoria have had a baby. The security of the marital relationship is exploded; in marriage, three is an uncomfortable crowd.

The triangular relationship between Victoria, Bill and Fred also anticipates that between the protagonists in Coward's *Design for Living*. But Gilda, Otto and Leo are artists with the off-beat mores of middle-class bohemia; Victoria's situation seems more threatening because she and her milieu are so conventional. The dilemma now is to decide who should stay married to Victoria. Conventional mores have no answers for such complex human situations. The simplest and most obvious answer would be to ask Victoria which of the two men she loves more. As is typical of Maugham, however, this romantic solution to the problem isn't even considered. The two men decide to behave like Englishmen and each agrees to bow down. It becomes obvious that both men are keen to extricate themselves from the selfish Victoria, described by Freddie as 'the white man's burden' and that each yearns for this unforeseen opportunity of freedom. The two men decide to draw lots: whoever chooses the slip of paper marked with a cross will remain Victoria's husband. But it appears that Victoria is the booby prize, as Freddie cheats by marking both pieces of paper with a cross. As an impasse has been reached and Bill threatens to emigrate to a farm in Canada if he is to remain married to her, Victoria decides that she should divorce both of them: 'The war is over now, and I think I've done my bit. I've married two D.S.O.'s. Now I want to marry a Rolls-Royce.'[34] She is keen to marry Leicester Paton, a 'wangler' who buys coal, chocolates and luxury goods on the black market and also happens to own a Rolls-Royce. Shocked by the unconventionality of having two masters in the house, all of Victoria's servants hand in their notice, but Freddie and Bill offer to share the cooking and cleaning between them.

The last act of the play is a satirical examination of the absurdities of the divorce laws. Once the arrangements have been made, Victoria goes off to lunch with Leicester Paton and the two men drink a toast to liberty. The play had begun in the intimacy of Victoria's bedroom and the dilemma had been who should share her bed. Having discussed who will play the role of Victoria's husband in the public rooms of the house, the play ends with the two men left alone together in an organized, domestic kitchen in the bowels of the house. Bill and Fred are now happily bonded to each other once more. Their former attachments to Victoria (and women?) are merely a bad dream, a temporary aberration, as they look forward to their new life (together??) in a woman-free misogynist's heaven.

Maugham's attitude to women is very ambivalent. His depiction of them in *Our Betters* and *Home and Beauty* is hardly flattering: they are greedy, selfish and deceitful. But though his portrayal of them is misogynous, Maugham does at least allow his women to get what they want, however much he might disparage their motivations or tactics. In *The Circle* and *The Constant Wife*, he redresses the balance and discusses marriage from women's point of view. Marriage is once again portrayed as a shackle, but Maugham's female protagonists are now empowered to manipulate their status within marriage or escape it altogether. Leslie Crosbie in *The Letter* is both an adulteress and murderess, but unlike Mrs Erlynne and Mrs Arbuthnot she avoids exile. The sanctity of marriage was finally exploded by the increase in the divorce rate after the First World War: 3,280 divorces were recorded between 1911 and 1915, which rose steadily to 20,100 between 1931 and 1935. In the 1920s and 1930s, a generation of women claimed the sexual autonomy which had always been assumed by their husbands and female infidelity became a commonplace. The Prince of Wales was known to have had a succession of affairs with married women before he met Mrs Simpson in 1930, but the British press, headed by Lord Beaverbrook, turned a blind communal eye. However, the legislation which policed marriage was clearly out of step with the social developments of the time. The absurdity that the law required proof of adultery as grounds for divorce was commonly satirized by writers such as Maugham in *Home and Beauty* and Evelyn Waugh in *A Handful of Dust* (1934). An extension to the divorce laws to include cruelty, insanity and desertion was made in 1937.

Anthony Curtis shrewdly observes Maugham's achievement in

portraying these twentieth-century daughters of Ibsen's Nora as they tasted the first flavours of liberation:

> Maugham understood women much better than any other play-wright of this period whether it was women of the political and social aristocracy, the wives of the professional middle-class or the common prostitute. He understood them much better than Shaw, for example, who merely created new stereotypes of his own by giving women many of the qualities of leadership and resourcefulness traditionally ascribed to men.[35]

Shaw's Major Barbara and Wells's Anne Veronica preach the Fabian-influenced philosophy of their creators, and their dilemmas rarely embrace the daily domestic challenges which face Maugham's female protagonists. But Maugham is also aware that he is chronicling the development of a new social and political female, who is the postwar embodiment of the New Woman of the turn of the century. In Elizabeth Champion-Cheney in *The Circle* and Constance Middleton in *The Constant Wife*, Maugham presented the dilemma of a whole generation of women. Though written shortly after *Our Betters* in 1919, *The Circle* was first performed in 1921 and its style seems extremely modern compared to the Edwardian tone of *Mrs Dot*, *Smith* or *Lady Frederick*. In *The Circle*, Maugham consciously echoes the situation of *Lady Windermere's Fan*. The two plays share many similarities of character and situation, but *The Circle* radically departs from the pattern of *Lady Windermere's Fan* at the denouement, reflecting the new social and political status of women immediately after the First World War.

The Circle

Arnold Champion-Cheney, a provincial MP, has a rather passionless relationship with his wife, the young, headstrong Elizabeth. Elizabeth is very curious about Arnold's mother, Lady Kitty Champion-Cheney, who like Mrs Erlynne had left Arnold and his father thirty years previously to live with Lord Porteous. In an echo of Wilde's ideal husband, Porteous had been Under-Secretary for Foreign Affairs and 'everyone was expecting him to be Prime Minister'. Lady Porteous had refused her husband a divorce, so the two lovers have had to live abroad in exile for thirty years 'in sin'. 'Naughty Lady Kitty' is a contemporary of Lady Windermere's, but unlike Lady Windermere, who faltered at the last moment, Kitty did actually leave her husband and abandon her child back in the 1890s. Like Mrs Erlynne, Lady Kitty has now returned to the scene of her sin.

Despite her husband's objections, Elizabeth has invited Lady Kitty and Lord Porteous for the weekend. As Arnold's father, Clive, also lives on the estate, she feels that she must inform him of his wife's imminent arrival, which he accepts without bitterness. In his conversations with her, it becomes apparent to Clive that Elizabeth has dangerously romanticized Lady Kitty in her imagination: 'she loved and dared', 'she gave up everything for love'. She imagines Lady Kitty to be the *femme fatale* of women's romantic fiction and wants 'Arnold's mother to be a mother to me'. When Lady Kitty and Porteous arrive, the reality is shocking. Lady Kitty is mutton-dressed-as-lamb, a 'tinsel' vulgarian, with dyed hair, 'outrageously dressed ... and behaves as if she were twenty-five'. Porteous is 'a grumpy, sodden old fellow with false teeth'. They are hardly the ideal romantic couple. Kitty, who had formerly been 'so gay and natural', has now become a 'ridiculous caricature of a pretty woman grown old'. Clive Champion-Cheney observes sadly that 'We are creatures of our environment. She's a silly, worthless creature, because she's led a silly, worthless life.'[36]

At bridge that afternoon, Kitty and Porteous bicker and argue, causing an unpleasant public scene, and Clive observes ironically that 'they might be married'. For Kitty and Porteous have sacrificed a great deal to be together and now, in their late middle age, the recriminations have begun and they blame each other for their losses. Now that physical beauty has faded and passion is spent, they have become rootless, aimless exiles embittered by what might have been. Kitty wonders whether she might not have been better off staying with Clive: 'for thirty years I've had to live in a filthy marble palace with no sanitary conveniences'.[37] Porteous swears that he might have become Prime Minister if his career hadn't been ruined by his elopement with Kitty. She, in turn, believes that with her charms and force of will she could have made Clive a Cabinet Minister if she'd wanted to, but Porteous claims that as Prime Minister he would only have rewarded Clive with some second-rate colony, such as Western Australia or Barbados, 'out of pure kindness':

KITTY	Nonsense! I'd have India.
PORTEOUS	I would never have given you India.
KITTY	You would have given me India.
PORTEOUS	I tell you I wouldn't.
KITTY	The King would have given me India. The nation would have insisted on my having India. I would have been vice-reine or nothing.
PORTEOUS	I tell you that as long as the interests of the British Empire – Damn it! All my teeth are coming out![38]

The scene is absurd, funny and cruel, exposing Lady Kitty's masculine hankering for the power which her gender has denied her. It is Clive, not Kitty, whom the King might have 'given' India. The argument also exposes the outrageous egotism and selfishness of their class, as they divide the Empire between them like some fancy cake.

The relationship between Porteous and Kitty is a warning to Elizabeth that a passionate romance might not be a secure basis for a life-long relationship. Though the play is dominated by the characters of Kitty and Porteous, Elizabeth is very much the focal figure. How is the example of Kitty and Porteous going to affect her? For even before the arrival of Lady Kitty, relations between Elizabeth and Arnold seem very cool. Clive suspects that Elizabeth's interest in the transgressions of Arnold's mother isn't very healthy and wonders about the sexual relationship between his son and daughter-in-law. When asked direct, uncomfortable questions, Elizabeth answers vaguely:

CLIVE	Are you happy with Arnold?
ELIZABETH	Why shouldn't I be?
CLIVE	Why haven't you got any babies?
ELIZABETH	Give us a little time. We've only been married three years.[39]

When Arnold Champion-Cheney first appears, he rearranges the ornaments on the mantelpiece, taking a rather fussy pride in the interior decoration and furnishings in the house. Early in the first act, he proudly shows his rather unenthusiastic father a new chair he has recently bought: 'It's exactly my period.' Clive exhibits a polite lack of interest in the chair, as interior design is not considered a 'masculine' subject of concern. Throughout the play, Maugham continually draws attention to Arnold's obsessive interest in home furnishings. He is outraged by the taste of some of the estate tenants:

ARNOLD   It's an almost perfect Georgian house and they've got a lot of dreadful Victorian furniture. I gave them my ideas on the subject, but it's quite hopeless. They said they were attached to their furniture.
CLIVE   Arnold should have been an interior decorator.
LADY KITTY   He has wonderful taste. He gets that from me.
ARNOLD   I suppose I have a certain *flair*. I have a passion for decorating houses.[40]

'Flair', indeed. A similar interest in interior decorating is shared by the effete Mr Dulcimer in *The Green Bay Tree* and the camp screamer, Bobbie Williams, in Frederick Lonsdale's *Spring Cleaning* (1925): 'What a perfectly gorgeous cushion. I must get some like this at once.' Such domestic nest-building interests are regarded as the province of women, and the development of a 'tasteful' sensibility discreetly but definitely calls Arnold's sexuality into question. He is the 1920s ancestor of the contemporary queen who regularly shops at Heal's, harbours a collection of early Bakelite and secretly covets a few good pieces by Clarice Cliff:

ARNOLD   You know, it does exasperate me the way people will not leave things alone. I no sooner put a thing in its place than somebody moves it.
ELIZABETH   It must be maddening for you.
ARNOLD   It is. You are the worst offender. I can't think why you don't take the pride that I do in the house. After all, it's one of the show places in the country.
ELIZABETH   I'm afraid you find me very unsatisfactory.
ARNOLD   *(good-humouredly)* I don't know about that. But my two subjects are politics and decoration. I should be a perfect fool if I didn't see that you don't care two straws about either.[41]

Arnold's marriage to Elizabeth is one of convenience, to provide a hostess for the house and the appearance of personal stability to support his political career: 'After all, a man marries to have a home, but also because he doesn't want to be bothered with sex and all that sort of thing.'[42] Not surprisingly, Elizabeth is beginning to look elsewhere for solace and passion. She had wanted to meet Lady Kitty, not so that Arnold could be reconciled with his mother, but because she wanted to meet a woman who had lived with the consequences of her transgression. Arnold had been reluctant for Elizabeth to meet his mother lest she be 'contaminated' by the morality of the older woman. Arnold's judgemental attitude towards his mother is reminiscent of Gerald Arbuthnot's priggishness towards his mother in *A Woman of No Importance*. As well as Porteous and Lady Kitty, Elizabeth has invited a young man called Teddie Luton as moral support during the weekend. Luton has neither fortune nor connections, but Elizabeth has been in love with him ever since their first meeting. She tells Arnold that she no longer loves him and that she wants a divorce. He refuses on the grounds that 'We've had enough divorces in our family.' He doesn't want Elizabeth to repeat the shameful pattern of his mother. But Arnold's concerns are less about the emotional fracture of Elizabeth's departure than the effect it would have on his political career.

Clive advises his son to affect magnanimity and allow Elizabeth to leave, with the hope that she will sacrifice her own feelings and return to her husband. As part of the scheme, Clive produces an album of photographs of 1890s society people such as Ellen Terry and Lillie Langtry. Clive shows the album to Elizabeth, who comes across a photograph of a beautiful young girl. She does not recognize it as Lady Kitty: 'Why didn't you tell me you looked like that? Everybody must have been in love with you.' Kitty looks at the photograph and breaks down. She comes face to face with reality, the passing of time and happiness and the fragility of beauty and love. But the photograph heals the rift between Kitty and Porteous, as they remember how desperately they loved each other thirty years before:

PORTEOUS   Do you remember how we used to sit on the terrace of the old castle and look at the Adriatic? We might have been the only people in the world [. . .]

KITTY   *(tragically)* And we thought our love would last for ever.[43]

Like Albee's George and Martha, Kitty and Porteous's relationship is fuelled by a deep unspoken sadness, part hatred and part dependency, evolved over decades of bickering and reconciliation.

Kitty and Elizabeth display many similarities and are drawn towards each other from the start. Clive tells Elizabeth that his wife 'was very like you . . . only she had dark hair instead of red . . . she had the most adorable little nose, like yours . . .'[44] But Lady Kitty's hair is dyed and her cheeks rouged; like Lady Frederick, she clings to the vestigial remains of her youth and beauty, employing fruitless attempts to stay the passage of time with make-up, dyes and wigs. Informed of Elizabeth's intention to leave Arnold, Lady Kitty determines to prevent her from repeating her own mistake. Kitty has learned in a 'bitter school' that life is hard for an adulterous woman and harder for upper-class women who have no earning power:

> They can make what laws they like, they can give us the suffrage, but when you come down to bedrock, it's the man who pays the piper who calls the tune. Woman will only be the equal of man when she earns her living in the same way that he does.[45]

Lady Kitty paints a sad, bleak picture of her life in exile. Cut by conventional society, she explains how they had to make do with any society they could get: 'Loose women and vicious men.' When Porteous began his infidelities, Kitty had only the power of a mistress and not a wife: she was forced to learn to turn a blind eye. Elizabeth is shocked by Lady Kitty's stoicism: 'One sacrifices one's life for love and then one finds that love doesn't last. The tragedy of love isn't death or separation. One gets over them. The tragedy of love is indifference.'[46]

Arnold continues to pretend to act the martyr and allow Elizabeth to divorce him with no stain on her character. For a moment she hesitates and decides to tell Teddie that she will stay with her husband after all. Teddie is open and honest: 'I don't offer you peace and quietness. I offer you unrest and anxiety. I don't offer you happiness. I offer you love.'[47] Recognizing the love that the young people have for each other, Lady Kitty and Porteous half-heartedly persuade Elizabeth to stay, whilst adding that they both think that Arnold is a bit of a prig. Elizabeth and Teddie decide to risk it together and accept the consequences. Kitty and Porteous offer their car and recommend places for them to see when they get to the Continent. The cycle of events has come full circle and Elizabeth has fulfilled her destiny in following the path taken by Lady Kitty. Wilde had his Lady Windermere return to her domestic responsibilities thirty years earlier, but Maugham's Elizabeth Champion-Cheney is a woman of the modern age and refuses to be defeated by the threat of social ostracism. Faced with the choice of a life of cold domesticity or an unstable existence governed by passion, however fleeting and unreliable it might be, Elizabeth chooses the insecure, romantic path of individualism.

The Constant Wife

The Constant Wife was produced in London in 1926, the same year as Coward's *Easy Virtue*. At twenty-seven, Coward was examining the society of his contemporaries; Maugham on the other hand was fifty-two, yet both wrote comedies about the new sexual freedoms of the flapper era. A great success in America, where it played for 295 performances, *The Constant Wife* was a failure in London, closing after only 70. The play returns to the Wildean preoccupation with the disparity between the moral code for men and women. Wilde had observed that 'The cultivation of separate sorts of virtues and separate ideals of duty in men and women has led to the whole social fabric being weaker and unhealthier than it need be.' The dilemma of *The Constant Wife* was actually anticipated by Wilde in a story he had discussed with George Alexander. A man of rank and fashion is married to a sweet country girl who is ignorant of society life. Bored with her, he invites a group of *fin-de-siècle* people to his country house and tries to persuade the wife to flirt with other men, thereby condoning his own indiscretions with other women. He deliberately invites one of her former admirers. After dinner, tired of the party, the wife seeks some peace in the drawing-room. She falls half asleep on the sofa and when her husband enters is surprised that he lowers the lamps and locks the door. To her horror, the wife realizes that her husband is accompanied by another woman, Lady X, to whom he begins to make love. The wife stays silent and listens to their lovemaking. Suddenly there is a knock at the door. Lady X's husband demands to be admitted. Lady X panics, but the wife rises, turns up the lamps and calmly opens the door. She apologizes to Lady X's husband and explains that the three had been experimenting with thought-reading. The husband is grateful for his wife's attempt to save his and Lady X's reputation. But the wife, having defended her husband, decides to leave him for her former admirer. Wilde was keen that the lovers should end up together happily, with 'No morbid self-sacrifice. No renunciation. A sheer flame of love between a man and a woman.'[48]

In *The Constant Wife*, Maugham similarly charts a woman's discovery of sexual freedom through her defence of a husband she knows to be unfaithful. But where the wife of Wilde's play would certainly have suffered socially for her actions, as Lady Kitty did in *The Circle*, Constance Middleton seems to embrace the new sexual freedoms of the 1920s without fear of ostracism. The play advocates absolute equality of sexual morality for men and women. Constance's modern values are contrasted with those of her mother, who represents prewar Edwardian women's attitudes towards infidelity. Constance, like her mother, is happy to turn a blind eye to her husband's infidelity; the difference between the two women is that Constance wants to be unfaithful too.

John Middleton, a successful Harley Street consultant, has been happily married to Constance for fifteen years. He is currently having an affair with his wife's best friend, Marie-Louise Durham. Constance's friends, her mother and sister wonder whether they ought to let Constance know about the affair. They believe that infidelity in men is an ordinary fact of marriage: 'so long as a man is kind and civil to his wife do you blame him very much if he strays occasionally from the narrow path of virtue?'[49] The women regard themselves as 'naturally faithful creatures' and collude in the maintenance of this double standard. Only Barbara Fawcett, the middle-aged widow, has chosen to live a life without men. She has to work for her living and

> When you work hard eight hours a day you don't much want to be bothered with love. In the evening the tired business woman wants to go to a musical comedy or play cards. She doesn't want to be worried with adoring males.[50]

Constance's mother hints to her daughter that she should turn a blind eye if her husband did ever turn out to be unfaithful, but she holds back from telling her the whole truth.

One afternoon, Marie-Louise's husband, Mortimer Durham, arrives and accuses Middleton of having an affair with his wife. As evidence he produces John's cigarette case. Constance intervenes and claims that she had left the case near Marie-Louise's bed. Mortimer begs his wife to forgive him for suspecting her. John is ashamed of himself and grateful that Constance has saved Marie-Louise's marriage and her reputation. Constance now reveals that she had known about the affair since it started and for the last six months had been desperately trying to prevent her friends and relations from telling her the 'ghastly secret'. Constance believes that she and her husband have been very lucky to fall out of love with each other at the same time. She certainly has no intention of divorcing him: though her desire for her husband has abated, she still enjoys his company. Besides, Constance has entered marriage as an economic bargain; she has delivered children and handed them over to others, more competent, to look after. Now that her husband no longer sexually desires her, she has become a 'parasite'. Constance is tired of being a 'modern wife', a 'prostitute who doesn't deliver the goods',[51] and uses the occasion of her husband's infidelity to reassess and restructure their relationship.

The last act of the play takes place a year later. Constance has gone into business with Barbara Fawcett. Like Syrie Maugham she has become a successful interior designer. After a busy and prosperous year, she is about to take a holiday. Before she leaves, she tells her husband that she has paid £1,000 into his bank account for her board and lodging during the past twelve months. Middleton is stunned, but Constance defends her actions: 'Now that women have broken down the walls of the harem they must take the rough-and-tumble of the street.'[52] Lady Kitty in *The Circle* had accepted that it was too late for her to make a bid for independence, but Constance has realized that the only freedom that really matters is economic freedom – not to be some man's chattel. Her economic freedom also entails sexual freedom and Constance informs her husband that she is going on holiday with an old flame and that they will be travelling 'as man and wife'. The affair is to last only for the six weeks of the holiday: Constance wants to have one last fulfilling sexual fling before her middle age. As she is only doing what her husband had done with Marie-Louise, Middleton has no choice but to grudgingly accept her bargain. Constance attempts to redefine the marital relationship so that each partner is equal. She liberates herself by, almost literally, buying her freedom. In the end, she has the best of both worlds, able to indulge in a one-off extramarital affair where she will fulfil herself sexually safe in the knowledge that she won't be jeopardizing the security of her long-standing relationship with her husband. It seems an ideal solution, a double life lived openly and above board, with sex and security very efficiently compartmentalized. But there's something slightly unreal, unbelievable, about Constance. She's so objective, so practical, even slightly removed from her emotions. Maugham's ideal marriage seems like a wish-fulfilment, uncomplicated by that illogical, uncontrollable emotion which haunted Maugham's own relationships as well as much of his fiction: that old green-eyed monster, sexual jealousy.

The Letter

An idle, sensuous woman. What good have you ever done in your life, I wonder? You go about seeking excitement, new experiences, anything to cheat you of your boredom, and you don't care what injury you cause to others. But this time, you've made a mistake. It's a risk to take strange men into one's house. I took you for a goddess and you're just a whore.[53]

The backstreets of Singapore and the humid jungle plantations of the tropical Malay peninsula are the exotic background for Maugham's tale of attempted rape, murder, adultery and blackmail in *The Letter*. The outpost-of-Empire setting and the adulterous relationship at its centre make *The Letter* a fairly representative example of Maugham's *oeuvre*. The stage version was written and performed in 1927, only a year after the story appeared in a collection entitled *The Casurina Tree*. Gladys Cooper produced the play having detected in the story of Leslie Crosbie a great potential vehicle for her own talent. The action begins with a spectacular *coup de théâtre* as Leslie shoots six bullets into the body of Geoffrey Hammond on the steps of her bungalow. It is an act of shocking violence. When her husband arrives with the District Officer, Leslie claims that Hammond had tried to rape her, so she shot him. Almost immediately Maugham dispenses with suspense. We know whodunnit and we know how. This is no typical murder mystery, for the interest of the play lies in Leslie's motivation and the action is a series of deceits and revelations which gradually expose her true character. Leslie is investigated by the men around her, for she herself is the mystery. All the male characters continually draw attention to Leslie's composure and self-control, the great assets of the English wife: 'Her self-control is absolutely amazing. She must have nerves of iron.'[54]

Leslie is sent to Singapore and charged with murder. But it looks like a very open and shut case: Hammond had a reputation for drinking and it is also revealed that he had a Chinese mistress. Popular opinion amongst the British is heavily in Leslie's favour and the trial looks like a foregone conclusion. However, the Crosbies' friend and lawyer Howard Joyce is approached by his Chinese assistant Ong Chi Seng, who tells him of an incriminating letter in the possession of Hammond's Chinese mistress. The letter was written by Leslie on the night of the killing, begging Hammond to come and see her whilst her husband is away. Leslie had claimed that she and Hammond enjoyed only a social friendship. The letter implies otherwise. Joyce confronts Leslie with the existence of the letter and she eventually confesses that Hammond had been her lover. She begs Joyce, for the sake of his friendship with her husband, to do anything in his power to prevent the letter from falling into the hands of the prosecution. Joyce feels uncomfortable about compromising his professional ethics, but ultimately buys the letter for a huge sum of money. Leslie is acquitted and returns home. Her husband announces that they should leave and establish their own plantation in Sumatra, where their only neighbours will be Dutch. For Leslie, this exile from her English compatriots would be a purgatory indeed, but Crosbie's plans come to nothing. Joyce is forced to tell him that because of the enormous price of the letter, Crosbie and his wife will be almost penniless; they will have to remain in the bungalow where the murder took place. Crosbie demands to see the letter and Leslie has no choice but to tell the truth. Joyce believes that Crosbie will eventually forgive his errant wife, but she cannot forgive herself for killing the only man she ever loved.

The Letter is typical in the literature of Empire in its focus on a story of rape. Ever since Caliban had attempted to rape Miranda on Prospero's pseudo-colonial island, the rape of the wives and daughters of colonists by natives has served as a metaphorical revenge for the economic and cultural ravishment of the Mother Country. The accusation of rape forms the bases of two of the most important twentieth-century critiques of British colonialism, Forster's *A Passage to India*, published just two years before *The Letter*, and Paul Scott's *The Jewel in the Crown* (1966). Forster's Adela Quested isn't actually attacked at all and her confusion is only part of a more wide-ranging spiritual crisis. Leslie Crosbie isn't raped either, but her accusation is a calculated deceit to cloud the reality of her own desires.

The Crosbies are typical products of Empire culture. The men have an idealized view of their wives as twentieth-century versions of demure Victorian matrons. Any woman who doesn't conform to such an ideal exacerbates the men's (and Maugham's) latent misogyny. Crosbie is a dull, trusting man married to a dissatisfied wife. He tells Leslie, 'You've been the best wife a man ever had,'[55] echoing the sentiments of Constance's only half-aware husband in *The Constant Wife*. Joyce has always found Leslie 'very reserved. I supposed she was shy'. But she is an ambivalent creature. During his investigation, Joyce becomes confused by the disparity between Leslie's reserved manner and the violence of Hammond's death (after all, she did shoot him in the back): 'I'm afraid you think me more cold-blooded than I am'.[56] The more he learns about her, the more Joyce becomes convinced that Leslie is exactly that: 'It suggests not so much panic as uncontrollable fury. Under the circumstances which your wife had described one would expect a woman to be frightened out of her wits, but hardly beside herself with rage'.[57]

Leslie takes her husband's gun, the masculine symbol of hunting and colonial culture, and shoots her lover. Leslie's duality is underlined by her name, which is, like Lady Frederick's, significantly masculine: Leslie is no typical woman and certainly not a typical wife. Beneath a veneer of respectability she harbours a clandestine sexuality. If the adulterous affair can be interpreted as one between Hammond and a male Leslie (Lesley), the tale reads like a metaphor of sexual choices. Hammond has chosen to live with a Chinese woman, a native of the country, rather than Leslie, the foreigner. He has made his sexual choice and rejected Leslie. Leslie/Lesley would rather see Hammond dead than allow him to leave her for somebody of a different (native/indigenous/Chinese/straight?) culture. By shooting Hammond in a jealous rage and exposing her relationship with him to detailed investigation, Leslie threatens the affair with exposure, a sort of unpremeditated, self-provoked 'outing'.

Leslie's composure disguises her passionate sexual nature. But the Crosbies as a couple are childless, locked together in a rather dull marriage, in which Crosbie is the simple, loving, domestic partner and Leslie rather 'mannish'. Leslie points out to her husband that the estate is 'like your child'. She seems all too aware of the close relationship between Joyce and her husband and that Joyce doesn't particularly like her: 'Oh you know what men are. They never care very much for the women their particular friends marry.' In compromising himself by saving Leslie, Joyce is actually more concerned about saving his 'particular friend' the humiliation: 'It's absurd how fond I am of Bob. You see, I've known him for so long. His life may very well be ruined too.'[58] The revelation of Leslie's deceit seems to confirm for Joyce his own misogynous feelings: 'It's strange that a man can live with a woman for ten years and not know the first thing about her. It's rather frightening.' For if Leslie Crosbie, the epitome of British womanhood, is an adulteress and murderer, how many other seemingly serene and contented wives in the colony might hide such dangerous secrets?

On the surface, Leslie's 'only accomplishment' is her lace-making, which is repeatedly referred to. Seemingly a very genteel occupation, the lace-making takes on a sinister quality as Leslie spins her web of lies and deceit. Almost the whole of the first act is taken up by Leslie's fictional account of Hammond's attempt to rape her and her performance as the injured victim. With great ease she manipulates the men's response to her, claiming that she firmly rejected Hammond's advances: 'Don't you know that I've never loved anyone but Robert and even if I don't love Robert you're the last man I should care for'. She keeps up the pretences: 'Oh it's horrible. I can't go on. It's asking too much of me. It's so shameful, shameful.' When she describes the rape she says 'his eyes were burning. He wasn't a man any more, he was a savage; I felt my heart pounding against my ribs. ... Don't look at me. I don't want any of you to look at me.'[59] Leslie plays the demure matron, ashamed of Hammond's unspeakable desires. But she has previously enjoyed his savage sexual play as an antidote to the passionless nights she spends with Crosbie.

When the letter is introduced to him by his assistant, Joyce finds himself manipulated by Ong Chi Seng, who has learned a variety of skills from the hypocritical British, including blackmail. There is an uneasy relationship between the Chinese and the British in the colony which is founded on a notion of racial superiority. Despite being one of the most popular men in the community, public opinion turns against Hammond because of his involvement with the Chinese woman. The very fact that he is living with a woman outside the British community convinces them that he was a man of 'notorious character' and almost deserved to be shot. But it is the colonists who are corrupt. 'In a civilised community a trial is inevitable', but the story of Leslie Crosbie, adulteress and murderer, reveals that the community isn't civilized at all, simply that they are practised and successful at deceit. Leslie's adultery is disguised by murder, which is in turn covered up by perjury. Justice is flouted, for the foundations of British rule are flawed by a blind and selfish hypocrisy. At least Hammond had the nerve to live openly with the Chinese woman and suffer the prejudice of his peers, rather than continue his hole-in-the-corner affair with Leslie whilst she preserved the appearance of propriety. Leslie shoots Hammond, not only because he no longer wants her but because she feels insulted that he should have left her for a woman of an inferior race. She resents the fact that they have equal status in their passion for Hammond, that they have both been his mistress. Leslie is particularly bitter in her description of her rival, describing her like a prostitute 'with her gold bracelets and her necklaces. . . . Horrible!' Leslie finds the very idea of the Chinese woman repellant and cannot bear or understand the fact that Hammond has chosen an alternative culture to the narrow British expatriate world which she herself represents: 'she was the only woman who really meant anything to him, and the rest was just pastime. . . . He couldn't have been more vile if I'd been a harlot on the streets.'[60] Ultimately Leslie must face the fact that she and the Chinese woman are levelled by sex and passion and that her disgust for the Chinese woman is actually an expression of her own disgust with herself:

LESLIE   What can I say? It wasn't me that loved that other. It was a madness that seized me, and I was as little my own mistress as though I were delirious with fever. It brought me no happiness, that love – it only brought me shame and remorse.[61]

Love for Maugham is far from ennobling; it is a disease which undermines reason over which the individual has no control. The jungle, representing unsullied nature, releases a passionate violence in Leslie. And though she will not actually suffer the exile of a Mrs Arbuthnot or Mrs Erlynne, her penance is to live the rest of her life with a husband who will never trust her again, sure in the knowledge that she alone is responsible for destroying any chance she may have had of happiness or fulfilment: 'My retribution is greater! With all my heart I still love the man I killed.'[62]

Maugham's retribution for his transgressors can be pretty severe. Kitty Fane in *The Painted Veil* is forced to accompany her husband to almost certain death in a leper colony. In his novella *Up at the Villa* (1941) Mary Paton, having shot her one-night-stand gigolo, is black-mailed into marrying the man who helps her cover up the murder. Such penances give the misogynist in Maugham the opportunity to make his heroines suffer for their sins. But these women are his heroines, rather than villains. *Footprints in the Jungle* is an example of a typical Maugham plot, in which the narrator observes a rather ordinary middle-aged woman as she plays bridge. It transpires that she has actually had her husband brutally murdered twenty years before in order that she could marry her lover, with whom she now lives in cosy middle-aged matri-mony. The crime is never discovered. Throughout Maugham's work the impression is created that the various outposts of the British Empire are colonized by some rather dangerous women who are certainly not to be trusted; men are poached, duped, cuckolded and sometimes killed by their wives and lovers.

In his early work, the characterization of Maugham's women is laced with a bitter misogyny, but as his vision darkens after the war, the strug-gles of women come to symbolize for him the struggles of the indivi-dual to achieve a sense of personal freedom. His women do seem to get away with murder, sometimes literally, but their future lives beyond their stories of adultery, elopement and killing look unsure and far from settled. Maugham's attitude to women is clearly informed by his own disastrous marriage to Syrie Wellcome: consequently, he finds women on the one hand threatening creatures who geld, restrict and kill men; on the other hand they are a convenient representation of individuals trapped by the circumstance of their gender, yearning to fulfil their sex-ual desires. It is this tension between misogyny and sympathy which characterizes Somerset Maugham's uneasy, unsettling tone of ambiva-lence towards his murderous and adulterous heroines.

Public Lives, Private Faces

Noël Coward's performance of a lifetime

When an all-male version of *Private Lives* was proposed, it didn't take long to reach a decision. No! Ditto *Fallen Angels*. Remembering the posters which advertised the fact that *The Boys in the Band* is not a musical! I shudder to think what they'd have done to us!

Graham Payn[1]

It was absolutely preposterous, the notion that gays were writing about gays, but disguising them as straights. Tennessee Williams knew the difference between men and women as well as I do. If you're writing about men, you're writing about men, and if you're writing about women, you're writing about women. But then rumour began that *Who's Afraid of Virginia Woolf?* was really about four men, which led to attempts at all-male productions of the play, which led me to close them down. For the same reason I don't allow all-female versions of *The Zoo Story*. Because they're incorrect. But somehow the sniping has never gone away.

Edward Albee[2]

To say that only a woman can portray the passions of a woman . . . is to rob the art of acting of all claim to objectivity, and to assign to the mere accident of sex what properly belongs to imaginative insight and creative energy.

Oscar Wilde[3]

As we slip into the next century, one wonders which of Noël Coward's seemingly slight creations will survive in the popular cultural imagination; the balcony scene from *Private Lives*, perhaps? 'Mad Dogs and Englishmen'? *Brief Encounter*? Madam Arcati? Perhaps his most complex creation and surely one of the iconographic figures of the twentieth century is 'Noël Coward' himself. As early as 1953, Kenneth Tynan recognized that 'Even the youngest of us will know in fifty years time exactly what we mean by a "very Noël Coward sort of person".'[4] Forty-four years later, Tynan's prediction seems to have been fulfilled; Diet Coke's Wimbledon '97 TV campaign had a Coward sound-alike trilling his way through a jingle which parodied 'Mad Dogs and Englishmen'. We don't need to see the dressing-gown or the cigarette-holder; we instantly know that the advertisement refers to Noël.

From the very beginnings of his theatrical career, Coward the performer was inextricably linked with Coward the author. He consciously fashioned and exploited this symbiotic relationship between his theatrical image and his public persona. Coward's were unashamedly commercial plays with starring roles intended for himself. In 1924, the then comparatively unknown Coward refused to compromise when the Everyman Theatre balked at the idea of his playing the lead in *The Vortex*; ultimately he had his own way and the play was a controversial success. He continued to promote himself through his work, from *Private Lives* in the 1930s and *Present Laughter* during the war years through to his final stage appearance in *A Song at Twilight* in 1965. As he matured, so too did the age range of his characters; their preoccupations developed from the ambitious and aspiring to the milieu of the successful and the famous. Coward's life infused his art and vice versa; consequently the autobiographical strain running through his work is very strong.

Though posterity will inevitably record Coward as a playwright of the 1930s, his first full-length play was completed at the end of the First World War. In *The Rat Trap* (1918) we are introduced to a bohemian couple, both writers, struggling to balance fluctuating fame and success whilst retaining the equilibrium of their relationship. The aspiring novelist Sheila Brandreth is warned by a friend on the eve of her wedding to aspiring playwright Keld Maxwell that one of them will have to make sacrifices if the relationship is to succeed: 'either you or Keld will have to sacrifice a certain amount of personality'.[5] Sheila relinquishes her writing in order to become a housewife, but leaves the now successful Keld when she discovers he has been having an affair with an actress. Ultimately Sheila returns to her writing and Keld returns to Sheila. But though pregnant and willing to take Keld back for the child's sake, Sheila declares that she no longer loves him. The theme of warring bohemian egos is further explored in *Design for Living* where Otto and Leo, an artist and a playwright, compete for Gilda as their fortunes prosper. When both have become successful, Gilda, feeling used up by her two lovers, marries the humourless Ernest, leaving Otto and Leo to find solace in each other. Eventually Gilda herself becomes a successful interior designer in New York and when Otto and Leo visit her, the three realize that they cannot live apart. Now that all three are successful, they settle for a *ménage à trois*. *Present Laughter* was written when Coward was forty, and examines the burdens of power and fame in the orbit of a star actor, his retinue and fans. It is a rather world-weary portrayal of the artist. The unproduced *Long Island Sound* is based on the satirical short story, *What Mad Pursuit?* It concerns a British playwright invited for a quiet weekend to escape the flurry of New York. But the protagonist finds himself relentlessly pursued by fans and well-meaning guests, who drive him to distraction. In a desperate effort to find peace and quiet he leaps out of the window, preferring the peace of death or injury; it's a classic Cowardian exit from chaos.

Coward's stage roles provide intermittent snapshots of himself in prose at various ages in his life. He observed later in his career: 'I've been a "personality" actor all my life. I've established in my early years the sophisticated, urbane type, which is in tune with my own personality.'[6] Even *Blithe Spirit*, though not originally performed by Coward, was written with himself in mind. Charles Condomine is a successful, sophisticated middle-aged writer with a talent for mixing cocktails as 'dry as a bone'. In tune, indeed.

Just as the caricatured visage of George Bernard Shaw as God-Author manipulates the puppet strings of Julie Andrews and Rex Harrison in the publicity for the original production of *My Fair Lady*, Coward played God in his own universe. He created the inner lives and motivations of his characters on the page and then went on to give them a physical, public reality as a performer on the stage. Consequently some of those roles, particularly Elyot Chase in *Private Lives* and Garry Essendine in *Present Laughter*, continue to resonate with shadows of Coward's performance, his inflections and mannerisms. Keith Baxter who played Elyot opposite Joan Collins in the 1990 West End revival of *Private Lives* remembers how difficult it was to get away from Coward's speech rhythms, which seem to be ingrained in the dialogue. Excerpts from the play were recorded on vinyl, an exceptional indication of success even in the 1930s, with Coward and Lawrence repeating their famous stage relationship for posterity. This recording continues to haunt subsequent productions with its definitive performances. Rather territorially, Coward formulated such definitive characterizations by establishing aspects of himself as elements of his stage characters. Well aware of the public's perception of him, Coward actually exploited it in self-mockery, as when the aspiring writer in *Present Laughter* accuses Essendine: 'All you do is to wear dressing-gowns and make witty remarks'. David Lean's film version of *Blithe Spirit* (1945) begins with a nursery rhyme, accompanied by a tune from a musical box:

When we are young
We read and believe
The most fantastic things.
When we grow older and wiser
We learn, with perhaps a little regret
That these things can never be.[7]

The screen then goes to black and we hear a familiar voice add: 'We are quite, quite wrrr-ong!' The inimitable trills and clipped consonants were Coward's trademarks. Even as early as 1945, before the proliferation of the media, Coward was sure that his celebrity was such that even without introduction or billing his vocal mannerisms would be immediately recognizable.

Coward surrounded himself, both privately and professionally, with a stock of trusted friends and colleagues. He wrote plays and parts not only for himself, but with particular actor friends in mind. *Design for Living* and *Quadrille* were written for Alfred Lunt and Lynne Fontanne, the golden couple of Broadway. He frequently claimed that he wrote a part in each of his plays for his close friend, Joyce Carey. Carey was the daughter of Lilian Braithwaite, who had created the role of the mother in *The Vortex*. Joyce Carey herself memorably played Mrs Bagot, the 'refained' refreshment-room manageress in *Brief Encounter*, and is particularly moving as the doomed working-class wife in *In Which We Serve*. Most famously, Coward wrote *Private Lives* and *Tonight at 8.30* as vehicles for himself (of course) and Gertrude Lawrence. In writing for known quantities, Coward was able to tailor-make roles. In creating his plays, he had no pretensions about textual 'sanctity', for text and personality were intertwined. Consequently, Coward was able to control other actors/characters' responses to his own performance. Coward's principal designer, Gladys Calthrop, was also a great personal friend and collaborated with Coward from 1922 onwards. His early financial affairs were taken over by his lover, Jock Wilson, who continued to look after them even when their relationship had ended. And who should replace Coward and play opposite Gertrude Lawrence in the 1948 American revival of *Tonight at 8.30*, that series of demanding vehicles written specifically for Noël and Gertie? It would be impossible to repeat the Coward/ Lawrence magic and anybody stepping into Coward's shoes opposite Lawrence would have a legendary partnership to live up to. Coward's roles were taken over by a young, little-known song-and-dance man called Graham Payn. He also happened to be Coward's lover; the revival was an unmitigated disaster.

The Coward circle seems close, perhaps even a little closed. But with his increasing popularity, particularly between the wars, it would have been necessary for Coward to rely on his friends' and associates' discretion in protecting and promoting his reputation. This warm, incestuous closeness is examined in detail in *Present Laughter*:

GARRY   You and Henry and Monica and Liz and I share something of inestimable importance to all of us, and that is mutual respect and trust. God knows it's been hard won. We can look back on years and years of bloody conflict with ourselves and each other. But now we're all middle-aged we can admit, with a certain mellow tranquillity, that it's been well worth it. Here we are, five people closely woven together by affection and work and intimate knowledge of each other.[8]

In his memoir, Graham Payn observes that 'A troupe of characters parades through the diaries like the cast of one of Noël's plays. He referred to them as the "Family".' Payn compares the ambience and characters of *Present Laughter* with the frenetic milieu at Coward's studio in Gerald Road, 'anytime from the early 1930's to the mid-50's'.[9]

Before the rise of the director in the postwar theatre of the kitchen sink movement, plays were often directed by the leading actor. Before the war, writers certainly didn't have the say in casting and rehearsal which they were to acquire in the 1960s. Coward's position as writer/

performer made him very powerful in the production of his own work and much of it he originally directed himself. With the current fashion of writer-directors like Terry Johnson, David Mamet and David Hare, it no longer seems so unusual, but in some ways Coward paved the way for them; he was the first living playwright to direct his own work at the National Theatre when he staged *Hay Fever* there in 1964. Script, design, casting, performance, direction: Coward had almost total control over the artistic presentation of his work from an early stage in his career, which he continued to exert until the end of it. Does such control imply a reluctance, or even a resistance, to interpretation by other theatrical practitioners? It was Kenneth Tynan who suggested that the National Theatre revive one of Coward's early works, and even in 1964 Coward was still regarded as the best interpreter of his own writing. It is only comparatively recently that Coward's work has been explored, examined and interpreted by other directors and designers and that performers have felt released from the traditional paraphernalia of a Coward play with its vowels, trills and cigarette-holders, a style very much associated with Coward himself.

Present Laughter examines the sexual intrigues surrounding Garry Essendine, a leading 'romantic comedian'. Essendine himself is rather promiscuous and his promiscuity is regarded very much as a matter of course by his servants and secretary. The action of the play is cyclical, opening with the young debutante, Daphne Stillington, who is Essendine's most recent conquest. She had lost her latchkey the previous evening and spent the night in the spare room. The loss of one's latchkey is adopted as a euphemistic excuse to stay overnight in Garry's bed. The key has a rather obvious sexual symbolism and the spare room is used by guests in the morning as a nod to convention. It also, very conveniently, would have countered any objections to the play by the Lord Chamberlain on grounds of immorality. Essendine's 'family' has been infiltrated by the vampish Joanna Lypiatt, who has married Essendine's business manager, Henry. She has also been conducting an affair with Essendine's accountant, Morris. In the course of the play, she reveals that these two relationships were calculated ways of getting to know Essendine better and that it is Garry she really wants; he willingly succumbs to her charms. Joanna is also consigned to the spare room after she eventually spends the night with Garry. The recurrent use of the spare room in the action underlines its symbolic function. The two off-stage areas continually used and referred to are the spare bedroom and the office, the arenas of private and public life, sex and stage. The play examines Essendine's self-imposed division between his sex life and his business life, a division under which Coward himself lived. The spare room is Coward's closet. In this world of bed-hopping between friends, and the lies and performances that follow, Garry claims to be the only character who is honest about his philandering. When Joanna propositions Essendine, he responds with lines from a play, a ploy which she duly recognizes. Such a tactic, she feels, is a proof of his emotional tepidness:

JOANNA   It proved that you are no more sincere emotionally than I am, that you no longer need or desire the pangs of love, but are perfectly willing to settle for the fun of love. It's an adult point of view and I salute it.[10]

Joanna's argument has little to do with love. She proposes an honest, purely sexual relationship, unhindered by the responsibilities of marriage or the trappings of romance. But Garry is appalled by the ease with which Joanna dupes her husband and her long-term lover. In his denunciation of Joanna, Morris and Henry's mutual and complicated sexual deceptions, Essendine observes that his own attitude to sex is comparatively straightforward:

To me the whole business is vastly over-rated. I enjoy it for what it's worth and fully intend to go on doing so for as long as anybody's interested and when the time comes that they're not I shall be perfectly content to settle down with an apple and a good book![11]

Coward sets up Essendine from the very beginning of the play as a heterosexual philanderer but with a homosexual's self-conscious anxiety about the maintenance of his public persona and reputation.* But Coward complicates the possibility of Essendine's sexuality by the introduction of a young writer, Roland Maule. Maule has sent Essendine a play that he has

---

*GARRY   I'm always acting – watching myself go by – that's what's so horrible – I see myself all the time, drinking, loving, suffering – sometimes I think I'm going mad – (*Present Laughter*, Act 1, p. 148).

written. It is a raw effort, rather serious and very uncommercial. Maule disparages Essendine's style of West End theatre and Essendine himself. Essendine tires of Maule's idealistic but naive views on theatre. He loses his temper and advises Maule to go and work in a repertory theatre where he might 'Learn from the ground up how plays are constructed and what is actable and what isn't.' Maule is overwhelmed by Essendine's vehemence and his attitude; he is quite hypnotized:

ROLAND   You've been a sort of obsession with me. .... I felt some-
                 how that I wasn't at peace with myself and gradually, bit by
                 bit, I began to realise that you signified something to me.
GARRY   What sort of something?
ROLAND   I don't quite know – not yet.[12]

Maule's devotion to Essendine is certainly that of the pupil for his guru. But Coward's calculatedly ambiguous way of exploring this devotion leaves sufficient room for speculation about Maule's erotic interest in that direction. Coward implies that Maule finally identifies his own sexuality and recognizes in Garry a similar sexual orientation. In a recent production of the play on Broadway,* Maule turns up at Essendine's flat naked under a raincoat and offers his body quite overtly to strains of 'Mad About The Boy'. That might well be taking dramatic licence over the hills and far away, but *Present Laughter* certainly dramatizes a theatrical environment where anything goes. Daphne doesn't believe that 'real love should be bound by Church or Law'; Joanna flippantly disregards her marriage vows and Liz and Garry 'never quite got round' to getting a divorce. The Essendine set are fashionably amoral and pay little heed to convention. It comes as no surprise that Essendine receives fan mail from young men he has only briefly encountered:

MONICA   Here's one signed 'Joe'. .... He seems to have met you in the
                 South of France.
GARRY   I do get about, don't I? *(looking at the letter)* Oh, it's Joe.
MONICA   *(patiently)* That's what I said.

---

* Directed by Scott Elliott and featuring Frank Langella as Essendine. See John Lahr, 'Mr Producer, I'm talkin' to you, Sir', *New Yorker*, 25 November 1996, pp. 123–25.

GARRY   Joe was wonderful. I met him in a bar in Marseilles. He's dark green and comes from Madras.[13]

Essendine also makes enthusiastic observations about the attractiveness of a young naval officer he had met who has a hankering for the stage, but it's neither the boy's nautical knowledge nor his thespian skill that Garry is interested in:

LIZ   What does he look like?
GARRY   Absolutely marvellous, if it's the one I think it is, vast strapping shoulders and tiny, tiny hips like a wasp . . .[14]

In the same way, Coward later implies Hugo Latymer's homosexuality by having him dwell on the physical attributes of his manservant, Felix, in *A Song at Twilight*: 'You look as though you should be a good swimmer yourself, with those shoulders.'[15]

Roland Maule visits the flat a second time the evening before Essendine is to leave for Africa. He recognizes that they both have been acting in real life (perhaps straight acting?):

GARRY   Listen, what exactly do you want, really?
ROLAND To be with you.[16]

Maule tries to seduce Essendine with the same intensity that Daphne has pursued him. Both want to accompany him to Africa. Their pursuit of Essendine is couched in exactly the same terms in two different scenes:

DAPHNE   You needn't be frightened – I won't make any demands on you whatever. I don't want you to marry me or anything like that.[17]

and

ROLAND You needn't be frightened that I shall get in your way or make demands on you.

To which Essendine responds comically 'You mean you don't expect me to marry you!'[18] At this point Garry has already pushed Daphne into his office and now Maule has locked himself in the spare room that has been the haven for all of Essendine's female conquests; Maule thereby identifies himself as one of them.

Garry Essendine lives a life of opportunistic promiscuity. Women, men, best friends' wives: all are fair game. Fidelity means very little. In order to resolve the confusion before his trip to Africa, Liz Essendine decides to take Garry back. Not out of love, but for 'the good of the firm', a real marriage of convenience. Essendine creeps out of the flat with Liz, leaving Maule locked in the bedroom and Daphne in the office (an indication that Garry can't fully compartmentalize the different aspects of his life and that sometimes the emotional takes over both bedroom and office?). *Present Laughter* is a cynical, unromantic study of human egotism, with Garry, the great individualist, continually in pursuit of personal pleasure, 'for as long as anybody's interested'.

Though obviously very aware of the attempts to reform the laws affecting homosexuals in the 1950s and 1960s, as his diaries indicate, Coward never 'came out' in public. Sheridan Morley was refused permission to discuss Coward's private life in his 1969 biography, *A Talent to Amuse*. When Coward was sent the proofs of Morley's book, he observed, 'I'm afraid Sherry has to do a bit more work [of expurgation]. There are still a few old ladies in Worthing who don't know....'[19] Coward, like Maugham, staunchly believed that 'One's real inside self is a private place and should always stay like that. It is no one else's business.'[20] Coward had actually written stories with homosexual protagonists, such as *Star Quality* and *Me and the Girls*, the latter of which is written in the first person by a sickly camp queen who manages a female dance troupe. He had also written the poem, 'Not Yet the Dodo', which is peopled by explicitly homosexual characters, but he seemed reluctant to discuss homosexuality directly in 'his' medium, the stage, until *A Song at Twilight* in 1966. Coward played the central character, an ageing writer with a homosexual past, but he did not expect audiences to interpret the piece as autobiography. Indeed, he went out of his way to imply that the character of Hugo Latymer was based on Somerset Maugham: *The Times* believed that the identification of Latymer as Maugham was 'beyond question'. As long as Latymer was regarded as a cipher for Maugham, audiences would not take the play as a thinly disguised confessional by Coward himself. In the 1920s and early 1930s Coward had 'joined Maugham in destroying the reputation of the well-born, the well-to-do and the well-educated'.[21] The two men became friends and Coward had often visited Maugham at his villa on Cap Ferrat, but after Maugham's attack on Syrie in 1962 and with the decline of his mental state, Coward's friendship with Maugham cooled: 'There's such a thing as *too* old', Coward observed. There was talk of libel suits against Coward over the similarity of Hugo Latymer to Maugham, but in 1965 Maugham conveniently died before the production opened.

A Song at Twilight examines Coward's own dilemma about the moulding and maintenance of his public reputation. Hugo Latymer is black-mailed by an old lover, Carlotta Gray, who has possession of a series of love letters Latymer had written to a former male lover, Perry Sheldon. Carlotta issues Latymer with a threat: 'Owing to your ceaseless vigilance your "bubble reputation" must be as solid as a football by now. You mustn't be surprised that certain people should wish to kick it about a bit.'[22] She claims that she isn't motivated by self-interest and that her intention is to make Latymer face up to himself: Carlotta is Latymer's self-appointed Nemesis. Latymer's love letters to Sheldon are genuine and passionate, written 'before your mind had become corrupted by fame and your heart by caution'.[23] But Latymer feels that the caution he has exercised in his life and work has been necessitated by the prejudices of the establishment and the reading public: 'It takes more than a few outspoken books and plays and speeches in Parliament to uproot moral prejudice from the Anglo-Saxon mind.'[24] Carlotta's most stinging sally is one which haunted Coward as well as Maugham and Rattigan: 'You might have been a great writer instead of merely a successful one, and you might also have been a far happier man.'[25]

Coward had spent over half a century developing his persona as the archetypal heterosexual dandy and was loathe to dispel the myth because of a change in social fashion or a modification in the law, for he had 'taken a lot of trouble with [his] public face'. The two most indelible images of Coward are aimed at promoting the same carefully con-structed image of 'The Master': successful, suave, single but straight. Photographic images were very important in constructing the Coward myth. There is the image of the precocious young man about town of the 1920s, complete with cigarette-holder and silk dressing-gown. And there is the older Coward, promoting his postwar cabaret shows in Las Vegas: drinking a cup of tea now, but still debonair, standing in a dinner-jacket out in the sun-baked Californian desert. The former image depicts the bard of the new bohemianism of the jazz age. The latter embodies the triumph of the sophisticate. Here is the older Coward, survivor of the changing fashions of the twentieth century, nonchalantly drinking the Englishman's drink, whilst the land dries up around him for lack of rain.

Coward had realized the importance of presenting the public with the image they expected to see. At the height of his fame, he met the aspiring Cecil Beaton on a transatlantic crossing and advised discretion in the public display of one's tastes and behaviour. Beaton recalls Coward's advice:

'It is important not to let the public have a loophole to lampoon you.' That, he explained, was why he studied his own 'facade'. Now take his voice; it was definite, harsh, rugged. He moved firmly, dressed quietly ... 'You should appraise yourself,' he went on. 'Your sleeves are too tight, your voice too high and too precise. You mustn't do it. It closes so many doors. It limits you unnecessarily, and young men with half your intelligence will laugh at you.' He shook his head, wrinkled his forehead and added disarmingly, 'It's hard I know. One would like to indulge one's own tastes. I myself dearly love a good match, yet I know it is overdoing it to wear tie, socks and handkerchief of the same colour. I take ruthless stock of myself in the mirror before going out. A polo jumper or unfortunate tie exposes one to danger.'[26]

The anxiety of 'indulging one's own tastes' in bed, whilst conveying a veneer of public 'respectability' is a tension which informed Coward's private life and provided a theme which he explored throughout his work. Whilst retaining a huge popular following, Coward was adept at manipulating his appeal to different audiences. For the ladies of Worthing, younger then, Coward presented a naughty, stylish, often hilarious exposé of the leisured, arty classes. But Coward's work was also littered with subtextual resonances for those who found the prevailing moral code difficult to live within or just plain wrong. The ambiguity of Coward's texts and performances, both on and off-stage, characterizes a style which he maintained to the very end of his career.

In two of his final film appearances Coward exploited the ambiguities of his own reputation. In both *Boom!* (1968, dir. Joseph Losey) and *The Italian Job* (1969, dir. Peter Collinson) Coward's contribution is very camp. *Boom!* is a version of Tennessee Williams's drama of sex, death and middle age under the Mediterranean midday sun, *The Milk Train Doesn't Stop Here Any More*. Supporting Elizabeth Taylor and Richard Burton, Coward plays the waspish Witch of Capri. But this character is female in the stage version. Was Coward exploiting the fact that the audience had guessed by now that he was gay and had tacitly accepted it? Or was he exploiting the knowledge of *some* members of the audience, attuned to reading ciphers and signals, in a private cinematic joke for those 'in the know'? Coward's final appearance on film was opposite Michael Caine in *The Italian Job*, a jaunty example of late 1960s Euro-froth. Coward plays Mr Bridger, a crime lord who runs his empire from a British prison cell. Despite his residence at Her Majesty's Pleasure, Mr Bridger is an impeccably turned-out gentleman awarded great privileges by the warders and Governor (John Le Mesurier) whom he treats with the courtesy of a duchess. Devoted to the British Royal family, he has covered the walls of his cell with pictures of them, particularly the Queen and the Queen Mother, and is singularly displeased when he notices that 'some of that mob in E block are not standing to attention when the National Anthem is played at the end of the nightly TV'. Coward himself was well acquainted with the Royal family and enjoyed a particular friendship with the Queen Mother. With his upper lip ever stiff and his manners ever polished, Mr Bridger is the epitome of the polite, deferential middle-class English gentleman, and not unlike the persona that Coward had been presenting in both his literary and public life since the 1920s. But Mr Bridger, the apparent personification of good manners, is also a criminal. The movie places Bridger at the centre of a successful criminal organization which he governs at arm's length. It seems unlikely that he would ever have made himself vulnerable enough to get caught, which begs the question *why* is he in prison at all?

Coward's presentation of the character defines Bridger as sovereign of the prison, more specifically, 'Queen' of the place. Throughout the film, Bridger gives 'the royal wave' to lesser mortals. When he is interviewing the Governor about Michael Caine breaking into his private lavatory for a chat, Bridger sits directly under a portrait of the Queen. (There is also the give-away lampshade in Bridger's cell: frilly and pink!) Bridger's sexuality, even for an audience unused to reading the symbols which a gay audience takes for granted, seems pretty obvious. He is continually accompanied by his fawningly camp companion, Keats. Keats is played by Coward's real-life lover, Graham Payn, who has had a long history of playing in Coward's work. Payn recalls in his memoirs, 'I found myself acting as film counterpart to my real-life role'.[27] Coward was playing a counterpoint to his real-life role as well: that of establishment icon harbouring a sexuality which had only recently been decriminalized and still provoked popular antipathy. In his presentation of Bridger, Coward suggests the character's homosexuality without explicitly stating it. It is a trick he had been turning in his writing for years: suggestive, sly, naughty, but never direct.

Such a style also depends on the collaboration of certain sections of the audience, as well as the relative ignorance (or innocence) of the rest. Alan Sinfield argues that Coward plays a dextrous balancing act in his work, exploiting a 'knowing subculture of privileged insiders in defiance of the respectable playgoers whose exclusion was both a necessary defensive manoeuvre and part of the joke'.[28] Sinfield observes that Coward reflected and promoted a very particular style, one that we now recognize as the twentieth-century gay/queer identity. Oscar Wilde had manipulated the figure of the dandy into the aesthete: effete, aristocratic and of independent means. It was only after the Wilde trials that effeminacy, an interest in the arts, leisure and wealth were for the first time equated with homosexuality. Wilde got away with it for as long as he did because his ambiguous public persona was simply carrying on a particular tradition within the leisured classes.

This is the homosexual culture that Coward inherited after his birth in 1899, just a year before Wilde's death. Coward had sprung from the genteel villas of Teddington and eschewed the iconography of 1890s aestheticism, which retained its Wilde-sullied reputation until the 1920s. Coward developed a new style of aestheticism for the 1920s: a world of silk dressing-gowns, chrome and white drawing-rooms à la Syrie Maugham. In the same way that Wilde found a mode of expression in dandyism or the aesthetic creed, Coward attached himself to the post-Great War movement: cynical, young bohemianism. Robert Graves observed in his remembrances of the inter-war years, *The Long Weekend* (1940), that bohemianism in the 1920s stood for a 'gay disorderliness of life, cheerful bad manners and no fixed hours or sexual standards'.[29] The 1920s were the decade of the 'bright young things', who railed against the Edwardian culture which had culminated in the First World War. Women lost the costumes which emphasized their hips and busts and had their hair bobbed; an androgynous, 'boyish' look was in fashion.

Cecil Beaton later recalled how this ambiguous, androgynous world evolved into a sensibility of camp:

> All sorts of men enjoyed imitating the exaggerated, clipped manner of certain leading actors and adopted the confident manner of those who were aware of their charms ... Noël Coward's influence spread even to the outposts of Rickmansworth and Poona. Hearty naval commanders or jolly colonels acquired the 'camp' manners of calling everything from Joan of Arc to Merlin 'lots of fun' and the adjective 'terribly' peppered every sentence. All sorts of men suddenly wanted to look like Noël Coward – sleek, shiny and well-groomed with a cigarette, telephone or cocktail at hand.[30]

Both Alan Sinfield and Philip Hoare examine Coward's use of the word 'gay' in his work of the 1920s and 1930s and how his manipulation of it has contributed to the word's popular usage in the late twentieth century. It is most prevalent in Coward's revue songs. Revue had a reputation for the risqué and tended to be allowed a greater licence than 'proper' plays. Coward's rather outrageous 'Green Carnation' song from *Bitter Sweet* seems pretty blatant today, overtly conjuring the world of the dangerous Oscar Wilde:

> Faded boys, jaded boys, come what may,
> Art is our inspiration,
> And as we are the reason for the Nineties being gay,
> We all wear a green carnation.[31]

In the sketch from *Words and Music* (1932) which introduced 'Mad About The Boy', a series of women – a society hostess, a schoolgirl, a cockney and finally a tart – sing about the object of their desire, a hero of the silver screen. The schoolgirl knows that 'Houseman really/Wrote *The Shropshire Lad* about the boy'. The tart nudges the subtext even further:

> He has a gay appeal
> That makes me feel
> There's maybe something sad about the boy.[32]

Are the women aware that their devotion can never be reciprocated, not only because their beloved is a Hollywood fantasy but also because, like many screen stars from Valentino to Rock Hudson, they are gay? According to Graham Payn a 'lost' verse was to have been added to the 1938 New York production, called *Set to Music*. A business man is discovered in a 'smart office setting':

Mad about the boy,
I know it's silly,
But I'm mad about the boy,
And even Doctor Freud cannot explain
Those vexing dreams
I've had about the boy.
When I told my wife,
She said:
'I've never heard such nonsense in my life!'
Her lack of sympathy
Embarrassed me
And made me frankly *glad* about the boy.
My doctor can't advise me,
He'd help me if he could;
Three times he's tried to psychoanalyse me
But it's just no good.
People I employ
Have the impertinence
To call me Myrna Loy.
I rise above it,
Frankly love it,
'Cos I'm absolutely
MAD ABOUT THE BOY![33]

The 'lost' verse was never included, but it provides a fascinating analogue to Coward's study of psychoanalysis and sex in *The Astonished Heart*, particularly the film version, in which a besuited writer consults his analyst about an obsessive homosexual relationship he is attempting to juggle alongside his marriage.

The word 'gay' certainly seems to have acquired its contemporary use relating to homosexual behaviour or manners in America, and Coward's transatlantic lifestyle in the 1920s and 1930s would surely have exposed him to the slang of theatrical circles over there. 'Gay' was used in its modern sense by British gay men at least during the Second World War, as the *Carry On* comedian Kenneth Willams's wartime diaries reveal. Coward's *Design for Living* was premiered on Broadway in 1933 with a scandalous reputation following the production's provincial tour. In *We Can Always Call Them Bulgarians*, an American study of gay plays on Broadway, Kaier Curtin notes that the adjective 'gay' was used in almost every review of the US production. Did it simply indicate that this dangerous play was a light comedy? Or were the reviewers using shorthand to describe the presentation on stage of a subversive sexual agenda? Studying the success of Coward's plays and songs on both sides of the Atlantic in this period as well as the development of the use of the word 'gay' in homosexual circles outside the theatre, Alan Sinfield concludes that the specialized usage of 'gay' as an adjective to describe homosexual behaviour 'gained currency through Coward's plays and the milieu that they helped to constitute'.[34]

Coward's way

Private Lives

> Thank God I'm normal.
> John Osborne[35]

> VICTOR   I'm glad I'm normal.
> AMANDA   What an odd thing to be glad about.
> Noël Coward, *Private Lives*[36]

The epitome of Coward's style and apex of his achievement is *Private Lives*. The structure of the play skilfully reflects its thesis: the world of Elyot and Amanda is a cyclical one. Once unhappily married to each other the two are now unhappily divorced, each spending their honeymoon with their respective new spouses, Sibyl and Victor. They meet on their terrace, as fate has decreed that they have honeymoon suites next door to each other. Realizing that they are still in love with each other, they run away to Amanda's flat in Paris, leaving Sibyl and Victor behind. After a brief period of bliss, Elyot and Amanda begin to get on each other's nerves as petty past jealousies and character traits exhibit themselves once more. They fall back into their old habits of bickering and fighting and are eventually discovered in a particularly violent scrap by the arrival of the bewildered Victor and Sibyl. The next morning Sibyl and Victor reconcile themselves to their respective spouses and in so doing begin to bicker with each other. Elyot and Amanda creep out of the flat in collusive silence, leaving Sibyl and Victor to their well-matched squabbling.

Private Lives is a pure distillation of one of Coward's favourite themes: the tension between restraint and its corrosive opposite, chaos. Coward explores a particular type of reticence and awkwardness, an embarrassment over emotional/sexual issues which is very English. When they first meet again, Elyot and Amanda attempt to communicate in the polite language of restraint in order not to reveal their true feelings:

AMANDA	What have you been doing lately? During these last years?
ELYOT	Travelling about. I went round the world you know after ...
AMANDA	*(hurriedly)* Yes, yes, I know. How was it?
ELYOT	The world?
AMANDA	Yes.
ELYOT	Oh, highly enjoyable.
AMANDA	China must be very interesting.
ELYOT	Very big, China.
AMANDA	And Japan ...
ELYOT	Very small.[37]

Such social chatter deflects, but doesn't disguise, their deep-rooted attraction to each other, which exhibits itself both in moments of desire (ELYOT There isn't a particle of you that I don't know, remember and want ...) and in moments of discord. They can neither live with nor without each other. Having got back together, they attempt to control and regulate their behaviour by imposing an invented phrase when arguments seem to be brewing, 'Soloman Isaacs'. But even this they corrupt to the vaguely indecent sounding 'Sollocks!' Amanda realizes that they must control themselves, restrain their natural impulse to argue, because 'it's the bickering that always starts it'. Coward had explored a prototype version of the Amanda/Elyot relationship in *The Rat Trap* as early as 1918. Like Elyot and Amanda, Keld and Sheila are caught in a cycle of arguments and reconciliation, where the bickering is regarded as a necessary part of the relationship:

KELD   I love every word you write I—

SHEILA   *(slowly)* You said all that last week when we'd just made up a quarrel, don't you remember?

KELD   Yes, perhaps I did, more or less, but really I can't see—

SHEILA   You'll say it again next week, and we shall kiss and be frightfully in love until the next time after that.[38]

Keld and Sheila, like Elyot and Amanda, are trapped in each other. Sheila realizes that the only way to break the cycle is to marry somebody who won't compete either professionally or emotionally, somebody without ambition: 'We're like two rats in a trap, fighting, fighting fighting. You need a commonplace, dull, domesticated wife with no brain and boundless, open-mouthed enthusiasm for every mortal thing you do.'[39]

Elyot and Amanda have acted on Sheila's advice, but find themselves married to completely unsuitable partners. When forced to compare their present relationships with their own in the past, the new ones are found wanting. In Sibyl, Elyot has found the perfect 'dull, domesticated wife with no brain'. Sibyl doesn't threaten Elyot and, consequently, he claims to have found contentment: 'Love is no use unless it's wise and kind and undramatic. Something steady and sweet, to smooth out your nerves when you're tired. Something tremendously cosy; and unflurried by scenes and jealousies. That's what I want.'[40] It sounds as if Elyot wants a cup of tea rather than a relationship. Love that's 'kind and undramatic' and 'steady and sweet' might be Earl Grey, but it certainly isn't passion. Elyot, like Amanda, really prefers storms in his teacup. Amanda admits to Victor that she loves him 'more calmly' than she had loved Elyot. The passion and violence of Elyot and Amanda's relationship is constantly compared to their cooler relationships with Victor and Sibyl in a series of contrasts that emphasize their natural compatibility and the unsuitability, even perversity, of their present matches. Elyot is described as a violent, passionate man who has struck Amanda 'More than once ... in several places' and would like to cut off the irritating Sibyl's head 'with a meat axe'. Amanda has been correspondingly violent to Elyot, having broken 'four gramophone records over his head'. Elyot and Amanda exchange their desire for each other in passionate exhibitions of temper and bickering. They provoke and stimulate each other. Victor and Sibyl are straightforward, simple and unprovocative:

SIBYL   I hate these half masculine women who go banging about . . . I should think you needed a little quiet womanliness after Amanda.[41]

Coward undervalued his achievement in the creation of Victor and Sibyl, dismissing them as 'puppets thrown in to assist the plot and to provide contrast'.[42] But they are an important touchstone of normality, good manners and ordinariness which offsets Elyot and Amanda's idiosyncrasies. They also complete the intricate cyclical pattern of the play: infected by Elyot and Amanda's standards they eventually begin to adopt their behaviour. At the beginning of the play, even the smallest details express their difference from Elyot and Amanda. They refer to their spouses with diminutives straight out of the nursery, 'Elli' and 'Mandy', further emphasizing the childlike and passionless nature of these new relationships:

VICTOR   You know I feel rather scared of you at close quarters.
AMANDA   That promises to be very embarrassing.[43]

Embarrassing and inappropriate to the honeymoon spirit. Neither Victor nor Sibyl likes sunburned women, not thinking it 'awfully suitable'. Amanda, however, is determined to turn a 'nice, crisp brown'. Coward and Gertrude Lawrence were part of the Riviera social set who made sunburn fashionable for the first time in the 1920s. Elyot and Amanda's love of sunburn is ultra-fashionable and also indicates a sense of gender equality which is alien to the rather pompous and old-fashioned notions about feminine beauty which Victor expresses and to which Sibyl is quite happy to conform. Neither do Amanda and Elyot care for 'heartiness' in men, rejecting the conventional gender roles which society would have them play:

ELYOT   If you think you'd like me to smoke a pipe, I shall try and master it.[44]

Elyot is quite content to be thought unmanly and effete, just as Amanda is happy to be thought 'half-masculine': conventional notions of gender really don't bother them. In contrast Sibyl is a 'completely feminine little creature' who 'likes a man to be a man'. In Act III Victor challenges Elyot to 'behave like a man', which Elyot finds 'very right and proper and highly traditional, but . . . won't get us very far'.[45] The contrast between Victor and Elyot, Sibyl and Amanda is the contrast of the uninitiated with those who are 'jagged with sophistication'. Sibyl and Victor are innocents in the complex emotional tangle of Elyot and Amanda's relationship. Unknowingly, they become drawn into the cycle of Elyot and Amanda's life. When Amanda wonders whose yacht she spies, Elyot can make a socially educated guess: 'the Duke of Westminster's I expect. It usually is.' When Sibyl sees the yacht, Victor can only 'wonder who it belongs to'. Elyot and Amanda share a social and emotional hinterland which is completely alien to their new spouses. These superficial contrasts serve to underline the differences of personal morality between Elyot/Amanda and Victor/Sibyl. When both Elyot and Amanda admit a compulsion to gamble in the casino on their respective honeymoon nights, their new spouses become rather alarmed: is this an indication of the tenor of their lives together, that their new partners prefer gambling to honeymoon romance? Elyot and Amanda reveal that they are resigned to the fact that chance rather than custom rules their lives.

Ultimately, the ability of Elyot and Amanda to control themselves and succumb to the vagaries of good manners fails and Act II ends famously with the pair of them writhing on the floor, *rolling over and over in paroxysms of rage*' with Amanda screaming 'Beast, brute, swine, cad, beast, beast, brute, devil.'[46] It is a savage parody of sexual coupling, with the confused Victor and Sibyl looking on voyeuristically; for, despite the cocktails and Molyneux dresses, sex is the motivating force of *Private Lives*, with the repartée and violent arguments only the tip of Coward's iceberg. Cecil Beaton remembered Gertrude Lawrence's ability to ooze sexuality as Amanda:

Though not a great beauty, she used her gifts to heighten her attractiveness and possessed the flavour and personality of the age to a high degree. She was a combination of remarkable contrasts. Her mellifluous voice was yet rather curdled. Her somewhat simian features were sunburnt. The long, loose-fitting dresses she wore suggested more than an indication of the vital, well-shaped figure beneath them; she could look remarkably provocative in a dress that covered her body almost completely. She smoked cigarettes with a nuance that implied having just come out of bed and wanting to get back into it.[47]

That 'just fucked' look characterizes the tone of the play, more so than the art deco paraphernalia which so often suffocates productions of it. The play advocates the supremacy of the sex instinct over all other considerations: legal, moral or religious. 'I'm apt to see [morals] the wrong way round',[48] Amanda admits to the uncomprehending Victor. Elyot and Amanda aren't complicated by familial responsibilities, neither by keeping up a family name nor by having to consider children of their own. They live for pleasure, for the experience of life. In many ways they are typical inhabitants of the hedonistic 1920s. Their lives are not conditioned by the desire or necessity to procreate and both have been sexually promiscuous. In 1930, it was only thirty years since the publication of Freud's *Interpretation of Dreams*, and his notion of the natural practice of non-procreational sex was in the process of becoming popularized. Like George and Martha in *Who's Afraid of Virginia Woolf* (1962), Elyot and Amanda will live in this dance of union and parting for ever. When they run off to Paris together, Amanda observes that they're now living in sin:

ELYOT   Not according to the Catholics, Catholics don't recognise divorce. We're married as ever we were.

AMANDA   Yes, dear, but we're not Catholics.

ELYOT   Never mind, it's nice to think they'd sort of back us up. We were married in the eyes of Heaven, and we still are.

AMANDA   We may be alright in the eyes of Heaven, but we look like being in the hell of a mess socially.[49]

Religion is manipulated by Elyot and Amanda to suit their social convenience and marriage is flippantly regarded as a social ceremony rather than a sacrament or spiritual commitment. The housekeeper in *The Rat Trap*, speaking from her own experience and from her observation of the deteriorating relationship between Sheila and Keld, sees marriage as only a 'snare', an unhappy convention that doesn't solve the problems of sharing a life with somebody: 'The one thing love never teaches you is how to manage each other.'[50] This is Amanda and Elyot's problem, but rather than seek the solution to their erratic relationship within themselves, Amanda blames the institution of marriage itself for destabilizing her relationship with Elyot: 'I believe it was just the fact of our being married and clamped together publicly that wrecked us before.'[51] Now that their renewed relationship will be a private one and necessarily lived outside society, they will have no such excuses to fall back on. When they dance to the gramophone they satirize the society they have now placed themselves beyond:

AMANDA   Is that the Grand Duchess Olga lying under the piano?
ELYOT   Yes, her husband died a few weeks ago, you know, on his way back from Pulborough. So sad.
AMANDA   What on earth was he doing in Pulborough?
ELYOT   Nobody knows exactly, but there have been the usual stories.[52]

They are funny and camp and apparently happy, but when they stop dancing they find that they are alone in their fantasy ballroom. Elyot and Amanda are a breed apart, the same sophisticated species. They have a shared culture, a shared language and a shared sense of humour. When they first meet, Amanda finishes the song Elyot is humming, a moment of their shared past revisited. Coward noted in *Present Indicative* that 'We [i.e. he and Gertrude Lawrence] had the parts, or rather, the part, as "Elyot" and "Amanda" are practically synonymous'.[53] Their relationship lasts as long as it lasts. It changes, they split, they re-form. This symbiotic relationship echoes Aristophanes's speech in Plato's *Symposium*: two halves of the same divided soul searching for fulfilment in each other.* In many ways, Elyot and Amanda's relationship dramatizes the Platonic theory of love: a search for truth and beauty by two people of the same

---

* In this period, classical writing which discussed 'the unspeakable vice of the Greeks' was important in the construction of homosexual identity. The *Symposium* was particularly important as a way for homosexual (usually educated) men to identify their sexuality. It was also often used by homosexual men as a relatively safe way of proclaiming their sexuality to others. Being ancient Greek, classical and therefore 'educational', the *Symposium* was almost absolved of its radical agenda and therefore a safe shared frame of reference. In *Maurice*, Clive repeatedly asks Maurice to read the *Symposium* in the vacation, as a way of making it clear what sort of relationship he would like to have with him. As well as discussing the position of various types of homosexual relationship in Athenian democracy, the *Symposium* also examines the cultural status of different forms of heterosexual relationships. In Diotima's speech on the nature of sexual love, Plato places procreation as the lowest form that Eros can take.

sex, inspired by mutual affection for each other. It is telling that the song that brings the two back together is 'Someday I'll Find You'. They find each other again because they are 'soul-mates'. Each of them recognizes that they are mutually to blame for the state of their relationship and both accept that blame. In Act I, Elyot admits, 'We made each other miserable' and that 'We lost each other'. Elyot and Amanda are not only synonymous but also inevitable.

In Coward's universe control, decency and manners are the antithesis of passion and individualism, and works as superficially different as *Private Lives* and *Brief Encounter* uphold the same agenda. Coward explores this thesis throughout the 1920s and 1930s in some of his most celebrated works – *Hay Fever*, *The Vortex*, *Design for Living* – all of which present characters who attempt to control their behaviour and capitulate to 'good manners', but who ultimately fail. Each of these works also explores some sort of unorthodox sexuality. In *Hay Fever* the Blisses respond outrageously melodramatically to the smallest declaration of affection, sending up the very idea of heterosexual relationships and romantic love as a game. *The Vortex* explores the world of drug dependency and Oedipal love. Coward's design for living in the play of that name is a bisexual threesome. As part of their rejection of the prevailing social and moral codes, Elyot and Amanda are typical of Coward's 1930s characters in their refusal to capitulate to the dictates of any religion:

ELYOT   You have no faith, that's what's wrong with you.
AMANDA   Absolutely none.
ELYOT   Don't you believe in—? *(He nods upwards.)*
AMANDA   No, do you?
ELYOT   No. What about—? *(He points downwards.)*
AMANDA   Oh dear, no.[54]

Elyot and Amanda inhabit the modernist universe of Conrad, Eliot and Forster. They share the bleak apprehension of human existence that Forster explored in *A Passage to India*, but laugh at the abyss that terrifies Miss Quested and Mrs Moore. In the Marabar Caves 'Everything exists, nothing has value'. Mrs Moore despises 'poor little talkative Christianity, and she knew that all its divine words from "Let there be light" to "It is finished" only amounted to "boum" ',[55] the cave's terrible, empty echo:

ELYOT   Let's be superficial and pity the poor philosophers. Let's blow trumpets and squeakers and enjoy the party as much as we can like small quite idiotic school-children. Let's savour the delight of the moment. Come and kiss me darling before your body rots and worms pop in and out of your eye sockets.[56]

Like Forster, Coward concludes that there is no solution to the dilemma of mortality: 'Death's very laughable. .... All done with mirrors.' The only option is to love, to live in the present. It is the pessimism that distinguishes Modernist literature; life for Elyot and Amanda is simply a cycle of 'Birth and copulation and death'.[57] Their separate travels around the world, their affairs and marriages are mere distractions in the dark and empty twentieth-century universe. As soon as they see each other again their fates are sealed. Elyot's attraction to Amanda expresses a simple, deep human need: 'You don't hold any mystery for me, do you mind? There isn't a particle of you that I don't know, remember, and want'.[58]

Private Lives differs from most of Coward's other comedies because it does actually explore the protagonists' lives as lived in private rather than the burden of fame and the adoption of a public persona. From *The Rat Trap*, *Design for Living* and *Present Laughter* to his final stage work *A Song at Twilight*, Coward explores how the public face complicates the private, and the uneasy relationship that exists between the two. Elyot and Amanda on the other hand don't care about their public face. They don't care about society and if they are exposed they will 'behave exquisitely'. Recognizing that their attitudes and behaviour aren't the norm, they cherish their ambivalence:

VICTOR   I'm glad I'm normal.
AMANDA   What an odd thing to be glad about. Why?
VICTOR   Well, aren't you?
AMANDA   I'm not so sure I'm normal.[59]

Leo, Otto and Gilda, in *Design for Living*, travel from Paris to London to New York in order to fit their 'abnormal' relationship into an established society. They try to reconcile themselves with the society of the major metropolitan centres of Western civilization. They, like Elyot and Amanda, discover that the only way to live outside society's conventions is to live without it. Amanda's knowledge of her own difference enables her to see just how different we all are and how absurd, therefore, are the plastic conventions of society:

> I think very few people are completely normal really, deep down in their private lives. It all depends on a combination of circumstances. If all the various cosmic thingummys fuse at the same moment, and the right spark is struck, there's no knowing what one mightn't do.[60]

Amanda admits the possibility of everything. There are no hard and fast rules. Such an all-embracing philosophy is full of opportunity and novelty. But it is also a philosophy of risk. In rejecting the safe tracks of convention, Amanda also rejects their security. But the acceptance of the mutability of relationships is regarded as par for the course, the price of liberty. Elyot and Amanda's acceptance of change and loss as part of life, particularly the death of love, is rather sad:

ELYOT	Things that ought to matter dreadfully, don't matter at all when one's happy, do they?
AMANDA	What is so horrible is that one can't stay happy.
ELYOT	Darling don't say that.
AMANDA	It's true, the whole business is a very poor joke.
ELYOT	Meaning that sacred and beautiful thing, Love?
AMANDA	Yes, meaning just that.
ELYOT	*(striding up and down the room melodramatically)* What does it all mean, that's what I ask myself in my ceaseless quest for ultimate truth. Dear God, what does it all mean?
AMANDA	Don't laugh at me, I'm serious.[61]

In the 1960s, Coward observed that the theme of *Private Lives* was 'two people who love each other too much. I wouldn't say it's a tragedy, but there's a certain sadness below it ...'. Elyot and Amanda are aware that things will never remain constant and that love, trust and dependency necessarily incur pain, mistrust and disappointment. It is no coincidence that Leo, the Coward-figure in *Design for Living*, scores his first success with a play called *Change and Decay*. It could be a subtitle for *Private Lives*. Like *The Importance of Being Earnest*, when first reviewed, *Private Lives* was dismissed as a triviality, a piece of fluff. Nearly seventy years later it reveals itself to be a superb black comedy of sexual manners masquerading as a light comedy. Marriage is discussed flippantly and fidelity within it is trivialized. The play is Coward's rallying cry in support of unorthodox ways of living. In the world of *Private Lives* there are no certainties other than death; and it is death alone that puts an end to physical pleasure, not laws, not morals and certainly not the inconstant conventions of society.

Blithe Spirit

> Sometimes in the corridors, I fancy I hear her just behind me. That quick, light footstep ... I've fancied I hear her ... calling to Mr de Winter the way she used to. Do you think she can see us now? Do you think the dead come back and watch the living?[62]

So asks the wonderfully obsessive housekeeper, Mrs Danvers, in Daphne du Maurier's hugely popular stage adaptation of her even more successful novel, *Rebecca*. Du Maurier's biographer, Margaret Forster, observes that the author was disappointed by early criticism of the novel in 1938 which focused on its gothic Brontë-like qualities. Du Maurier had intended the novel as a psychological examination of the second Mrs de Winter's jealous obsession with her husband's dead wife, Rebecca. Du Maurier's stage version opened in the West End in April 1940. Celia Johnson played the second Mrs de Winter and Margaret Rutherford played Mrs Danvers. Coward's *Blithe Spirit* opened at the Piccadilly Theatre in July 1941, with Rutherford playing Madam Arcati. The two plays were amongst the most successful of the war, and *Blithe Spirit*'s run of 1,997 performances was only surpassed by that of *The Mousetrap*. Though both *Blithe Spirit* and *Rebecca* were written, as well as produced, during a major world conflict, neither directly mentions the war. However, both plays examine narratives in which people in their prime have unexpectedly died and in so doing are able to discuss death and the operation of grief. Margaret Rutherford, who created the role of Madam Arcati, genuinely believed in spiritualism and only took on the part when she had been assured that it was not to be a send-up: 'I regard this as a very serious play, almost a tragedy. I don't see it as a comedy at all.'[63] Coward and du Maurier do explore wartime anxieties about death, but do so in the English way, with discretion. Though Rebecca remains unseen throughout the drama, she forms the same sort of *ménage à trois* that Charles, Ruth and Elvira do in *Blithe Spirit*. Rebecca is not a ghost, but rather a psychological manifestation in the mind of the second Mrs de Winter. Elvira, on the other hand, does come back and 'watch the living', haunting both Charles and his second wife, Ruth.

Elvira's appearance as a ghost and the ensuing supernatural pranks are wonderfully theatrical. But like *Rebecca*, *Blithe Spirit* is as much a play about sexual jealousy as it is about mortality. The title quotes Shelley's 'To a Skylark':

> Hail to thee, blithe Spirit!
> Bird thou never wert,
> That from Heaven, or near it,
> Pourest thy full heart
> In profuse strains of unpremeditated art.

Shelley's poem provides more than just a sexy title, though, as it actually reflects the darkly humorous tone of the play:

> Our sincerest laughter
> With some pain is fraught;
> Our sweetest songs are those that tell of saddest thought.

Coward had gone to the Welsh village of Portmeirion with Joyce Carey in order to write the play. Portmeirion is Clough Williams-Ellis's bizarre fantasy version of a Mediterranean village, a mass Italianate folly, and perhaps the absurdity of the surroundings contributed to the strange tragi-comic humour of the play. Carey was intending to write a play about the young Romantic poet, John Keats, and his beloved Fanny Brawne, and the discussion of the work of the Romantics between the two friends seems to have been absorbed into Coward's play. Shelley's contemporary and fellow champion of Romanticism, William Words-worth, had written a companion poem, 'To the Cuckoo', which also reflects Coward's title:

> O blithe New-comer! I have heard,
> I hear thee and rejoice.
> O Cuckoo! shall I call thee Bird,
> Or but a wandering Voice;

Cuckoos, of course, are traditionally believed to steal other birds' nests. When Madam Arcati opens the windows to take some air before the seance, it is not the skylark she hears but a cuckoo: 'That cuckoo is very angry.'[64] Ruth has stolen Elvira's 'nest' as well as her mate. Charles and Ruth Condomine have both been married before and each of their respective spouses has died. Like the second marriages of Elyot and Amanda in *Private Lives*, the Condomines' relationship is much calmer than their first marriages. Both have experienced a certain promiscuity and have now settled into a comfortable, not particularly passionate, relationship:

RUTH   We've neither of us led exactly prim lives, have we? . . . Careless rapture at this stage would be incongruous and embarrassing.[65]

Even before the arrival of Madam Arcati for the seance, Ruth asks, 'Was she more physically attractive than I am?' The fact is that Elvira *was* more attractive than Ruth. Just as Elyot and Amanda talk about their former spouses just a little too much for comfort on their second honeymoons, Ruth insists on comparing herself to Elvira. It seems that Charles is no more happy with Ruth's cool, comfortable love than Elyot is with a love that's 'wise and kind and undramatic'. After Elvira's arrival, Ruth becomes 'glacial' and 'increasingly domineering'. Charles talks of her 'gentle comradely hand'. With Elvira to compare her to, Ruth is 'granite . . . sheer, unyielding granite'. Elvira is simply the catalyst who reveals Charles's dissatisfaction with Ruth to himself.

Charles is a writer who is keen to gather material for his new book, *The Unseen*, which is to be about a charlatan spiritualist. He wants to pick up some tricks of the trade first hand and has consequently invited a local medium to dinner, Madam Arcati. After dinner Madam Arcati, the Condomines and their guests, the sceptical Dr Bradman and his wife, settle down to a seance. After the seance, Madam Arcati senses that there has been some sort of psychic happening, and indeed Charles's first wife has materialized but only Charles can see and hear her. The deceased Elvira enters the Condomines' living-room as if she has just left a cocktail party, albeit one that is attended by Joan of Arc, Merlin and Ghenghis Khan. Manners and breeding still count: 'It's considered vulgar to say "dead" where I come from.' The other world doesn't seem so very different from the one Elvira has left. In order to revisit Charles, Elvira has had to 'fill in all those forms and wait about in draughty passages for hours', as if she were applying for a wartime travel permit. Like the American troop song popular during the war, Elvira's new 'home' is referred to as 'over there' or 'on the other side' as if she had recently returned from a cruise on the *Queen Mary*. When asked where she actually comes from Elvira replies that she has 'forgotten'. As in *Private Lives* death is 'laughable, such a cunning little mystery. All done with mirrors.' There is little metaphysical speculation in *Blithe Spirit*. Heaven and Hell are only mentioned as expletives. The ease with which Charles and Elvira talk to each other on their first supernatural meeting reflects the same sort of comfortable familiarity that Elyot and Amanda displayed on their first meeting since the divorce. Though she can neither drink nor eat, Elvira can, of course, smoke. Much of the comedy of Elvira is that she is so ordinary and familiar – so lively, in fact.

Madam Arcati implies that Elvira's materialization must have been inspired by Charles's wishful thinking. For Charles, there isn't a particle of Elvira that he doesn't 'know, remember and want'. Even before she appears, Charles has been haunted by her memory. When she challenges him, Charles says that 'I shall always love the memory of you'. He yearns to touch her, as their previous relationship had been physical and passionate, even violent: 'you hit me with a billiard cue'. Charles is haunted by the memory of desire. In Elvira's return, like Leontes in *The Winter's Tale*, Charles has been offered the fulfilment of a fantasy, the resurrection of a loved one, the opportunity for a second chance. Charles asks Elvira, 'Is it cold – being a ghost?', just as Leontes touches the statue of Hermione and finds that 'she's warm'. A touching frustration exists between Charles and Elvira, as they can both see and hear their object of desire, but cannot fulfil their yearning to touch each other:

ELVIRA   I loved you very much.
CHARLES   I loved you too. . . . No I can't touch you – isn't that horrible?[66]

The return of Elvira from beyond the grave initiates a bizarre 'astral' *ménage à trois*. The triangular relationship is a favourite Cowardian device in which he challenges the apparent security of conventional relationships. Charles's relationship with Ruth is passionless in contrast with the very physical relations he had enjoyed with Elvira. His relationship with

Ruth now cold, and unable to physically consummate his relationship with his dead wife, Charles is in a peculiar state of sexual stasis, a sort of erotic limbo.

The structure and much of the comedy of *Blithe Spirit*, like *Private Lives* and *Design for Living*, is cyclical. When Ruth becomes exasperated by Charles's insistence that Elvira has materialized, she shouts, 'To Hell with Elvira!' But Elvira has only recently arrived from wherever she is resident 'over there'. When Elvira soothingly seduces Charles she dismisses Ruth in Ruth's own language: 'To Hell with Ruth.' Like Mrs Arbuthnot in *A Woman of No Importance*, Elvira dismisses her rival with the language of the enemy. Her understanding of Ruth and her language, the language of the living, is part of her danger. She is both familiar and 'other'.

Cowardian comedy is like a formal dance, a never-ending game of exchanging partners. These characters live for the moment and pay little heed to mortality. Without children to occupy them or oblige them to stay together, and with little serious regard for marriage vows, these relationships last as long as desire lasts. Structurally and thematically the characters are caught in cycles of their own making – of bickering and making up and bickering again. When Ruth and Elvira are finally being dematerialized, Elvira venomously admits that she had slept with Captain Bracegirdle whilst on her honeymoon with Charles adding that she 'couldn't have enjoyed it more . . .'. Like Rattigan's Alan Howard in *French Without Tears* and Maugham's dual heroes in *Home and Beauty*, Charles Condomine now frees himself of the tenacious grasp of the female sex. Charles realizes that he has been 'hag-ridden' all his life, first by his mother and then by Elvira, Ruth and the voracious Mrs Winthrop Llewelyn. He now delights in his new-found, woman-free liberty and though he knows that the three are bound to meet again one day, vows 'to enjoy myself as I've never enjoyed myself before'. Charles, like Elvira, is talking about sexual enjoyment. Having rid himself of the two women in his life once and for all, we wonder just who he is going to enjoy himself with? Perhaps Charles thinks he'll be lucky with women third time round? Or perhaps his new freedom will involve the boys this time?

The final scene in the 1945 film version has Charles leaving the house, with the unseen poltergeist spirits of Ruth and Elvira rather too helpfully sending him on his way. Charles drives off in his car. Elvira and

Ruth stand on the bridge where Ruth had died and wait for Charles's booby-trapped car to crash. Charles's ghost drops between the two female spirits. Theirs will be a supernatural *ménage à trois*, where they can bicker and reconcile their differences for eternity. Like George and Martha and Elyot and Amanda, the three ghosts are trapped with each other in a compulsive and never-ending cycle. The ending of the play offers Charles a temporary freedom as the two female ghosts destroy the house between them and he exits from the ensuing chaos, sarcastically quoting from *Romeo and Juliet*, the archetypal tragic romance: 'parting is such *sweet* sorrow!' Romeo and Juliet are united in death because of their devotion for each other, and eventually Charles will be reunited for eternity and in enmity with both Ruth and Elvira. But the last line is also an ironic reference back to Shelley's 'To a Skylark', further stressing the bitter-sweet tone of the play.* The ending of the film speeds up the whole process and we catch a glimpse of Charles's eternal fate. Anticipating Sartre's conclusion to his black comedy, *Huis Clos*, Charles discovers that hell really is other people, or, reading both Coward (and Sartre) less sympathetically, that hell is an eternity trapped by women:

INEZ	So here we are, for ever. *(laughs)*
ESTELLE	*(with a peal of laughter)* For ever. My God, how funny! For ever.
GARCIN	*(looks at the two women and joins in the laughter)* For ever and ever, and ever.
	(They slump on to their respective sofas. A long silence. Their laughter dies away, and they gaze at each other.)
GARCIN	Well, well, let's get on with it . . .[67]

---

* Shelley, 'To a Skylark', 'Our sweetest songs are those that tell of saddest thought.'

Sentimental Education

First Episode and *French Without Tears*

My salad days,
When I was green in judgement, cold in blood,
To say as I said then.
      Shakespeare, *Antony and Cleopatra*[1]

The English are not a sexual nation and you cannot easily persuade them that a man will sacrifice anything of importance for love. I do not think an English audience ... ever really accepts the story of Antony and Cleopatra as credible. It is this difference of attitude towards sexual passion that makes foreign plays so improbable to us.
      Somerset Maugham[2]

Terence Rattigan achieved his first huge financial and critical success with the ebullient comedy, *French Without Tears*. He was twenty-five. The play was first presented in 1936 and ran for three years, notching up over one thousand performances. His reputation as a popular comic writer was thus confirmed early; it was also to haunt him for the rest of his career. Though he achieved fame and fortune with an apparently vacuous frivolity (in the words of *The Times*, 'A world in which nothing matters except to be entertained'), he was to return throughout his career to the dramas 'of character' in which he created his richest, most resonant work. Rattigan's oeuvre exhibits a broad diversity of genres, ranging from historical epic to drawing-room comedy. It is a diversity which belies his later reputation (anointed by Kenneth Tynan, the critic and self-appointed champion of the angry young men) as a staid, unadventurous crowd pleaser. His character studies encompass iconographic figures such as Nelson, Alexander the Great and Lawrence of Arabia as well as that focus of *News of the World* sensationalism, Alma Rattenbury. But despite this breadth of genre and subject matter, Rattigan's work has a thematic consistency that can be traced from his apprentice work in the 1930s to his final offerings of the 1970s. Time and again, Rattigan betrays his preoccupation with the human heart, often exploring his own emotional dilemmas through his work. Rattigan's world is a particularly English territory where individuals struggle with the middle-class mores of the mid-twentieth century. It is a world of seaside boarding houses, public schools and hotel lounges where individual freedom is checked by the pressures of gentility. It is a rich territory inhabited by those crippled with paranoia about sex, frustrated by the cruelties of age and isolated in their own painful, solitary English world.

Rattigan had determined to become a playwright from his youth. By the time he went up to Harrow in 1925, he had already written several juvenile works with melodramatic titles of the Pinero school, such as *Shoot to Kill* and *Lady Hermione's Secret*. Whilst at Harrow, Rattigan was reputed to have read all the plays in the school library, including Barrie, Galsworthy and Shaw: 'one could get a copy of *Plays Unpleasant* which was not supposed to be shown to boys under seventeen, and was kept under lock and key.'[3] In his first term, Rattigan's French class were set the task of writing a short play as an exercise. The young T. M. Rattigan produced the full-blooded final scene of a tragedy of adulterous desire, incest and revenge. The Comte de Boulogne, mad with jealousy over his wife's passion for a young policeman, storms into her boudoir and announces that the young man is none other than her long-lost brother. The policeman is hidden in the Comtesse's wardrobe at the time. Despite his inadequate linguistic skills, Rattigan came up with a choice curtain line:

COMTESSE   *(souffrant terriblement)* Non! non! non! Ah non! Mon Dieu non!

His French master gave the burgeoning playwright two marks out of ten and commented prophetically, 'French execrable; theatre sense first class.'[4]

Whilst at Harrow, Rattigan developed tastes which were to dramatically influence his life and career. As well as exploring his passion for the theatre, he also had the opportunity to explore his sexuality. Not unusually for public schools of the period, homosexual activity was discreetly tolerated. In his classic study, *Enemies of Promise*, Cyril Connolly observes that the homosexual behaviour inherent in public-school culture greatly influenced the culture of the English upper and middle classes:

The experiences undergone by boys at the great public schools, their glories and disappointments, are so intense as to dominate their lives and to arrest their development. From these it results that the greater part of the ruling-class remains adolescent, school-minded, self-conscious, cowardly, sentimental and in the last analysis homosexual.[5]

Certainly, Rattigan's life, taste and art were formed by and reflected public-school culture and public-school values. One of his greatest achievements, *The Browning Version* celebrates both the potential of the public-school system, in the character of Taplow, the enthusiastic schoolboy, as well as the damaging effects of that culture in the emotionally fractured schoolmaster, Crocker-Harris. In his last play, *Cause Célèbre* (1977), Rattigan discusses homosexual behaviour at public school in the mid-1930s very much as a matter of course. Tony Davenport and his best friend, Randolph Browne, are classmates at Westminster School. In a discussion of the sexual excesses of the Rattenbury murder case, they reflect on their own sexual predicament:

TONY   Who is it now?
BROWNE   Shuttleworth.
TONY   I don't know him.
BROWNE   He's in the choir.
TONY   God, you are disgusting! Randy by name, randy by nature.
BROWNE   That's right. Anyway, a chap's got to do something, hasn't he? Or else he'd go raving mad.
          There is a pause.
TONY   It's hell, isn't it?
BROWNE   Oh, I don't know. It'll do till something better comes along.
TONY   But when will that be? God, it's frustrating. To be seventeen is hell – I mean, seventeen and English and upper-class and living in this century is hell ... I wonder what our parents think we do between the ages of thirteen and twenty-one?[6]

From the end of the summer term of 1927, apparently not satisfied with the midnight offerings of the dormitory, Rattigan embarked on an affair with Geoffrey Gilbey, the racing correspondent of the *Daily*

Express. The couple had been introduced by Rattigan's philandering father. From now on, Rattigan was to mix more and more in homosexual circles. The drag performer Douglas Byng became a great friend. Jimmy Stow, a contemporary of Rattigan's at Harrow, remembers, 'Terry rather liked all that, the groups of homosexual men. He always used to say that the Greeks had a good attitude towards sex, which the British people didn't apparently have. He was always after the Greek ideal.'[7]

By the time he went up to Oxford, Rattigan was obsessed with the theatre, voraciously consuming the fare of Shaftesbury Avenue. Though ostensibly at Trinity College to read history as a pathway to the diplomatic service, Rattigan spent much of his time at the Oxford University Dramatic Society (OUDS), then as now a seed-bed for careers in the theatre. Amongst his contemporaries were the novelist Angus Wilson, George Devine, later to head the English Stage Company at the Royal Court, Peter Glenville, who would direct the premières of *The Browning Version* and *Separate Tables*, and Frith Banbury, who would direct the original production of *The Deep Blue Sea*. After a year of living in college rooms, Rattigan opted to lodge in digs from the autumn term of 1931. Together with a law student, Philip Heimann, he moved in to the fashionable Canterbury House in King Edward Street. Heimann, a tall, fair-haired South African, was just a year older than the twenty-year-old Rattigan. They became very great friends.

Oxford in the 1930s was almost entirely a society of men. Of 1,750 undergraduates only 250 were women. Many freshman undergraduates, like Rattigan, had progressed straight to university from public schools. Consequently, the social environment at Oxford was in many ways an extension and development of that of Eton, Marlborough, Rugby and Harrow. The culture of homoerotic bonding at Oxford between the wars is memorably described in Evelyn Waugh's *Brideshead Revisited*. In the 1920s, Harold Acton, the inspiration for Waugh's outrageous Anthony Blanche had inspired a generation of aesthetes, whose influence was still strongly felt in the 1930s. In *Degenerate Oxford?*, Terence Greenidge examines the schism between athletes and aesthetes. He challenges the popular conception of an aesthete as 'untidy, lank, pale, decadent and degenerate, the sort of man who produces doubtful Elizabethan plays in the name of art'. But Greenidge admits that 'queer deeds may occasionally get done among those who come from over-emancipated public schools'. He explores the attraction of men for men and terms it 'Romanticism' ('homosexuality I do not favour. For it sounds very sinister.').[8] 'Romanticism' seems to be an extension of the ideal 'Greek' relationship developed at the public schools. Even the athletes are not immune to 'Romantic' feeling: 'I have been present at many a hearty blind; even in athletic Magdalen, where the behaviour of the most unlikely people showed evidences of tender feeling.'[9] Greenidge quotes a homophobic old colonel who declares that 'Romanticism' in the atmosphere of Oxford is both current and to be expected: 'You won't stop Romanticism till you stop young men being beautiful'.

Homosexuality, or the appearance of it, was part of the Oxford aesthetic culture. The aesthetes' cosmopolitan tastes also included flamboyant costume and a flirtation with other taboos, such as pacifism. At an Oxford Union debate in 1933, Rattigan was one of 275 who voted for the motion 'That this House will in no circumstances fight for King and Country'. The motion was passed and those who supported it were condemned by the *Daily Telegraph* as 'woolly minded communists, practical jokers and sexual indeterminates'.[10] Central characters in Rattigan's first two plays are defiantly, and for the period unfashionably, pacifist. By the time he reached Oxford, Rattigan seems to have been exclusively homosexual and though he was as cautious as any homosexual man in this period, according to Frith Banbury Rattigan's sexuality does not seem to have caused him any great anxiety. He was certainly 'out' to his circle of friends. Anthony Powell, who shortly afterwards worked with Rattigan as a staff scriptwriter for Warner Brothers in Teddington, remembers Rattigan as 'tall, good-looking, elegant in turnout, somewhat chilly in manner. He had been a cricketer of some eminence at Harrow. His homosexuality, of which he made no particular secret, probably unswerving, was not at all obvious on the surface'[11] Though 'not at all obvious on the surface' seems to indicate that Rattigan wasn't effeminate, he was by no means averse to playing camp. Rattigan entertained his OUDS contemporaries at the all-male 'Smokers' with a bitchy character called Lady Diana Coutigan. Her name may have been inspired by the current 1930s phrase, 'queer as a coot'. She prefigures the controversial character of Aunt Edna whose voice Rattigan adopted in the 1950s. Aunt Edna defended Rattigan's 'well-made' Shaftesbury Avenue theatre against the threat of the kitchen-sink revolution. In creating Lady Diana and Aunt Edna, Rattigan adopted an ironic, self-mocking stance which gay men from the 1930s to the present day would recognize as a familiar form of camp gay culture.*

Despite their affection and attraction for each other, Rattigan's relationship with his house-mate Philip Heimann seems to have remained platonic; theirs was an ambiguous but intense friendship. Not that Rattigan languished in a state of lovesick catatonia; Heimann seems to have been well aware of the nature of his appeal to Rattigan, and Rattigan himself was very honest about it. It was a relationship that was not and could never be fully mutual. Rattigan was experiencing, possibly for the first time, the difficulty of an ill-matched relationship which he was to explore in his great works. Geoffrey Wansell quotes a contemporary friend of both men who remembered Heimann talking about a truth game they enjoyed playing as undergraduates. On one occasion, the question they had all asked each other was ' "Who in this room would you most like to kiss?" Rattigan didn't hesitate: "Oh Philip, definitely." '[12] Rattigan was only too aware that his devotion was not reciprocated and that the heterosexual Heimann was happily having an affair with a female undergraduate called Irina (aka Va-Va) Basilewich. At the age of twenty-six she had already been married and divorced and had the reputation of a siren. Rattigan began to explore this jealousy and sexual frustration in the form of a play. It was to be a complex variation on the familiar theme of the eternal triangle.

First Episode

While Rattigan was working on this play, George Devine became president of the OUDS, and invited John Gielgud to direct their spring production of *Romeo and Juliet*. Gielgud had established himself as the leading young classical actor of his day, but had never directed before. As women were not allowed as members of the OUDS at this time, Gielgud invited Peggy Ashcroft to play Juliet and Edith Evans to play the nurse.

---

* In 1924 Noël Coward had adopted a female persona, Hernia Whittlebot, and published a volume of poems entitled *Chelsea Buns*, parodying Edith Sitwell. Sitwell, not famous for her sense of humour, refused a reconciliation until 1962. A strong vein of the camp that we understand today has its roots in the popular culture of the 1920s and 1930s, when Coward's popularity was at its zenith and Rattigan's in the ascendant. In the 1960s Joe Orton carried on the tradition with his creation of Edna Welthorpe (Mrs).

Christopher Hassall was to play Romeo, Devine took the part of Mercutio and Rattigan played a walk-on role with just one line. This production, together with the continuing triangular relationship between Va-Va, Heimann and Rattigan, eventually took dramatic shape in Rattigan's play. For the first time, Rattigan used a play as a way of examining his own emotional crisis, a therapy he would continue to use throughout his life, dramatizing his own concerns on the stage. Rattigan discussed the play with Heimann at great length and ultimately both took joint credit for it. Like Loevborg and Mrs Elvsted's book in *Hedda Gabler*, the text had a symbolic value, uniting the two men in a way they could never be in reality, much in the same way as Wayne Koestenbaum discusses his theory of literary collaboration between men:

> When two men write together, they indulge in double talk; they rapidly patter to obscure their erotic burden, but the ambiguities of their discourse give the taboo subject some liberty to roam . . . men who collaborate together engage in a metaphorical sexual intercourse.[13]

A 'metaphorical sexual intercourse' might seem rather far-fetched, but the play certainly did give the subject of intense relationships between young men 'liberty to roam'. Significantly, Rattigan and Heimann's play was originally called *Embryo*. Not only was the play a sort of shared child but it also exhibits the embryonic themes, dilemmas and characters that would be the meat of Rattigan's work for the next forty years.

The two young men completed the script on holiday in Germany. Retitled *Episode*, the play was accepted and successfully produced at a small theatre in Kew, eventually reaching the West End in January 1934 under the title *First Episode*. The play explores the preoccupations of privileged undergraduate life: sex, alcohol, gambling and shirking tutorials. Four final-year students share a house in an all-male college, presumably Rattigan's Trinity. Tony Wodehouse is producing the university Dramatic Society production of *Antony and Cleopatra*. He is also playing Antony opposite a celebrated professional actress from London, Margot Gresham. Though he is already attached to a younger actress, Joan Taylor, Tony falls in love with his serpent of the Nile. Margot, however, is wary about having an affair with such a young man. She relents, but shortly into the affair Tony becomes irritated by Margot's demands.

Her attractions pall for Tony, despite her increased ardour for him. Tony's friend David Lister is a misogynist and insists that Margot is ruining Tony's chances of getting a degree. David takes no part in the Dramatic Society production and idealistically intends to become a journalist when he graduates. David plays the Rattigan figure to Tony's Heimann, with Margot a composite of several women including Va-Va Basilewich and Peggy Ashcroft. When Margot's relationship with Tony breaks down, Margot blames it on David's influence, ultimately accusing him of 'degeneracy'. Having lost Tony, she betrays David's philanderings with Joan Taylor out of college to the university authorities and he is sent down. At the end of the play, Margot returns to apologize to David for her actions and to say goodbye to Tony. Tony ignores her, but David now feels a certain bond between himself and Margot. In essence, they have both been bruised by Tony's first experience of love and both have lost him.

Despite Rattigan's later sympathy with older women in love, his early work reveals an antipathy towards women, which occasionally flares up into blatant misogyny. Either the male protagonists declare positively antagonistic opinions about women, with little deflating irony, or the female protagonists are depicted as stupid or as seductive, venomous man-eaters. In *First Episode*, both David and Tony have a reputation for treating women badly and are frequently disparaging about women's value other than for sex:

DAVID   Are you talking about a woman with a mind? It's a contradic-
         tion in terms.[14]

In this hearty environment Tony and David are regarded as slightly unusual. Their oafish house-mate Bertie informs David that 'you and Tony are getting rather unpopular in College because you won't play games'.[15] Like Jean Brodie's special brood, Tony and David loathe team sports associated with traditional male bonding, in preference for the 'gentler' pursuits of golf and tennis: unlike rugby or cricket, these were games that women also pursued in the 1930s. David is also the president of a university Pacifist Club. In 1931 Heimann himself had proposed a motion at the Oxford Union that 'Pacifism is the only true form of Patriotism'. There is a suggestion in *First Episode*, as there was in the *Daily Telegraph*'s report of the OU debate, that pacifism simply disguises the cowardice of the unmanly and effete. Rattigan returns to the issue of pacifism and associates it with misogyny and homoerotic bonding in *French Without Tears*, when the Rattigan character in the play discusses the plot of his novel about two conscientious objectors drawn together by a woman they both come to despise.

Tony and David's feeling of superiority and resentment towards women suggests a certain anxiety or even fear of the feminine. The house, the Dramatic Society and the college that encompasses them are bastions of maleness. The world of *First Episode*, like that of *French Without Tears*, is characterized by a public-school camaraderie in which the men seem secure in their traditional gender roles. The women who infiltrate and almost fracture this camaraderie in *First Episode* are both treated very much as outsiders, foreign and strange. The women begin to invade the young men's environment by first infiltrating the rehearsals for the play. The off-stage rehearsals of *Antony and Cleopatra* echo the on-stage dilemmas of *First Episode*. Just as the Romans disparage Cleopatra and the East as corrupt, sensual and feminine, it is Joan and Margot's difference, their femininity, that threatens the *status quo* at Oxford. Shakespeare's play presents a great cultural, political and romantic clash. It also consistently draws attention to a confusion of gender. Eunuchs appear on-stage, Cleopatra famously predicts that her role will be played by boys on the Renaissance stage and Antony is accused of being 'unmanned' in his seduction by the East. He finds himself trapped in two emotional triangles. First between Cleopatra and the chaste Octavia, which mirrors Tony's relationship with the sexually experienced Margot and Joan, the girl who won't go 'all the way'. But *Antony and Cleopatra* is also haunted by the ambiguous figure of Antony's best friend, Enobarbus. A strange voyeuristic figure throughout the play, he eventually kills himself rather than fight his friend, uttering the words 'O Antony! O Antony!' Tony is playing Antony in the college production of the play. Though David takes no part in the production, he certainly shares Enobarbus's deep feeling for this particular Antony and a very ambiguous attitude to Margot/Cleopatra.

Women are at odds with the masculine undergraduate world of *First Episode*. Invited only to act in the play, they have no serious, academic purpose in the life of the college. Their gender excludes them. This despite the fact that the male undergraduates are depicted as mostly lazy and even stupid in the case of Bertie. The women must leave before curfew, and if they wish to return, must climb furtively through the window. They are denied an official, dignified entry into this environment. It is Margot who first has to enter and exit through Tony's window in order to rehearse 'the love scene'. Near the end of the play, when David makes his hasty exit from Joan's room at The King's Head Hotel, he does so through the window, thus identifying himself as an outsider and therefore with the women in the play. Rattigan reserves much of his anti-female bile for his characterization of Joan Taylor and her treatment by Tony and David. Joan is slow-witted ('Oh, she's all right. I wish she wasn't so dumb, that's all'). She initially appears as Tony's girlfriend, but when Tony falls for Margot Gresham he literally hands Joan over to David:

TONY   Do you want to have an affair with Joan?
DAVID   Do ducks want to swim?
TONY   Well it's a long time since I gave you a present – you can have her.[16]

Whilst Tony is obsessed with Margot, David occupies himself with Joan. Poor Joan, who is too thick-skinned, or just too thick, to realize that she is callously being used as a surrogate Tony. In the same way Charles Ryder respectably transfers his homoerotic affections for Sebastian Flyte to Sebastian's sister, Julia, in *Brideshead Revisited*. It is Sebastian whom Charles is in love with, but his middle-class mores prevent him from acting on his impulses. Julia Flyte, like Joan Taylor, is the next best thing. Likewise it is Joan's previous intimacy with Tony that makes her attractive to David. David's attitude towards her is quite heartless:

TONY   You'd be happy with a cow if it had the right shape.
DAVID   If you're alluding, Sir, to Miss Joan Taylor – you're perfectly right.
TONY   Do you see much of her nowadays?
DAVID   Not in the daytime if I can help it.[17]

Eventually Joan meets her perfect match in David and Tony's dim-witted house-mate, Bertie. Her series of incestuous attachments with three men living in the same house pre-empts the man-hunting career of Diana Lake in *French Without Tears*. There are also hints of Diana in the character of Margot Gresham. She too is regarded, and regards herself, as a man-eater: 'A woman of my age should keep away from a university town' (Margot is all of thirty-five). In Margot and Tony, Rattigan explores the prototype obsessive relationship of the older woman for a younger man who is less interested in her. The sympathetic characterization of Margot anticipates the portrayal of the female protagonists of *The Deep Blue Sea* (1952), *Variation on a Theme* (1958) and *Cause Célèbre* (1977). Margot's concerns about her age and fading charms occasionally have the familiar ring of the Rattigan who will give voice to the anguish of Hester Collyer or the Williams who will create Blanche Dubois:

MARGOT   Nothing matters much when you're twenty. Somehow I think one's heart doesn't beat at twenty, it just lies waiting to get hurt like some dumb thing that must suffer without crying out.[18]

But unlike the later works where the dilemma of the female protagonists preoccupies Rattigan, in *First Episode* it is clearly the undergraduate Tony's emotional development which is the heart of the play. This development is shaped and guided by Margot and David. In his early work, Rattigan focuses on the emotional lives of young, inexperienced men such as Tony Wodehouse or the young men in *French Without Tears*. As he approaches his maturity as a writer and as a man, Rattigan begins to focus on the emotional lives of the women who love, sacrifice and suffer, like Hester Collyer and Alma Rattenbury. In essence, as his career progressed Rattigan transferred his sympathies from the younger man with his life ahead of him to the older woman who is beginning to recognize that time is passing and physical beauty fading. Margot knows that she and Tony are not suited but desperately hopes that she is wrong. The relationship cannot work. In the classic Rattigan conundrum, without him she will be unbearably lonely but with him she will be destroyed by his indifference. In a life of such invidious choices – 'when you're between any kind of devil and the deep blue sea' – it's not very surprising that sometimes the deep blue sea 'looks very inviting'.

What makes *First Episode* unusual in the Rattigan canon is the complication of Tony's relationship with David. Unlike the traditional eternal triangle, it is not Margot whom the two men fight over. On the contrary, David and Margot fight for the affections of Tony. Rattigan was not to explore such a complex emotional triangle so explicitly again until *Variation on a Theme* in 1958, where Rose Fish fights for the affections of her younger lover with his homosexual dance tutor. Though the relationship between Tony and David is not (apparently) physical, it is certainly homoerotic. David betrays his affections for Tony when he recognizes that Margot is a real threat and that their relationship seems to be 'serious'. He exhibits an intense jealousy in his antagonism towards Margot, which is excused, not very plausibly, as his concern that Margot is distracting Tony from his degree. He accepts Joan Taylor, both as crumbs from his beloved's table and as a way of vicariously achieving intimacy with him by sleeping with her. David finds Margot's power over Tony threatening. David's influence over Tony is equally unsettling to Margot and she eventually reaches her own conclusions:

MARGOT   The friendship of young men can be very selfish.
DAVID   But so impregnable.[19]

Battle lines are drawn. With her experience of the world, and particularly a liberal theatrical world, Margot senses the nature of David's affections for Tony and articulates it in a way that the two young men would never dream of doing:

MARGOT   I'm not afraid of you, you can't fool me – because you're
          just a filthy degenerate!
DAVID   God! How dare you! You who come down here and seduce
          a boy half your age. . . . You who've done your best to ruin
          his life for him; he's up to his neck in debt and he'll go
          down without a degree, and all because of you – you talk
          about degeneracy.[20]

Margot recognizes David's devotion to Tony as homosexual and is as explicit as the language of 1930s stage conventions would allow. Margot's accusation of degeneracy only confirms the series of ambiguous hints which call David's sexuality into question: his pacifism, his loathing of team games, his jealousy of Margot, his misogyny. David Lister is ultimately sent down after being discovered in Joan Taylor's room. It's possible that Rattigan wants to show David attempting to prove his heterosexuality to himself by going to Joan's room. It is also a convenient way of reassuring a 1930s heterosexual audience that David, though quirky, is really a harmless red-blooded young man who gets very drunk and then feels frisky enough to risk his degree and future career for a quick shag with Joan. But the impulse and development of the story demand a more logical and truthful conclusion which Rattigan avoids.* Having had his degeneracy articulated for him by Margot, David would then act on it. Betrayed by Margot, he would be discovered in the room of another man and then expelled from the university under a cloud. This scenario would prepare us better for the final reconciliation of David and Margot, who recognize the similarity of their positions:

DAVID   Let's forget about last night, Margot. I don't think it was your fault any more than mine. Don't blame yourself too much for anything that's happened . . . wasn't it inevitable? Tony's only a boy. We're just two unlucky people in his first episode. It's something we must both get over.[21]

David and Margot both learn about themselves from the episode and about the damaging effects of love. Margot certainly realizes the 'impregnable' strength of relationships between young men. She is defeated by it and ultimately resigns herself to it. When she returns to say goodbye to Tony, he will not speak to her directly. Once again the three find themselves in a triangular relationship where David is both pander and voyeur:

DAVID   *(Kindly)* You brought a lot of happiness to Tony – that's something to remember. Let's forget the rest.
            Tony turns away a little embarrassed.
MARGOT   *(going to David)* I'm glad you're Tony's friend.
DAVID   *(taking her hand)* That makes up for a lot.
MARGOT   May I say goodbye to him?
DAVID   Tony.
TONY   Yes, David?

---

* Perhaps Rattigan felt that he was appealing 'over the head of the Lord Chamberlain', as he explained a similar 'heterosexualizing' in *Separate Tables* years later.

DAVID	Margot's waiting to say goodbye to you.
	Tony comes to Margot. They kiss. It is a kiss of farewell.
DAVID	Has she gone?
TONY	Yes – she's gone.[22]

The stage directions for this scene vary in different manuscripts of the play. The fuller stage directions are very telling and expressive. Once Margot has left, no more words are spoken and we are left with an ambiguous ending. Does Tony fully understand David's affection for him, as Heimann did Rattigan's? Or has Tony recognized a mutual feeling for David and is now devastated to lose him? Whatever Rattigan's intentions, it is clear that given a choice between his relationship with Margot and his relationship with David, Tony chooses David:

> *The tension between the two boys is very great. David pretends to go on with his packing, but watches Tony out of the corner of his eye. Tony crosses to the gramophone and puts the needle down to start it without looking to see what record is in. As the gramophone starts he goes to get a drink. The record on the gramophone is the 'signature tune' of the play and as Tony realises it, he puts his drink down and crosses and changes the record to a lively jazz tune. This done he crosses to the window as if to see the last of the disappearing Margot. David remains at the trunk, but he realises all that is passing through Tony's mind, but not a word is said. The curtain falls.*[23]

The 'signature tune' of the play is associated with Margot. In changing the record, perhaps we witness Tony making the choice between a life with the Margots or Davids of the world, and ultimately resigning himself to his true homosexual nature. As David is leaving the university, a relationship with him is not an option, but it's almost as if the struggle between David and Margot has forced Tony to address the uncomfortable issue of his sexuality. As in the articulation of many gay relationships both on and off stage in this period, the final expression of Tony and David's relationship is silent. The 'unspeakable vice' is not spoken, voiceless, but present in Rattigan's manipulation of the subtext. Tony and David do not end up happily together; at the end of the play both men are isolated and Margot goes back to London alone. The only couple who do seem to be content together in the play are Bertie and Joan. They are ideally suited as they are both equally dim. Rattigan implies that only the stupid can ever be happy in love. When Bertie announces that he and

Joan are going to marry, David comments typically acidly: 'Well good luck to both of them. They'll need it. Fancy those two having to sit opposite each other for the next forty years.'[24] The image anticipates the last scene of *The Browning Version*. After the bitter recriminations between them, Millie and Crocker-Harris sit down to eat another interminable meal. They are condemned to live an unhappy, frustrated existence, together in resentment, for the rest of their lives. It's a bleak and bitter view of conventional marriage.

First Episode was disastrously revived on Broadway in 1934, the critics complaining that an unsophisticated farce had suffocated 'a disarmingly poignant drama'. The play has never since been revived and remains out of print, though readings of the play have recently been organized by a group of enthusiastic young actors at the Green Room Club (19 July 1995) and Salisbury Playhouse (26 September 1996) in an effort to provoke a restaging. Though a fascinating antecedent to his later work, *First Episode* is flawed by Rattigan's indecision about the genre of the play. He can't quite decide whether it's a youthful comedy or a more serious discussion about a young man's emotional development, complicated by his latent homosexuality. Rattigan had no such confusion about his next play, which he very clearly intended to be a comedy. He later claimed that his study of Chekhov's comedies had much influenced *French Without Tears*, both in structure and characterization. Forgoing the undergraduate larks of *First Episode*, Rattigan now developed a comedy of character and situation through which he continued to explore themes initiated in the earlier play: men's anxiety about women, the ambiguous friendships between young men and the conflict between reason and passion.

French Without Tears

As with *First Episode*, Rattigan drew on his own experiences in *French Without Tears*. Rattigan's father was determined that his unwilling son should follow him into the diplomatic service. Consequently Rattigan was sent on residential language courses to Germany and France during the long summer vacations, to polish his languages to the standard required by the diplomatic service. In the summer of 1931, Rattigan attended a crammer in Wimereux near Boulogne. It was presided over by a Monsieur Martin who practised the 'direct method': French was spoken at all times, and all meals were to be supervised by M. Martin, who also required a daily tutorial with each pupil. In *French Without Tears*, Rattigan transfers the action to the climatically more attractive west coast of France, though utilizing the general set-up at Wimereux. Four young men are attempting to learn French, with varying degrees of success. They are 'Babe' Lake, Kit Neilan, Brian Curtis and the Hon. Alan Howard. Howard, like Rattigan, is trying to evade his father's intentions of sending him into the diplomatic service; his ambition is to become a novelist (David Lister, the Rattigan figure in *First Episode*, wanted to become a famous journalist). They are joined by Lieutenant-Commander Rogers from the British navy. Babe Lake's sister, Diana, is also staying at the Villa Miramar because 'her people live in India and she's got nowhere else to go'. Diana is a self-confessed serial man-hunter. Despite her knowledge that M. Maingot's daughter Jacqueline is in love with him, Diana has captured Kit Neilan's affections. When Commander Rogers arrives she seduces him as well and plays Kit and Rogers off against each other. During the festivities for Bastille Day, Diana's flirtatious machinations are exposed and she is challenged by Alan to reveal whom she really loves. She declares that it is actually Alan she is in love with and he, in turn, is mortified. When Brian admits that he had tried to seduce Diana and that she had slapped him, Alan decides that he will try the 'direct method' and attempt to seduce her as well. If she lets him, he will stay and become a diplomat. If she refuses, he will return to England to become a novelist. Diana refuses and he goes off to pack. Learning that a new student, Lord Heybrook, is arriving the next morning, Diana then sets her sights on this blue-blooded catch. Her scheming is scuppered, however, when he turns out to be a fifteen-year-old schoolboy. She quickly changes her plans and determines to catch up with Alan's boat.

Much of the humour of the play arises from the cultural and linguistic differences between the English and the French. French is a romance language and it is in the romantic idiom, the language of love and desire, that these young men are found wanting. An honest expression of love or sexual desire is alien to the traditionally cool and understated British. Rattigan's young Englishmen experience at Miramar the same sort of cultural and emotional education that E. M. Forster's young people do in Edwardian Italy. In the same year as the première of *French Without Tears*, Forster wrote in his 'Notes on the English character' about the nature of the 'undeveloped heart', observing that the products of the public-school system graduate into a 'world of whose richness and subtlety they have no conception'.

> They go forth into it with well-developed bodies, fairly developed minds and undeveloped hearts. And it is this undeveloped heart that is largely responsible for the difficulties of Englishmen abroad. An undeveloped heart – not a cold one. . . . For it is not that the English-man can't feel – it is that he is afraid to feel.[25]

Like Forster, Rattigan explores the English reticence to feel and the vulnerability and fear of potential humiliation of those who dare to express feeling, either physically or verbally. Rattigan is particularly interested in the faltering attempts at the expression of feeling. Language itself is a problem. From the beginning of the play, the linguistic definition of the world of 'richness and subtlety' is problematic. The theme is initiated in a comic tone. Brian tries to help Babe Lake translate the phrase 'She has ideas above her station'. He famously mistranslates it as 'Elle a des idées au-dessus de sa gare'. It is, of course, 'not that sort of station'.[26] In the world of this play, the simplest things evade definition; the subtleties of feeling are even more complex. Of course Rattigan exploits the stock British discomfort with and distrust of other tongues; it can be traced from the Princess of France's *double entendres* in *Henry V* to television comedies such as *'Allo,'Allo*.

In exploring his protagonists' difficulties with language, Rattigan also suggests the poverty of words to express thoughts and emotions, particularly of love and desire. Such a metaphorical use of the young men's inability to acquire French alerts us to their inability to express sexual or emotional feelings in English. The young men use the 1930s slang typical of their age and class which M. Maingot doesn't understand: 'Qu'est-ce que c'est ça, po-faced?' Sex is continually referred to as 'hanky panky', as if by describing it in the language of the dormitory they can deflate their anxieties about it. Commander Rogers feels isolated as he understands neither French nor the slang that the young men use. In Act III, he admonishes his colleagues for their coldness when he first arrived: 'plumped down in a house full of strange people, all either talking French, which I couldn't understand, or your own brand of English, which was almost as hard'.[27] The only character in the play who neither speaks French nor expresses any desire to learn it is Diana Lake. Diana is the huntress of classical myth, but she is also (ironically in this case) the patroness of chastity. But Alan deflates the resonances of a name associated with the groves of Arcady by referring to her hobby as 'the machinations of a scalp-hunter'. Rattigan's elliptical style and his suggestive subtext, enable him to refer to the unthinkable, unreadable and unspeakable:

ALAN   I've warned him against you.
DIANA   You warned him? What did you say?
ALAN   I told him what you are.
DIANA   *(quietly)* What's that?
ALAN   Don't you know?[28]

Diana is that which cannot be defined, or like Maurice's definition of himself, that which cannot be named, the 'unspeakable'. This confrontation reverses that between Margot and David in *First Episode*, as Diana, like David, is accused of hunting and capturing young men. Diana is variously described as a 'bitch' or a 'cow'. As in *First Episode*, the men reveal an inherent misogyny, especially when drunk. They regard women as creatures with a different moral code than their own: 'You can't judge women by our standards of right and wrong'.[29] The novel which Alan is writing and which is continually being returned to him ends in an idealistic, woman-free relationship between two men. The plot, focusing on two young conscientious objectors, echoes the triangular relationships which resound through Rattigan's plays. When war breaks out, rather than fight and betray their principles, the two main characters leave for Central Africa. One of the men is accompanied by his wife, who ultimately makes love to the other man. The two men fight over the woman and realize in doing so that their impulses are as animal as those that are involved in fighting a war. They return to England to fight for their country. But their ideal of non-violence is not proved wrong just because they were unable to live up to it. When the two men return home together, they leave the wife behind in Africa, having discovered that she is a 'bitch'. Ultimately, Commander Rogers and Kit find themselves performing the roles of the two men and concluding that Diana (and perhaps Woman generally) is indeed a bitch. But Rogers had been warned about Diana's siren tendencies as soon as he had arrived when Alan sang the 'Lorelei'.

ALAN   I ask you, what sailor would be lured to his doom after he had been warned of the danger?[30]

Diana even refers to herself as a 'scheming wrecker of men's lives': a lake might look placid, but men can still drown there. The Commander is literally at sea. In a recent production of the play at the Palace Theatre, Watford, the action took place in a disused swimming pool and in Diana's (Sara Crowe) final pursuit of Alan (Louis Hillyer), he became stranded in the deep end of the pool, literally out of his depth.[31] Aquatic images abound, for Diana is a siren. She doesn't need to learn French for she requires neither language nor wit in order to communicate; she has sex:

DIANA   I'm not clever and I can't talk intelligently. There's only one thing I've got, and I don't think you'll deny it. I have got a sort of gift for making men fall in love with me.[32]

Diana is unashamed of her 'gift' and practises it relentlessly. Alan claims that both he and Brian are 'immune' to Diana's infectious affections. Brian is learning French for 'commercial reasons'. He needs to know just enough to get the best prices for casual sex with prostitutes in town. When Brian receives a telephone call from one of them, he needs Alan to translate for him in order to make the arrangements. Brian, like Diana, can communicate on a sensual level. When M. Maingot asks who the telephone call is from, Brian unwittingly puts his finger on it: 'Une jeune fille je connais dans le ville'. M. Maingot bursts into 'stentorian laughter':

ALAN   A fille doesn't mean a girl, Brian.
BRIAN   It says so in my dictionary. What does it mean then?
ALAN   A tart.
BRIAN   Oh! *(He considers a second.)* Well, I hate to have to say it, old boy, but having a strict regard for the truth that's a fairly neat description of Chi-Chi.[33]

Like Bertie and Joan Taylor in *First Episode*, Brian is stupid, but happy. He has successfully avoided Diana's wiles and has apparently solved the dilemma of sex. He segregates his sexual feelings from the rest of his life. He is not interested in romance, nor is he keen to develop relationships. Brian, like his colleagues, fears intimacy. He responds simply and directly and refuses emotional intimacy altogether:

JACQUELINE   I think [Brian's] too stupid to be bad tempered.
KIT   No, Brian may be stupid but he's right-minded. He's solved the problem of living better than any of us. It seems a simple solution too. All it needs apparently is the occasional outlay of fifty francs. I wish I could do the same.[34]

Brian has avoided, rather than solved, the dilemma. Kit has tried to follow his example, but failed. The 'problem of living' seems to be the integration of sex into life, rather than compartmentalizing it. Years later Rattigan returned to this theme explicitly in *Who Is Sylvia?* This 1950 comedy follows the sexual career of Mark St Neots from 1917 to 1950. Mark goes through life in love with 'the same face'. Dedicated with an apology to Rattigan's philandering father, the play explores the dilemmas of a man who lives a double life – one domestic, the other sexual:

MARK   [. . .] I may well have stumbled on the whole secret of successful living... to divide the illicit from the domestic, the romantic and dangerous from the dull and secure – to divide them into two worlds and then to have the best of both of them.[35]

The inability of Rattigan's characters to reconcile their sexual activities with the rest of their lives is a characteristic of their Englishness. But through this English reluctance to wholeheartedly submit to sexual love, Rattigan is able to explore the dilemma of those who cannot thus reconcile their lives because their sexuality is 'illicit' and 'dangerous'. In exploring the dilemma of the double life in his light plays, Rattigan was following a comic tradition that harked back to Wilde's Mr Bunbury. After a visit to the casino on Bastille Day, Alan drunkenly expresses the fears of all the young men at Miramar when he observes that 'love is only sublimated sex'. Alan advocates sexual honesty and deplores coquetry:

ALAN   How simple everything would be if that sort of so-called vir-
         tue were made illegal – if it were just a question of will you or
         won't you. No one ought to be allowed to get away with that –
         'I'd like to, but I mustn't'. It's that that leads to all the trouble.[36]

Diana leads the men on, but she will not sleep with them. Sex in the 1930s was not just a question of 'will you or won't you'. The restrictions of polite convention on Diana's behaviour – willing but unable – echo the dilemma of gay men in the period, restricted as they were by law. Alan claims to be frustrated by the conventional mores of his class and background, but does not realize that he also upholds certain of the very conventions he purports to resent. It seems that he doesn't like Diana because it is she who pursues men, unsettling the 'natural' order. She refuses to conform to the conventional modes of behaviour that the young students have brought with them from England. Alan recognizes that on foreign soil the young men are disorientated and confused. Diana certainly wouldn't get away with her flirtatious behaviour in England, but in the relative French freedom of Miramar, she is dangerous because she has the power to make men forget good sense and be led by their sexual instincts. Ultimately, when Diana claims that she is in love with Alan, he responds in particularly Miltonic terms: 'I shall fall. Oh God! I know it, I shall fall.'[37] Having spent most of the play disparaging Diana's attractions, Alan admits that he has succumbed to her charms. He knows he must avoid Diana at all costs, but is unsure whether his sexual attraction to her will get the better of him. But Diana and Brian have also been drinking that evening and she had given Brian 'the old green light'. Seeing it as an opportunity not to be missed, Brian then 'handed out an invitation to the waltz, if you follow me'. Diana was not up for that sort of dancing and belted Brian in the mouth. It is at this point that Alan decides that his future will depend on the way that Diana responds to him. If she is willing to be made love to, he will stay on at Miramar, continue his studies and become a diplomat. If she refuses him, he will go back to England to become a novelist. Diana refuses Alan's advances and he begins to pack. Once again Diana retains her power over the men. Alan's future is in her hands and he allows her the power to dictate it. His sexual rejection by Diana will mark the beginning of his life as an artist, possibly even provide the fuel for it. But Alan has been exposed as a hypocrite. Diana, at least, had always been honest about her intentions: she enjoys leading men on and isn't ashamed of it.

Rattigan's attitude to Diana is ambivalent. On the one hand, she represents a snare to entrap young men and intervene in the development of relationships between them. On the other, she advocates sexual freedom of a type not generally associated with the English. Her behaviour is unorthodox by English standards and her attitude towards sex a good deal healthier than that of the repressed and anxious young men.

The most mature love in the play is that of the long-suffering Jacqueline Maingot for Kit Neilan. Unlike Diana, Joan and Margot in *First Episode*, Jacqueline is not regarded as an outsider. She is a native French speaker and takes the young men for tutorials. She also, rather maternally, assists in the domestic tasks at Miramar. Jacqueline sets Kit an exercise in which he must translate *La Bruyère*. He is only able to translate the text literally, and he cannot interpret Jacqueline's true feelings for him either. In his faltering way he attempts to translate the extract and Jacqueline corrects him. When he translates the title as 'Of the Heart', which could be the title of a medical textbook, Jacqueline points out that the correct translation is 'Of Love'. As in *The Browning Version*, when Crocker-Harris corrects Frank Hunter's translation of Taplow's inscription, the ability to precisely translate a literary work doesn't necessarily indicate pedantry, but a heartfelt understanding of the text to be translated. Kit translates 'Friendship can exist between people of different sexes, quite exempt from all grossness'. A friendship can exist between Jacqueline and Kit, because her gender appears not to threaten the young men. She is treated casually and is almost always referred to as the rather masculine 'Jack'. Unlike the predatory Diana, Jacqueline is neither threatening nor seductive. De-feminized by the men around her, she is treated as one of the lads:

KIT	I like you so much that it's sometimes quite an effort to remember that you're a woman at all …
JACQUELINE	Oh. I thought you liked women.
KIT	I don't think one likes women, does one? One loves them sometimes, but that's a different thing altogether. Still, I like you.[38]

Love is only used in a sexual context ('Love is only sublimated sex, isn't it?'). The characters in *French Without Tears* choose not to use the word ambiguously. Diana is loved but not liked; whereas Jacqueline is liked but not loved. Diana tells her, 'You're the sort of person that people like. But nobody likes me.' Liking does not involve erotic attraction or desire and is therefore safe. Alan describes the sort of girl he would like to fall in love with: she must have 'all the masculine virtues and none of the feminine vices'. His ideal picture of a woman is a description of Jacqueline. But Kit declares, 'Love and Jack. They just don't seem to connect.'

The confusions of language and desire reach their height on the night of Bastille Day, the annual celebration of French liberation. Once a year, rather like Midsummer Night, normal behaviour is turned on its head. At Miramar the festival initiates an evening of licence and excess, where conventions are relaxed, a great deal of alcohol is consumed and the students begin to speak of their feelings more openly and honestly. It is an evening of revelations. The festivities begin with everybody dressing up for a costume ball. National identities become confused, with Maingot dressing as a Scot, Jacqueline as a Bavarian and Kit as a Greek. Alan, as usual, wears a German jacket. Just as there is a confusion of national identities so is there a confusion of gender. Both Kit and Maingot wear skirts as part of their costumes. Babe Lake wears a sailor suit, a uniform of camp 'butch drag' for gay men. Kit borrows his Greek costume from Babe. It is deliberately referred to as a dress, rather than the less gender-specific 'costume': 'Could I get into this dress of your brother's?' Commander Rogers observes, 'you look so damned funny in that get up – like a bedraggled old fairy queen'.[39] The confusions of costume prepare the way for a series of revelations about Diana's behaviour, which will force the men to reassess their attitude both to her and towards each other. Learning of Diana's machinations, Rogers and Kit begin to forget their differences and develop a certain camp camaraderie, recalling the meeting of Gwendoline and Cecily in *The Importance of Being Earnest*:

KIT   I say, I may call you Bill, mayn't I?
ROGERS   Oh, my dear Kit.[40]

The men leave Diana to her own devices and go to the casino, returning home very drunk. In their drunkenness they become sentimental and very affectionate with each other. This is the closest that the men get to making declarations of affection for each other. The poignancy of the play comes from this very English inability to articulate feelings of love and affection. The most apparent unspoken loves of the play are those of the two women. Diana secretly loves Alan, but dissuaded by his misogyny towards her has said nothing and seeks solace elsewhere. Jacqueline suffers in silence as she listens while Kit complains about the way Diana treats him. But there are also unspoken attractions between the young men which are never articulated. Alan admires the swaggering, straightforward masculinity of Brian. Kit and Rogers, having fought over Diana, evolve a relationship of their own. Most curious is Babe Lake, a strange figure who quietly haunts the play and yet takes no part in the sexual power play. As Diana's brother, he looks very similar to her. He insists that Alan helps him with his French and is terribly disappointed when he won't go to the ball with him. When Alan leaves Miramar, Babe is very upset: 'Alan, must you go? ... I don't think you know what you're doing.'[41] But Alan seems oblivious to Babe Lake's regard for him, which suggests something more than hero-worship. Like the two heroes of his novel, Alan finally escapes the clutches of women. Rattigan's original conclusion to *French Without Tears* is significantly different from the version eventually performed, but was changed only at the last minute. Rather than the arrival of a fifteen-year-old Lord Heybrook, Rattigan had introduced a 'blond swishy queer':

KIT	*(calling)* Diana! Lord Heybrook!
JACQUELINE	*(leaning over Alan's shoulder)* What does he look like, Alan?
ALAN	I can't see.
	The crowd round the window disperses as a taxi-man comes in carrying two suitcases. Maingot follows.
MAINGOT	*(to taxi-man)* Apportez-les en haut. Tenez. Je vous monterai sa chambre. *(calling)* Par ici, Milord.
	Lord Heybrook comes in. He is a pale, slender man with golden hair. He has a borzoi on a lead.
MAINGOT	D'abord je vous monterai votre chambre. Les présentations après.
	He opens the door at back. Lord Heybrook goes towards it. Before he reaches it, Diana comes in in a bathing dress and wrap. She flashes him a brilliant smile, but he appears not to notice her.
LORD HEYBROOK	*(to the Borzoi, sibilantly)* Come along, Alcibiades. Follow your master.[42]

If the dyed hair or the camp lisp hadn't given it away, Alcibiades was one of the most outrageous queens of ancient times and turns up at Socrates's dinner party in the *Symposium*. Lord Heybrook is to occupy the place at Miramar vacated by Alan. Superficially different, are they in essence interchangeable? And isn't there surely a resurgence of the misogyny of *First Episode* in having the promiscuous Diana's designs thwarted by the arrival of an effeminate homosexual? In an interview shortly before his death, Rattigan reflected on the play:

> I think it's a bit more serious than anyone has ever allowed. It's not simply a lot of young men romping about. It's not a farce. I regard it as a comedy of mood and character.[43]

But surely the play can be about 'a lot of young men romping about' and still be a 'bit more serious'. As Margot warned in *First Episode*, the friendship of young men can be impregnable, and yet also strangely, tantalizingly (frustratingly for some of us) ambiguous.

Brief Encounters

Two films by Noël Coward: *Brief Encounter* and *The Astonished Heart*

JULIA   I'm torn between my better self and my worst self. I never
realised there were two of me until this moment so clearly
defined. I want terribly badly to be a true, faithful wife and
look after Fred and live in peace, and I want terribly to have
violent and illicit love made to me and be frenziedly happy
and supremely miserable.
Noël Coward, *Fallen Angels*[1]

LAURA   Do you know, I believe we should all behave quite differently
if we lived in a warm, sunny climate all the time. We shouldn't
be so withdrawn and shy and difficult.
Noël Coward, *Brief Encounter*[2]

I might just as well come out about this now as later: I never tire of watching *Brief Encounter*. There, I've said it. Part of its appeal to me is my own very ambivalent attitude to it, for it seems to me to represent all the most attractive and most repellent aspects of English culture. It promotes on the one hand a nostalgic world of decency and niceness, suffused by the comforts of home, and on the other a repressed, class-ridden culture suffocated by its own nostalgia and characterized by emotional sterility and quiet self-sacrifice. I'm also aware of the 'deadly respectability' of the film's reputation and that in defending it I'll probably be condemned as a secret wearer of cardigans, slippers, brushed-cotton pyjamas and God knows what other horrors. But as we move further away from *Brief Encounter* as a document of contemporary life, and the film joins the mythology of 'Englishness', its conventions seem to me as foreign but its emotions as fresh and direct as a Restoration comedy or a Victorian sensational novel.

Despite his enormous success in the theatre and the rather more symbiotic relationship of theatre and film between the wars, Noël Coward
made surprisingly few forays into film. Compared to the theatre, where
Coward was indisputably 'the Master', film-making is a much more collaborative medium, dominated by technicians rather than performers. As I
have discussed earlier, Coward went to great lengths to see his vision realized very precisely on stage and might have been anxious about relin-
quishing artistic control in the cinema. Since Britain's entry into the war
in 1939, the patriotic Coward had wanted to make a 'lasting contribution'
to the war effort, but was refused any position of responsibility in the
services. Winston Churchill advised him to 'go and sing to them while
the guns are firing'. So Coward performed his way through the war, giving a lengthy series of concerts to the troops abroad. But in 1942 he finally
found his role in the war, writing, producing and starring in his paean to
the Royal Navy and British resilience, *In Which We Serve*. The film follows
the fortunes of three crew members of *HMS Torrin* at sea and the domestic
stories of their families at home. Through this divided narrative, the film
articulates the different lives experienced during the war by the men away
on active service and the women attempting to live a semblance of a normal life at home during air-raids, food shortages and daily anxiety about
their loved ones. There is a deeply melancholic feeling to the film due to
the fact that the story of the *Torrin* is told in a flashback after she has gone
down fighting off the coast of Crete. The flashback was a favourite device
of Coward's in his films, and it establishes a sense of loss from the start.
Commended at the time for its documentary-style realism, the film today
is a fascinating examination of a still watertight class system headed by
Coward's Captain 'D', based on Lord Mountbatten, who had been a friend
of Coward's since the 1920s. The stories of a working-, a middle- and an
upper-class family are woven into a film united by patriotic feeling and
national suffering. But the destruction of the *Torrin*, with her crew of dis-
parate classes left clinging to life-rafts, is an image which pre-empts the
immediate future of a once-great sea-faring nation which needs must re-
evaluate her international status. The war will explode the deferential class
system on which commanders like Captain 'D' had relied.

Though Coward is credited with co-directing the picture, he also
starred in it and consequently left much of the directorial work to the
young David Lean. They then collaborated on *This Happy Breed* (1944), an
evocation of lower-middle-class family life between the wars, as well as

Blithe Spirit (1945) and *Brief Encounter* (1945). Coward adapted his own stage works for the screen and Lean directed. A core of regular performers were drawn on, including John Mills, Kay Walsh, Joyce Carey, Stanley Holloway and Celia Johnson. It seems clear that Coward certainly had the skill and opportunities, particularly after the enormous popular and critical success of *In Which We Serve* and *Brief Encounter*, to explore his interests in film further. But unlike Terence Rattigan, who spent a successful and lucrative sabbatical in Hollywood running off scripts and accepting the money (*The Yellow Rolls-Royce*, *The VIPs*), Coward's environment remained the theatre. His only other screen-writing credits were adaptations from his series of short plays, *Tonight at 8.30* (1936). *Meet Me Tonight* is a rather unsuccessful, stage-bound conglomeration of three of the plays. When Coward saw the film in September 1952 he was appalled by it: 'Absolutely awful – vilely directed and ... abominably acted';[3] it hasn't improved with time. Fortunately the same can't be said of the fascinating, if flawed, film version of *The Astonished Heart* (1949). In considering Coward's expression and manipulation of his authorial voice and his public persona, it is fascinating to examine aspects of his cinematic work in order to probe his dilemma as a gay writer working in popular commercial forms. The British cinema of the 1940s and 1950s was not one that embraced difference, but Coward was still able to produce provocative, richly resonant work, which explored the dangers and dilemmas of forbidden love.

Though Coward's lasting reputation will probably rest on his comedies, his few dramas reveal an equally adept talent for examining the everyday tragedies of the middle classes. In his serious plays, Coward avoids the society and bohemian milieu of his comedies. He examined the temptations, dangers and pains of transgression in two related works from the *Tonight at 8.30* sequence: *Still Life* and *The Astonished Heart*. As stage works, they are related in theme and tone and stimulated Coward to return years later to both texts, adapting each of them for the screen. Coward almost suffocates *The Astonished Heart* with his centrality to it, whereas in *Still Life*, filmed as *Brief Encounter*, his personal preoccupations haunt the film more subtly and much more successfully. A comparison of these two films sheds a fascinating light on Coward's continuing dilemma, exploring his own emotional territory as a gay man in a pre-liberation culture, whilst at the same time maintaining his public image of ageing playboy and heterosexual dandy.

Both films chart the development, crises and ending of adulterous heterosexual affairs. In *Brief Encounter*, Laura Jesson (Celia Johnson), a 'happily married woman', meets Alec Harvey (Trevor Howard), a general practitioner, when he takes a piece of grit out of her eye in the refreshment room at Milford Junction station. They continue to meet, at first accidentally, every Thursday for seven weeks, going to the pictures and having tea. Laura and Alec realize they have fallen in love and after a trip to the country Alec invites Laura to the flat of his colleague, Stephen Lynn, to consummate the relationship. After initially refusing, Laura capitulates, but the couple are interrupted by Lynn's unexpected return and Laura is forced to make an undignified exit down the back stairs. Shamed by the furtiveness of the affair and drawn by motives of self-respect and decency, Alec and Laura agree to end their relationship. Alec accepts a job in Johannesburg. When he is about to leave for the last time, their parting is interrupted by the arrival of Dolly Messiter, a gossiping acquaintance of Laura's. The lovers' farewell is reduced to a polite goodbye and the light squeeze of Alec's hand on Laura's shoulder.

The milieu of *The Astonished Heart* is very different from that of *Still Life/ Brief Encounter*. Laura Jesson's world is provincial and middle class. She shops weekly in Milford, changes her library book at Boots and enjoys a mid-week matinée. Christian and Barbara Faber in *The Astonished Heart* are sophisticated metropolitans, living in a new block of service flats overlooking Hyde Park. They are comfortably off and cosily married. Christian Faber (played on stage and film by Coward), 'only one of the most celebrated psychiatrists in the world', falls in love with Leonora Vail (Margaret Leighton), a glamorous school-friend of his wife, Barbara (Celia Johnson). Leonora is quite a siren and makes a deliberate attempt to seduce the doctor. The liberal and long-suffering Barbara, having guessed about the affair, magnanimously suggests that Faber and Leonora go abroad and let the relationship run its course. But Faber becomes anxious about Leonora's flirtatious manner and jealous about her past relationships; the affair begins to deteriorate. When they return to London, the relationship ends with bitter recriminations. Faber commits suicide by leaping from a roof, but manages to whisper his wife's name just before he dies. In essence, *The Astonished Heart* is a bitter comedy of three modern, intelligent people attempting to apply their modern intelligence to an age-old emotional problem and arriving at the usual tragic result.

Both *Brief Encounter* and *The Astonished Heart* are told as long flash-backs. Though Barbara Faber initiates the flashback in *The Astonished Heart*, inviting Faber's assistants, Susan (Joyce Carey) and Tim (Graham Payn), to remember the moment a year before when Leonora entered the room for the first time, the tone throughout is much more objective than that of *Brief Encounter*. The audience is presented with the dilemmas of all three of the main characters. We travel abroad with Faber and Leonora, but we also see Barbara alone at home. We follow Faber to his suicide and also observe the action after his death. Laura Jesson's flashback in *Brief Encounter* is shot specifically from her subjective point of view. Her voice-over tells the story as she sits at home with her husband Fred on the evening that Alec has left her for ever. She is nervous and tense and her memories of the affair are inspired and accompanied by the romantic strains of Rachmaninov on the wireless. The tone of the voice-over is very intimate, like a confession. Laura attempts to shrive herself of her pain and guilt over the affair by going through it in her mind. She shares her grief with the audience, but ultimately nobody actually listens to her painful story. Her love and the affair are literally unspoken. But the final exchange of the film indicates that Laura's husband has understood the reason for her apparent distress:

FRED   Laura . . .

LAURA   *(Turning her head slowly and looking at him – her voice sounds dead.)*
           Yes, dear?

FRED   Whatever your dream was – it wasn't a very happy one, was it?

LAURA   *(in a whisper)* No.

FRED   Is there anything I can do to help?

LAURA   Yes, my dear – you always help . . .

FRED   You've been a long way away?

LAURA   *(nodding – her eyes fill with tears)* Yes, Fred.
           Fred moves a little closer to her and quietly rests his face against her hand.

FRED   *(with a catch in his voice)* Thank you for coming back to me.[4]

Through the narrative of Laura Jesson's 'dream', Coward explores the excitement and trauma of forbidden love and the burdens of duty, decency and respectability with great intensity. Like Christian Faber, Laura is torn between the known comforts of home and family and her natural emotional impulses, or as Coward named it elsewhere, her 'secret heart'.

Brief Encounter might seem a surprising film to appeal to gay men, compared to the histrionic Hollywood movies of the 1940s which have a more obvious camp appeal. Celia Johnson's style is far removed from that of screen queens like Bette Davis, Joan Crawford and Barbara Stanwyck in films like *Now, Voyager* and *Mildred Pierce*. *Brief Encounter* has some similarity to these 'women's pictures' in that it focuses on the emotional life of the female protagonist and was originally aimed at a predominantly female audience. But the style which characterizes the Hollywood melodramas of the 1940s is very much one of excess. Laura's dilemma, and Johnson's interpretation of it, is a study in restraint. This self-harnessing of emotion in both the narrative and the performances is one of the reasons that contribute to the film's continued gay following. The complex relationship of *Brief Encounter* to its gay audience has been wittily examined by Richard Dyer in his study of the film. He notes the camp appeal of dialogue such as 'There go me Banbury's all over the floor' and ' My dear, I've been shopping till I'm dropping', as well as Joyce Carey's wonderfully 'refained' accent: 'Time and taide wait for no man, Mr Godby'. But camp aside, it is surely the emotional depth of the film and its allegorical representation of forbidden love at a time of intense legal homophobia which have appealed to generations of gay men.

Brief Encounter, like the movies of Crawford and Davis, was typical of the Saturday matinée fodder which I used to watch on television throughout the 1970s. It is through television, before the age of video and 'revival' cinemas, that a generation of gay men were first introduced and attracted to the performers and stories which they would later identify as part of a shared gay subculture. I remember being very surprised, but delighted, that a university friend of mine quoted the film in a letter of farewell to his estranged boyfriend: 'I didn't think such violent things could happen to ordinary people'. Surprised, because I had thought that I alone had identified the resonances of Laura Jesson's dilemma as relevant to my own, and delighted, because I realized that mine wasn't a perverse reading of the film, that it could be interpreted from a gay perspective and by young gay men in the mid-1980s, seemingly so divorced from the world described in *Brief Encounter*. Dyer observes that 'The subject matter – forbidden love in ordinary lives – makes an obvious appeal to gay readers, as do fear of discovery and settling for respectability

(Laura's home is her closet).'[5] Andy Medhurst concurs that the film 'explores the pain and grief caused by having one's desires destroyed by the pressures of social convention and it is this set of emotions which has sustained its reputation in gay subcultures'.[6]

Both Dyer and Medhurst admit that the film upholds patriarchal British culture in that Laura ultimately renounces her feelings of passion and returns to the comforting arms of her dull husband, Fred. Laura is the heart of the film and whether we love or loathe it depends primarily on our attitude to her. Many readers find Laura's dilemma and cut-glass accent difficult to tolerate, even laughable, establishing her as a privileged, gutless housewife who capitulates to the strictures and comforts of patriarchy. But this is not a new post-feminist response to the film. When previewed in Rochester in 1945 it was laughed off the screen. David Lean recalled the occasion: 'A woman in the front began laughing and pretty soon the entire audience was hysterical. I wanted to burn the print, I was so humiliated.'[7] In the 1960s, when writing his diatribe against the 'scratch and mumble' school of new British playwrights like Wesker and Osborne, Coward challenged the contemporary bigotry of assuming that 'reasonably educated people who behave with restraint are necessarily "clipped", "arid", "bloodless", and "unreal"'.[8] Just because Laura refuses to submit to her desires doesn't mean she feels them any less intensely than Madame Bovary or Anna Karenina. In fact, Coward consciously invokes Tolstoy's tragic heroine when Laura threatens to throw herself under an express train. Unlike Laura, Anna Karenina succeeds. Is Laura's pain any less intense because she doesn't aggrandize herself with death?*

Despite Lean's initial reservations and the disbelief of the German audience who couldn't understand why Alec and Laura just didn't get to bed and have done with it, *Brief Encounter* went on to receive the Prix Internationale de Film at Cannes in 1946 and continues to resonate in

---

* Indeed, the much-disparaged, contemporary 'Aga-sagas' of Joanna Trollope and Mary Wesley deal with the same basic dilemma that confronts Laura Jesson – home versus personal freedom. The literary press's snobbery towards them is possibly as much because of the gender of their protagonists (and their core readership) as their popularism. The heroine of Joanna Trollope's *The Rector's Wife* is called Anna Bouverie, in an echo of Flaubert's dissatisfied provincial housewife, Emma Bovary.

contemporary film-making. Richard Kwietniowski reworked the story from a gay perspective in *Flames of Passion* (1990), the title taken from the film that Alec and Laura walk out of during their romance. In Kenneth Branagh's recent film, *In the Bleak Midwinter* (1995), a group of resting actors are almost defeated in their attempts to put on a production of *Hamlet* over Christmas. The central character is the director (Michael Maloney), who ultimately questions the point of trying to achieve anything in life, or even to live it. Vernon, one of his fellow actors, tries to give him a reason for living: 'That bit in *Brief Encounter*. And *Brief Encounter* actually – that makes life worth living. I'll buy you the video for Christmas.'[9] C. A. Lejeune, a perceptive female critic of the period, lauded the film and identified some of the reasons that continue to attract successive generations to it:

> I don't think it will be everybody's film, but I'm sure there'll be people here and there who'll find it intensely moving . . . it seems to me to catch in words and pictures so many things which are penetratingly true. The whole colour, the spring, the almost magical feeling of the discovery that someone's in love with you, that someone feels it's exciting to be with you; that is something so tenuous that it's hardly ever been put on the screen. And yet it's here. And then the feeling of home; the warm kindly harbourage of familiar things; and the understanding of a person who's fond of you with whom you've lived for many years and who doesn't need to ask questions before he can get answers.[10]

Dyer and Lejeune, writing fifty years apart and with diverse cultural agendas, concur that one of the greatest strengths of the film is Celia Johnson's interpretation of Coward's character. Lejeune defined Johnson's ability as 'the sort of acting the French have been taught to understand: confessional acting from the inside outwards'. According to Kate Fleming's biography of her mother, the lifestyle and persona of Laura Jesson the suburban housewife had much in common with that of the private world of the actress, Celia Johnson. On first receiving the script from Coward, Johnson was enthusiastic about it in a letter to her husband:

> It's about a woman, married with two children who meets by chance a

man in a railway waiting room and they fall in love. And it's all no good ... it will be pretty unadulterated Johnson and when I am not being sad or anguished or renouncing, I am narrating about it.[11]

Coward's great successes turned on the symbiosis of performer and character: Coward/Elyot, Gertrude Lawrence/Amanda and Margaret Rutherford/Madam Arcati. Thus were created indelible, iconographic performances. The marriage of Celia Johnson and Laura Jesson creates a sense of honesty and authenticity which, despite the accent and the ridiculous hats, continues to move us, because we do more than sympathize with her, we identify ourselves with her predicament. As Richard Dyer admits, 'I have often wished I knew – or was – Celia Johnson, but of course what I meant was that I'd like to have known or been Laura Jesson.'[12]

Passion contained and controlled, together with a sense of passion that has passed, contributes to the sad, elegiac quality of *Brief Encounter*. From the very start it is infused with a sense of loss because our first encounter with Laura begins with the end of her affair. We know that the relationship is doomed and every frame leads us further towards an inevitable parting. Part of its appeal is its nostalgia. Nostalgic for Laura as she reflects on her recent past, but also for us with its vanished world of Kardomah tearooms, Boots' lending libraries and steam engines. Alison Light detects in the film 'an infatuation with a fading image of national life'.[13] The very mores of *Brief Encounter* are the mores of a world now past. But there is something in this fictional world of timetables, order and strict social codes, where individuals agonize over their responsibilities, that seems so secure, so attractive. In our contemporary age of impersonal internets and anger, where strangers are to be feared in the street as well as in bed, there is great comfort in the gentle good manners of Laura and Alec, who are prepared to act 'sensibly' and 'decently', refusing to hurt the people they love, even if it is at their own expense. Like the carefully arranged apples and Bath buns on the refreshment-room counter, Alec and Laura succumb to the pressures of ordered society, ultimately capitulating to 'stifling conformity'. But Alec and Laura prefer stability to chaos. Dyer observes that

Part of the pleasure of *Brief Encounter* is simply the recognition of the way that restraint, not wanting to hurt, wanting to be nice, desiring comfort, stymie emotional abandon. . . . There is an extra pull for me too in what I think of as nostalgia for ordinariness: unlike some gay men, I have never wanted to be marginal or outcast, but have no option. In this perspective the very dowdiness of *Brief Encounter* evokes the cosy lure of normality.[14]

But even in 1946 the film shared a certain nostalgia with its contemporary audience. Though the costumes seem contemporary mid-1940s, the world of Milford and Ketchworth is that of the late 1930s, and is certainly prewar. The stage play, *Still Life*, had taken place over a year from April 1936 to 1937, but *Brief Encounter* occurs over seven weeks during the winter of 1938–39. During the filming, dummy bars of chocolate and plastic cakes were used because of wartime shortages, but Alec and Laura buy chocolate and buns with coupon-free abandon. This sense of indulgence in food, casually but so tantalizingly displayed on the screen, but denied to the audience in reality, was similarly exploited by Evelyn Waugh in *Brideshead Revisited*.* *Theater Arts* congratulated Coward and Lean for their 'extraordinary feat of projection by setting the picture in pre-war days and providing – out of the rigors and shortages of post-war life – all the proper accoutrements of the past, including chocolate, buns and a peculiar brand of pre-war soldier'.[15] Celia Johnson, 'down to one of everything and yearning for some splendid clobber', was desperate to keep some of her costumes: 'I long to have even the mackintosh, but no.'[16]

Just as the war affected the production, the anxieties of wartime make themselves felt in the completed film in subtle ways. The contemporary audience in 1945 would certainly have recognized the nostalgia in the film for the comparative innocence of the 1930s. Fred and Laura discuss entering their son for the Navy, which they seem to regard as an extension of the Boy Scouts, rather than the major military force it's about to become: 'he'll have a wife in every port and be able to see the world.' Dolly Messiter unknowingly prattles on that 'Wild horses

---

* The preface to *Brideshead Revisited* (1959) reads: '[1943] was a bleak period of present privation and threatening disaster – the period of soya beans and Basic English – and in consequence the book is infused with a kind of gluttony, for food and wine, for the splendours of the recent past, and for rhetorical and ornamental language . . .'

wouldn't drag me away from England, and home and all the things one's used to'; in a matter of months, however, England is about to be thrown into a cataclysmic world conflict where individuals would be wrenched from their loved ones and scattered across the globe. Even Laura's living-room at Ketchworth advertises the prewar luxury of open curtains and no blackout: a lovely, detailed domestic touch. And at the cinema, Alec jokes that 'The stars can change in their courses, the universe go up in flames and the world crash around us, but there'll always be Donald Duck.'[17] As Antonia Lant observes, this joke would have been 'divested of its humor by 1945'.[18]

The film is infused with a sense of ending. Just as we know that the affair is doomed almost from the beginning, we are also aware that the world the film portrays, this naive, unknowing provincial life, is finite, but with a very definite ending in September 1939. Without directly referring to the war, the film examines the confusions of an unfamiliar world where strangers are haphazardly thrown together, and ephemeral relationships take on a desperate intensity. In this context it is not the death of relationships which is examined, but the emotional wrench of parting which in the war years had become such a way of life. For a woman of Laura's background, as well as for the audience, the world is changed. The old certainties don't necessarily hold good any more and the chance of a brief, intense affair might outweigh the security of a lifetime's comfortable companionship. The end of filming *Brief Encounter* coincided with the end of the war in May 1945. Having experienced the relative social and sexual freedom of wartime Britain, many women found the post-war pressure to return to the conventions of the 1930s a great strain; Laura's dilemma, therefore, seemed to express the dilemma of a whole generation of women.

Like Hester Collyer in Rattigan's *The Deep Blue Sea*, Laura experiences passion for the first time. The experience overwhelms her and changes her life. Her story explores the awakening of her sexuality, which has lain dormant in her relationship with her comfortable husband, Fred. The sexual desire Laura feels is a disorientating emotion which calls into question many of the received ideas and rules by which she lives her life and thereby defines herself. Laura finds that passion is at odds with the foundation of her other life, decency. Things matter other than love: 'self-respect matters, and decency'. 'Decency' and 'niceness' are the fabric of the film, complicating Laura's sense of morality with their close relations, guilt and shame: 'Why didn't you tell [Stephen Lynn] we were cheap and low and without courage.' Laura lies to her husband for the first time and goes to great lengths to secure an alibi that involves buying his birthday present. But even as she realizes the triviality of the lie, she recognizes that her sense of morality has altered. She actually considers consummating her relationship with Alec at Stephen Lynn's flat. It is fate which bids Stephen Lynn to return and bring their tryst to an end. But Laura has made the choice, even if she hasn't physically consummated the affair: she *is* prepared to risk her home and family for this unstable, insecure adulterous affair. In *Still Life*, not bound by the British Board of Film Censors, Laura and Alec do actually consummate their affair. In the film version, the unexpected arrival of Stephen Lynn saves Laura from her desire, but there's something unsettling about him. He is described in the screenplay as 'a thin, rather ascetic-looking man'. As played by Valentine Dyall, Lynn is very knowing ('I am the most broad-minded of men') and very camp: 'You know, Alec, my dear, you have hidden depths that I never even suspected.' He pointedly observes that the restaurant downstairs 'caters for all tastes' as he picks up a scarf that Laura has left behind. Coward subtly implies Lynn's homosexuality, and then has Lynn equate Alec's sexual transgressions with his own.[19]

Laura's metamorphosis leads her ultimately to consider suicide. In Laura's world, suicide is regarded as both sinful and illegal and in contemplating it in the darkest moment of her despair, she sets herself apart from the bastions of middle-class society, church and state. Twice in the narrative, Laura feels herself supervised by representatives of God and the law. After her first meeting with Alec, she experiences the 'first awful feeling of danger' sweep over her and enters the train compartment feeling 'as though they could read my secret thoughts. Nobody was looking at me except a clergyman in the opposite corner. I felt myself blushing and opened my library book and pretended to read.'[20] Laura almost expects to look physically different because she is beginning to feel a sense of difference. She experiences the guilt of aberrant behaviour and is starting to appreciate that such a life is built on deceit and pretence (reflected here in her pretending to read). When she has hastily left Stephen Lynn's flat, Laura telephones home and tells another lie: 'It's awfully easy to lie – when you know that you're trusted implicitly – so very easy, and so very degrading.'[21]

She wanders around the wet streets and eventually comes to rest at a war memorial, a potent symbol of both frowning masculinity and Empire. The memorial commemorates the First World War, but would have had a greater resonance for audiences in 1945 of the more recent conflict. Laura's transgression, and that of women like her, threatens the world that men have died for. She sits and lights a cigarette and reminds herself that her husband disapproves of women smoking in the street. At every turn and in the subtlest ways Laura is shaking herself free of her former 'ordinary' self. When a policeman approaches her 'rather suspiciously' their exchange is very ambiguous. The policeman addresses her as an unmarried woman, and she doesn't correct him. There is a strong sense that a woman alone, smoking in the street at night, might be a prostitute:

POLICEMAN	Feeling all right, Miss?
LAURA	Yes, thank you.
POLICEMAN	Waiting for someone?
LAURA	No, I'm not waiting for anyone.
POLICEMAN	You don't want to go and catch cold you know – that would never do. It's a damp night to be sitting about on seats, you know...
LAURA'S VOICE	I walked away – trying to look casual – knowing that he was watching me. I felt like a criminal.[22]

Laura's previous sense of morality did not encompass deceit and sexual transgression. In the same scene in *Still Life*, Laura does explicitly state that she left Lynn's flat 'feeling like a prostitute'. The disintegration of Laura's middle-class morality reaches its nadir in her attempted suicide. Here she is not only risking censure in her own cul-de-sac but the immortal future of her Anglican soul. Ultimately she can't go through with it, and recognizes that her reasons for doing so are selfish:

LAURA'S VOICE	I meant to do it, Fred, I really meant to do it – I stood there trembling – right on the edge – but then, just in time I stepped back – I couldn't – I wasn't brave enough – I should like to be able to say that it was the thought of you and the children that prevented me – but it wasn't – I had no thoughts at all – only an overwhelming desire not to be unhappy any more – not to feel anything ever again.[23]

Laura barely recognizes the new self who has tasted passion: she is alien to herself. In *Still Life*, Laura feels that she is leading a double life:

Loving you is hard for me, it makes me a stranger in my own house. Familiar things, ordinary things that I've known for years like the dining-room curtains, and the wooden tub with a silver top that holds biscuits and a water-colour of San Remo that my mother painted, look odd to me, as though they belong to someone else – when I've just left you, I'm more lonely than I've ever been before. I passed the house the other day without noticing and had to turn back, and when I went in it seemed to draw away from me – my whole life seems to be drawing away from me ... I love them just the same, Fred and the children I mean, but it's as though it wasn't me at all – as though I were looking on at someone else.[24]

This list of tangible objects – the biscuit barrel, the watercolour of San Remo – reek of familiarity (of the family), but are now alien to Laura. They represent the cosy, suffocating world of conventional heterosexual middle-class life. There's a melancholy to this world, particularly for gay men: the attraction of the comfortable ordinariness which we can never fully achieve. As Philip Larkin observed, home can be so sad:

Look at the pictures and the cutlery.
The music in the piano stool. That vase.[25]

The sense of objective self-policing, which Laura exhibits, occurs throughout Coward's work, expressing the continual vigilance of the homosexual, who inhabits the world but feels detached from it. Coward had famously advised Cecil Beaton in the 1930s to develop this sort of extreme self-consciousness: 'I take ruthless stock of myself in the mirror before going out.' In *Present Laughter*, Garry Essendine declares, 'I'm always acting – watching myself go by – that's what's so horrible – I see myself all the time, eating, drinking, loving, suffering – sometimes I think I'm going mad.' In the 1970s Coward had identified himself directly with this sort of estranged, divided personality: 'Garry Essendine is me'.

Alec and Laura's restraint is a particular responsibility of the middle class. Throughout the narrative their relationship is counterposed by the flirtations and innuendoes of Myrtle Bagot, the refreshment-room manageress, and the ticket inspector, Albert Godby. Young Stanley also finds excuses to pop into the refreshment room and flirt with Beryl, Myrtle's assistant. The sexual lives of these working-class characters seem much easier and more natural than Alec and Laura's. The refreshment room harbours an atmosphere of sauciness – 'Just in time – or born in the vestry' – as well as naughty indulgence: the tea, Bath buns, rock cakes, brandy and 'Nestle's nut milk'. Just as Albert points out that passengers with third-class tickets cannot travel in first-class carriages on the trains, the narrative explores the difference in ways of loving between the middle and working classes. In Scene II of *Still Life*, Stanley winks at Beryl and Myrtle asks, 'Got something in your eye?', an echo of the romantic first meeting of Alec and Laura. But Stanley, saucily and unromantically replies, 'Only a twinkle in it every now and again'.[26] Unlike Alec and Laura, Albert, Myrtle, Stanley and Beryl harbour no guilt about their sexual feelings and are happy to indulge in a bit of uncomplicated 'slap and tickle'.

Laura's middle-class, middle-aged, Anglican, Home Counties morality is essentially English. She wonders whether 'we should all behave quite differently if we lived in a warm, sunny climate all the time. We shouldn't be so withdrawn and shy and difficult'. But these inhibitions do not seem to affect Myrtle or Beryl. Laura's is a specifically middle-class culture in which poetry and romance are reduced to the clue for a crossword puzzle:

FRED   'When I behold upon the night-starred face, huge cloudy symbols of a high' – something – in seven letters.
LAURA   *(with an effort)* Romance, I think –yes I'm almost sure it is . . .
FRED   No, that's right . . . it fits in with 'delirium' and 'Beluchistan'.[27]

Keats's poem, 'When I have fears that I may cease to be', is particularly pertinent to Laura, considering she has recently contemplated suicide:

And when I feel, fair creature of an hour!
That I shall never look upon thee more,
Never have relish in the faery power
Of unreflecting love! . . .

Keats's posthumous poem is one of lost opportunity, a reminder that life does not repeat its chances: fame and love 'to nothingness do sink'. Keats was one of Coward's favourite poets and the poem obviously had a particular appeal for him, as he was to quote it again in his novel *Pomp and Circumstance* (1960)[28] and was also to return to it in his own final poem, a parallel of Keats.[29] It is this deeply felt poem of loss and death that prompts Laura to turn on the wireless, which in turn leads to her reverie which is the core of the film.

In *Still Life*, Laura reveals a yearning for freedom and experiment which had always been part of her persona, but which has lain dormant until released by her romance with Alec:

LAURA   May, that's my sister, and I used to climb out of our bedroom window on summer nights and go down into the cove and bathe ... I'd never have dared do it by myself, but sharing the danger made it all right ...

ALEC   But there must be a part of you, deep down inside ... some little spirit that still wants to climb out of the window – that still wants to splash about a bit in the dangerous sea.[30]

Laura has repressed her natural instincts. Alec, like the voice of her heart, appeals to her to succumb to the 'urgent and real' love that all their 'instincts are straining after'. But Laura fantasizes about their relationship together on Pacific beaches, at the opera, in Venice ('like a romantic school-girl, like a romantic fool!'), a world away from the dour world of Milford and Laura's domestic responsibilities. It is the romantic ideal of love which Laura has read of in her Boots' library books as well as the sort of romance that Christian and Leonora try to distract themselves with in *The Astonished Heart*: 'It was one of those absurd fantasies – just like one has when one is a girl – being wooed and married by the ideal of one's dreams – generally a rich and handsome Duke.'[31] Laura has visions of another life of possibility and fulfilment with Alec, but like Wilde's heroines, Laura discovers a huge chasm between the ideals in her 'silly dreams' and the reality of her existence. Her fantasy is truncated, just as the palm trees of her imagination change to the bleak pollarded willows by the level crossing, and Laura must return to the comforts, strains, responsibilities and disappointments of married life.

In *Brief Encounter* it is Alec who initiates the idea of sex in Stephen

Lynn's flat. But we feel that the burden of guilt and shame falls on Laura. We have met her husband and children and share her domestic life. As we never actually see them, we don't feel that Alec's family will be hurt by his adultery in the way that we would feel for Fred and the children. In *Still Life* Laura asks Alec about guilt: 'Do you know what I mean? Or is it easier for men –.'[32] Laura is a prisoner of her own conventional attitude to her gender and attacks Alec's masculine philosophy of risk. Such a life would be characterized by furtiveness, shame and guilt, and Laura believes it 'better not to love at all': 'What is there brave in it – sneaking away to someone else's house, loving in secret with the horror of being found out hanging over us all the time.'[33]

Rather than 'loving in secret', the adulterous affair in *The Astonished Heart*, which is consummated, continues despite the fact that all the main characters know about it. Like *Brief Encounter*, the film is related in flashback and we are introduced to the characters at a point near the end of the story. Unlike Laura Jesson, Christian Faber does have the courage (or is so unbalanced by his emotions) that he is ultimately successful in his suicide attempt. Coward isn't interested in creating suspense; we know what the denouement is at the beginning of both *Brief Encounter* and *The Astonished Heart*. We know that Laura and Alec will part and that Christian Faber will return home to his wife. It is the development of the dilemma, the journey through pain that Coward is keen to explore. The two films are related thematically and structurally and they are in many ways the flip side of each other.

The screenplay of *The Astonished Heart* was adapted by Coward from his own play of the same name. Michael Redgrave was originally to have played Christian Faber, but when Coward saw some of the rushes, he was unhappy with Redgrave's performance and took over the leading role himself. A married bisexual, Redgrave was nine years Coward's junior and had been romantically involved with Coward whilst he was in the Navy during the war. Celia Johnson, a Coward regular, had played Coward's wife in *In Which We Serve* and had been miscast as Ethel Gibbons in the film version of *This Happy Breed*. She had last worked with Coward five years earlier on *Brief Encounter*. Joyce Carey makes an inevitable appearance as Coward's faithful friend and assistant, and Graham Payn plays the devoted secretary, once again repeating his real-life role on screen. Author, screenwriter and leading actor, the film is suffused, even suffocated, by Coward's presence; he even wrote the music. C. A. Lejeune, a huge admirer of both Coward's and Celia Johnson's work, was disappointed that the film failed 'to touch the emotions at any point'. Laura Jesson returns to her husband, not because of any logical reasoning, but because that is what she feels in her heart she ought to do. The characters in the love triangle at the centre of *The Astonished Heart* attempt to reason their way through their dilemma. The territory of *Brief Encounter* is that of the heart and moves us deeply, whereas the domain of *The Astonished Heart* is that of the mind, and even though the denouement is apparently more tragic than that of *Brief Encounter*, it fails to gain our sympathy. Christian Faber's problem is that, though he is a doctor of the mind, he has no understanding of the operation of his own heart.

LEONORA   What's a psychiatrist then?
BARBARA   Someone who cures diseases of the mind.
LEONORA   Oh, repressions and inhibitions and all that sort of thing.[34]

Faber is a typical repressed and inhibited Englishman with the Forsterian 'undeveloped heart'. Leonora asks Barbara, 'Does he know all about himself right from the beginning? Is everything cut and dried and accounted for?' But Chris's tragedy is that he doesn't know himself, nor is he aware of how to learn. The Fabers are childless and have separate bedrooms, unlike Laura and Fred Jesson, who might not share a bed but do sleep in the same room, and have two children to their credit. Barbara admits that she and Chris don't have sex any more: 'It would be tiresome to go on being emotional after twelve years of marriage.' Faber's comfortable platonic love for Barbara is challenged by his passion for Leonora and the strain of these two loves induces a nervous breakdown. The understanding Barbara suggests that he go abroad with Leonora: 'Unless you put a stop to this agonizing battle between your emotions and your intelligence, you'll break completely.' Faber has apparently always been obsessed with work and is also sexually frustrated in his relationship with Barbara. Leonora, who advertises her sexuality very openly, 'astonishes' Faber. The Damascus-like revelation of electric sexual attraction between them is devastating. Faber ultimately finds himself a casualty of the battle between reason and passion, unable to reconcile the two.

Coward's protagonist, like Bunyan's pilgrim, is called Christian. But

Faber's twentieth-century world of science and logic offers no solutions to his emotional dilemma. Barbara is liberal-minded and professes not to be worried by any sexual jealousy for Leonora. But Coward is very sceptical of attempts to be clinical and objective about desire. In his characterization of Christian Faber, Coward further develops the scene in *Brief Encounter* in which Laura falls in love with Alec Harvey, another doctor, as he waxes lyrical about 'preventive' medicine. The strange and foreign-sounding names confuse Laura, but she understands a passion beneath the words which doesn't need to be explained. Alec and Christian both discover that neither physical nor psychiatric doctors can cure or prevent the sickness of love.

The Astonished Heart takes its title from Deuteronomy: 'The Lord shall smite thee with madness and blindness and astonishment of the heart'. Faber wants to refer to the quotation during a lecture on psychiatry, but nobody in the flat has a Bible and one has to be obtained from the cook: the sophisticates may have divorced themselves from the touchstones of traditional morality but are no better at solving their moral problems. Coward's story does have the quality of a contemporary parable about what Rattigan called the 'English vice': 'not flagellation or pederasty. . . . It's our refusal to admit to our emotions. We think they demean us, I suppose.'[35] Faber suffers a breakdown and ultimately kills himself because he fails to analyse his own 'secret heart'. Leonora is the catalyst who will make Chris see the truth: that he and Barbara do still have a strong emotional love for each other and that his relationship with Leonora was primarily a sexual infatuation.

One of the main differences between the film and the original stage version of *The Astonished Heart* is that we are allowed to share in Faber's consultations with his psychiatric patients, none of whom appear in the play. The film is punctuated by sessions with a variety of patients, all of whom believe that they have some sort of aberrant sexual feelings. Mr Bowman has problems relating to his mother, and Mrs Gaythorne has become obsessed with her son's young colleague in the Navy who bears a strong resemblance to her son. Her desires are clearly Oedipal:

MRS GAYTHORNE   The situation is grotesque, insane. But I can't help myself. I can't get him out of my mind, out of my heart.

In the first half of the film, Faber is professional and objective. When his own affair flounders, however, he becomes distracted and useless as a psychiatrist. He becomes a patient himself. The longest psychiatric session in the film has Faber examining a middle-aged man, Philip Lucas. Lucas is the only patient named in the cast list of the shooting script and is described by Coward as 'one of Christian Faber's patients *whose problems are similar to his own*' (my italics):

COWARD/FABER	You finally confessed everything to your wife?
LUCAS	Yes. I couldn't bear the thought of deceiving her any longer.
FABER	You resent her efforts to understand, don't you? They irritate you?
LUCAS	Sometimes. Yes they do.
FABER	This new attraction is far stronger than any of the others?
LUCAS	Yes.
FABER	What have you come to me for, really?
LUCAS	To cure me, of course.
FABER	Of your desires?
LUCAS	I suppose so.
FABER	You're an intelligent man. A writer, a creative artist. I've read a great deal of your work. It struck me, all of it, as being intensely personal. Its whole quality seems to depend on the accuracy of your own observation through the medium of your own experience. Do you really want to be cured of the instincts and urges and impulses which go to form that experience?
LUCAS	I want peace of mind – the conflict within me is torturing me too much. I'm afraid of breaking down completely.
FABER	These other loves which rob you of sleep, threaten to wreck your home. They bring you no happiness, nothing but remorse and despair?
LUCAS	Yes . . . no, not exactly.
FABER	I'll do everything in my power to help you.

It is a dexterous, subtle style of writing. Coward carefully avoids the gender of Lucas's extramarital lover ('this new attraction', 'these other loves'). Lucas is a married homosexual, attempting to divide his sexual life from his home and work life. But Faber/Coward implies that it is exactly this tension, this schizophrenic existence, that feeds Lucas as an artist. Lucas, like Coward, Charles Condomine and Garry Essendine, is 'a creative artist' and Coward's work, like Lucas's is 'intensely personal', a reflection of the author's interests and preoccupations. Faber's conversation with Lucas anticipates the ending of his own affair with Leonora, when he too wants to be 'cured' of his desires. Both Lucas and Faber are married men, seeking sexual solace elsewhere, both their hearts have been 'astonished' and their lives can no longer continue as 'normal.' Does this connection between the two men suggest that we might read Leonora as something of an allegorical figure? She is certainly the dominant partner in the relationship and when she first appears Barbara remembers that she had played King Lear at school. There are many such nuances in the film, hinting at a broader agenda, and yet it doesn't quite work; it's neither emotionally nor intellectually convincing.

One of the major flaws of *The Astonished Heart* is Coward's performance itself. It is impossible to imagine his clipped, impeccable persona falling even for the seductive Margaret Leighton. The love scenes are cold and hollow, for Coward doesn't provide Faber with the wit or camp of an Elyot Chase. Essentially, he is unconvincing in the role of a heterosexual man galvanized by lust. John Gassner, in his review of the film, saw a parallel between Coward and Faber:

> [as a playwright] his values are those of a Harley Street doctor who knows that the old virtues of clean living and plain thinking – home, hearth, exercise and good diet – are the best no matter how often his profession keeps him in touch with the aberrations.[36]

There is a sense of 'no-nonsense' about Coward, a man who had successfully compartmentalized various areas of his life and was playing a wonderful public role which he had constructed for himself. Faber, on the other hand, is a man wrecked by the duality of his nature. Bearing in mind his moving portrayal of the dried-up, frustrated and probably gay schoolmaster in *The Browning Version*, which was filmed only a year after *The Astonished Heart* in 1951, I wonder what the troubled, but brilliant, Michael

Redgrave might have done with the part of Christian Faber, if the film had gone ahead as originally planned? Now *there* might have been a performance to shake Coward's closet doors and a film to rank as an equal companion to *Brief Encounter*, rather than a fascinating but frustrating shadow of it.

Between the Devil and the Deep Blue Sea

Three dramas by Terence Rattigan

Terry is a most curious mixture. His appearance and ordinary dialogue are deceptive. He is light, sweet, ready to giggle, incredibly
silly over his emotional life, weak and stubborn at the same time –
they usually go together – and yet capable of writing *The Deep Blue Sea*,
Separate Tables, *The Browning Version*, etc., plays so richly impregnated
with human understanding and compassion.

> Noël Coward[1]

I suppose out of that brilliant playboy talent have come two important plays, *The Browning Version* and *The Deep Blue Sea*. The rest seem to
me full of moral evasions. Perhaps any homosexual dramatist who,
during a time of secrecy and blackmail, presented his own emotional
life in his work as if he were a woman, suffered some terrible disabil-
ity. Tennessee Williams was the most successful, but then he was a
woman right through. I think the problem with Rattigan was that
even if he had the opportunity for frankness, his whole repressed
class background, the stiff upper lip of Harrow, would have made it
impossible for him. Deception and restraint are at the heart of that
kind of Englishman. I suppose it's at the heart of me, heterosexual as
I am.

> Peter Hall[2]

Few careers in the theatre express the cruelties of theatrical and cultural
fashion more than that of Terence Rattigan. Rattigan was a huge success
from his youth with *French Without Tears* enjoying a three-year run in the
1930s. Despite and partly because of his popularity at the box office, his
career in the 1950s and 1960s was beset by criticism from the champions

of the new wave of British drama which had been launched from the Royal Court Theatre and the Theatre Royal Stratford East. Britain in the 1950s was a very different nation than the one which Rattigan had reflected in his early work. In *French Without Tears* Rattigan had examined the linguistic and emotional education of the young men who would one day go out and police the outposts of the British Empire. After the war and the decision to quit India the British Empire was severely contracted. As early as 1901 Lord Curzon had observed that 'As long as we rule India we are the greatest power in the world. If we lose it we shall drop straightaway to a third-rate power.'[3] The Suez Crisis of the 1950s certainly drove Britain's third-rate status home to the nation.

The cultural response to Britain's revised status in the world was examined by a new generation of writers who had been in their teens during the war and were now in their twenties and thirties. These new 'kitchen sink' writers examined the confused postwar Britain where class and gender barriers had been severely shaken. Working-class writers discovered their voice and publishers began to print their work. A fashion or school was born. Novelists such as John Braine, Alan Sillitoe and Lynne Reid Banks, playwrights like Shelagh Delaney, Arnold Wesker and Brendan Behan contributed to a rich, young, cross-class examination of contemporary British society. In the theatre the fashion was ushered in with John Osborne's *Look Back in Anger* in 1956. Rattigan attended the opening night of the play and planned to leave after the first interval but was persuaded to stay until the end by the critic, T. C. Worsley. Questioned by a *Daily Express* reporter about his opinion of the play, Rattigan rather flippantly remarked that Osborne was saying, 'Look ma, I'm not Terence Rattigan.'[4] This off-the-cuff comment fuelled the schism between Rattigan and the Angry Young Men, which the press gleefully leaped on and exploited. Rattigan later had a long and intense discussion about the play with his old Oxford contemporary George Devine, the genius behind the Royal Court. Rattigan argued for two and a half hours that the play could never be a success. Devine kept stating that it already was. 'Then I know nothing about plays,' Rattigan answered. Devine retorted, 'You know everything about plays but you don't know a fucking thing about *Look Back in Anger*.'[5]

The first two volumes of Rattigan's *Collected Plays* had been published in 1953. Perhaps unwisely, Rattigan had decided to take on his critics and promoted in his preface to Volume Two the cause and tastes of a character

called Aunt Edna. Rattigan thought he had created an amusing character, with a tongue-in-cheek tone, never imagining that his critics would
take her as seriously as they did. Rattigan's editor at Hamish Hamilton,
Roger Machell, later recalled that neither Rattigan nor his colleagues
were at all aware of the potential harm that Aunt Edna might do to Rattigan's reputation: 'I never thought for a moment that it would be used as
a stick to beat him with. I've kicked myself ever since.'[6] Aunt Edna represents what Rattigan believed to be the 'core' audience: 'a nice, respectable, middle-class, middle-aged, maiden lady with time on her hands
and the money to help her pass it'. In the iconoclastic 1950s, Rattigan
had set himself up as an easy target. A generation ago, his work was
dismissed as the middle-of-the-road products of a middle-class crowd
pleaser. In the 1990s his reputation is in the ascendant after a clutch of
well-received revivals, in particular the film director Karel Reisz's production of *The Deep Blue Sea* at the Almeida Theatre in 1993. Reisz directed
one of the key texts of the 'angry' movement, the 1960 film of Alan Sillitoe's *Saturday Night and Sunday Morning*, and the production resonated with
echoes of his earlier 'kitchen-sink' work: the English difficulty of recon-
ciling sex with domestic life, postwar disillusion and the struggle for
individuality in a culture still ingrained with class differences. With
hindsight, Rattigan's play revealed itself to be much more in tune with
the spirit of the early 1950s than it had previously seemed to be. As the
century turns, Rattigan seems to have finally confirmed his status as one
of the great British dramatists of the century.

The Deep Blue Sea

The same thing happened over and over: I would catch sight of some
flawless man off in the distance but as soon as he moved close, I immediately saw he wouldn't do at all.[7]

In February 1949, whilst touring with *Adventure Story* in Liverpool, Rattigan received a message that a young actor called Kenneth Morgan had
committed suicide. He was devastated. On Rattigan's recommendation,
Morgan had appeared in the film version of *French Without Tears* in 1939.
Around that time the two men began an affair. Morgan subsequently
went on to appear with Frith Banbury in Rattigan's ill-fated anti-Nazi
satire, *Follow My Leader*, which closed after fifteen performances. Hardly

an auspicious West End debut for Morgan. Banbury recalls that 'Kenneth was a wide-eyed kiddiwink really at that time, and very much Terry's type – he liked chaps that looked as though they were in their late teens ... but were actually well into their twenties – which I think Kenneth Morgan then was – and could make intelligent conversation after the event.'[8] B. A. Young observes that Michael Franklin, a later lover of Rattigan's, also had a 'notably boyish face'. Young regarded Rattigan's relationships with these Peter Pan types as that between 'a senior schoolboy with a younger'.[9] Rattigan's experiences at Harrow continued to haunt and affect his life.

The relationship between Rattigan and Morgan continued on and off throughout the war. But Rattigan thought Morgan unreliable and continually rebuked him for persistent infidelity. This was in spite of the fact that Rattigan himself continued to have both serious and casual affairs with other men. He never, however, allowed his lovers to live in his home or to stay overnight, preferring to keep his domestic life and sex life carefully segregated. By late 1948 Morgan had grown tired of playing the role of occasional sidekick to Rattigan's society playboy. He announced that he was leaving Rattigan for good to live with another young actor in a small flat in Camden Town. Rattigan wasn't sure how to respond. He wanted to continue the relationship but was unsure what step to take next. Morgan's new relationship turned out to be very unsettled. Six weeks after moving in with his new lover, Kenneth Morgan was found dead. He had taken a bottle of pills and when these didn't appear to be working fast enough, had placed a tea towel over his head and held himself over a small gas ring until he lost consciousness. This rather sad, 'kitchen-sink' story was the genesis of one of Rattigan's finest plays, *The Deep Blue Sea*.

Though it is still rumoured that Rattigan wrote a 'homosexual' version of *The Deep Blue Sea*, Frith Banbury, the director of the original production, is adamant that whilst Rattigan may well have contemplated the idea, his better judgement and knowledge of the theatre would have prevailed. Rattigan was a commercial playwright and would have known that such a play would never be granted a licence by the Lord Chamberlain and consequently stood little chance of being produced by a West End manager like Binkie Beaumont. During the writing of *Separate Tables*, he had reached the point when the homosexual Major's offence was to be revealed before he realized that he would have to find a way of getting past the Lord Chamberlain if he wanted the play to be produced in the West End. Even if it were produced in a club theatre it wouldn't make any money and might even damage Rattigan's future commerciability. Rattigan did, apparently, toy with the idea of converting the text into a gay story at a later date. Geoffrey Wansell quotes a letter Rattigan wrote years later to John Osborne, after the demise of the Lord Chamberlain's powers of censorship:

> At last I can write about my particular sins without Lord Chamberlain-induced sex-change dishonesty. . . . But my own sins bore me terribly, which may be the lethargy of old age creeping over me, or just the disinclination to join in the chorus of voices endlessly shouting the love that once dared not speak its name, from every house top in the country. Perhaps I should rewrite *The Deep Blue Sea* as it was really meant to be, but after twenty years, I just can't remember why I made all that fuss.[10]

After the publication of the Wolfenden report and the staging of *A Taste of Honey* in 1958, Rattigan was tempted to replace Hester with Hector, but he was dissuaded by his friends and colleagues and the project was abandoned. But Hester Collyer's story continues to resonate for gay men. She rejects her known, ordinary life in favour of a predominantly sexual relationship with a virile younger man. Her new-found discovery of her own sexuality completely changes her life and how she regards herself.

Whilst Rattigan's bio-epic about Alexander the Great, *Adventure Story*, had been touring in 1949, the West End was playing host to genteel dramas like Lesley Storm's *Black Chiffon* and traditional small-cast domestic thrillers such as *The Late Edwina Black*. In October of 1949 a new play by a little-known American dramatist opened at the Aldwych Theatre. Despite hugely enthusiastic audiences, the play was viciously reviewed in the press: 'Unrelieved sordidness' (*Daily Herald*), 'geared to bring out as much sexual detail as is permissible on the stage' (*Daily Express*). Tennessee Williams's *A Streetcar Named Desire* was a breakthrough in American and world theatre. Stanley Kowalski removes his sweaty shirt in front of his sister-in-law, Blanche Dubois, and in doing so becomes a new male icon: 'My clothes're stickin' to me. Do you mind if I make myself comfortable?' Stanley's exposed naked torso is the object of the female gaze, decades before taut pectorals would advertise everything from underwear to ice-cream. Williams examines Blanche's sexuality very explicitly.

She has been run out of her home town for her addictive dalliances with the local army, but talks of her past without shame and even with a certain pride. We watch her flirt outrageously with her brother-in-law and seduce a young teenage boy: 'It would be nice to keep you, but I've got to be good and keep my hands off children.'

A Streetcar Named Desire is radical in its discussion of promiscuous sexuality in women and of homosexuality, as well as its implied connection between the two. But Williams's Blanche is also a representative figure of a culture in transition. Blanche, the English teacher and promoter of the values of civilized old Europe, is challenged by 'the brutes', the new 'one hundred per cent American' second-generation immigrants embodied in Stanley. But Blanche's fantasy world is too brittle to resist Stanley's strength and she retreats into madness. In the destruction of Blanche, Williams charts the transition from a civilized Jamesian America to a postwar multicultural world of aggression and self-interest. Williams chose his epigraph for the play from a posthumously published poem by the fragile gay poet Hart Crane:

And so it was I entered the broken world,
To trace the visionary company of love, its voice
An instant in the wind (I know not whither hurled)
But not for long to hold each desperate choice.[11]

Blanche's alcoholism and sexual liaisons are desperate, snatched moments of oblivion with which she tries to block out the ugly truths of the past and the harsh reality of the present. Rattigan's Hester Collyer is also a casualty of 'the broken world'. *Streetcar* and *The Deep Blue Sea* are parallel stories of changed postwar cultures on opposite sides of the Atlantic. The world of *The Deep Blue Sea* is the new post-Empire Britain. First performed in 1952, the play reveals itself with hindsight to be a transitional work for Rattigan as well as for British drama. It is certainly his richest full-length play, testing both his skills as a mature dramatist as well as his ability to explore elements of his own personal history in his work. Like Blanche, Hester inhabits an age of confusion and reassessment. The priorities and mores of the 1930s are no longer secure. The war has undermined the class system and women have been empowered both sexually and as a labour force. It has enabled middle-class women like Hester to identify their needs and to question their traditional domestic role.

The environment that Rattigan describes is a world away from the comfortable West End apartments with which his work was so long associated. Hester's cheap furnished flat is part of a 'gloomy Victorian mansion' built at the zenith of the British Empire, but has been converted 'after World War One' when the Empire, like the house, began to disintegrate. The house is now surrounded by a 'badly-blitzed neighbourhood' and has 'so obviously "come down in the world" ';[12] Hester's world is indeed broken. As such, the setting of the play is not dissimilar to Jimmy Porter's Midlands bedsit in *Look Back in Anger*. In many ways *The Deep Blue Sea* is the examination of the fall from grace of a typical heroine of the 'well-made' school directly into the kitchen sink.

Hester, the daughter of an Anglican clergyman, has left her husband, a judge, for a young test pilot, Freddie Page. She and Page had initially gone away to Canada, but have recently returned to England and are living as man and wife in a slightly decaying rented flat in Ladbroke Grove. Money is scarce and Freddie is not working. Hester believes that 'his life stopped in nineteen-forty' when he was in the RAF. The play opens with Hester lying unconscious in front of the gas fire. She has attempted suicide with gas and an overdose of aspirin, but the fates have intervened and the gas meter has run out. Hester has realized that Freddie doesn't love her with the same intensity that she loves him. The catalyst for her suicide attempt is that Freddie had forgotten her birthday. Hester is discovered by the landlady and two young tenants, Mr and Mrs Welch. They fetch another tenant to revive Hester, a Mr Miller, who is a struck-off doctor. Without her knowledge, Philip Welch informs Hester's estranged husband about the incident. Sir William Collyer visits Hester at once to see if there is anything he can do to help. After he has left, Freddie returns from golfing at Sunningdale and finds Hester's suicide note in the pocket of her dressing-gown. Shocked by the revelation, Freddie proceeds to get very drunk and embarrasses Hester in front of his friend, Jackie Jackson.

Freddie meets up with a South American who offers him a job as a test pilot in Brazil. He informs Hester that he will be going to Brazil without her. Hester begs him to stay with her for one night longer, but Freddie leaves to go out drinking. Later that evening, Hester receives another visit from her husband. Freddie has dropped him a note indicating that his relationship with Hester is over and that Collyer and Hester might make another go of their marriage. Collyer suggests that

Hester return to him, but she refuses. Freddie has been to a club with Philip Welch whom he sends to pick up his belongings. Hester forces Welch to tell her where Freddie is and then phones the club to ask him to stop by and pick up his things himself. Freddie hangs up on her. Hester locks the door and decides to kill herself once and for all. Mr Miller observes her putting a rug under the door and demands that she unlock it. In despair, Hester wonders why she should continue living without hope. Miller tells her that 'the only purpose in life is to live it'. Freddie finally does return to say goodbye and Hester makes no attempt to get him to stay. He leaves, she packs his clothes, turns on the gas and lights the fire.

The Deep Blue Sea, like *The Browning Version*, is a near tragedy. Near tragedies, because neither Hester, nor Crocker-Harris are permitted the easy comfort of death. Like Chekhov's Vanya, they must face life, despite their despair. Postwar Britain is a destabilized culture and its inhabitants are still coming to terms with the novelties and confusions ushered in by Atlee's Labour victory. Hester is a typical middle-class product of the interwar years with no real education or skills; now she feels at sea. The daughter of a clergyman who married 'the first man who asked her' has now fallen in love with 'the first man who gives her the eye'. In the 1930s she would have repressed her desires, but now Hester has actually acted upon them. She has embraced the choice and freedom which the war has inspired among women, but finds herself ill-equipped, both emotionally and practically, to live in this brave new world. Hester's father had 'believed in spiritual values . . . and the pettiness of the physical side' of relationships. Consequently she had not expected passion in her marriage. As a typical product of her class and culture, rather like Laura Jesson in *Brief Encounter*, Hester had settled for a loveless, significantly childless marriage to Sir William Collyer. Collyer insists that he still loves Hester, but she disagrees:

> You weren't in love with me on our wedding day, Bill. You aren't in love with me now and you never have been. . . . Oh, I'm not denying you married for love – for your idea of love. And so did I – for my idea. The trouble is they weren't the same ideas.[13]

Rattigan explained to Laurence Olivier that 'The phenomenon of love is inexplicable in terms of logic. That was the theme of *The Deep Blue*

Sea.[14] The complex love relationships between Hester and Freddie and Hester and Collyer inspire a debate within the play about different kinds of love, a distillation of one of Rattigan's major themes. This debate extends to the other characters in the play. Even the young couple, the Welches, rather like the Gilberts in *The Browning Version*, exhibit unsettling differences which don't bode very well for their future together. Kenneth Tynan defined the theme of the play as 'the failure of two people to agree on a definition of love'. But the play explores a situation in which *nobody* seems able to agree on a definition of love. In Freddie, Hester has discovered sexual love for the first time, with an intensity that destabilizes her own view of herself. Since she has met him, Hester is 'no longer the same person'. Her love for Freddy is firmly rooted in her sexual passion for him. When Freddie first enters, Rattigan's stage directions are very clear:

> *He walks forward and kisses her. Instantly she responds, with an intensity of emotion that is almost ugly.*[15]

'Ugly'? Because of its intensity? Because she is a woman and such sexual aggressiveness is 'unsuitable'? Because of the age difference? Because she has just tried to kill herself? Perhaps a combination of them all. But the passion does not seem to be reciprocal. Now that she has finally discovered it, Hester is much more enthusiastic about sex than Freddie is:

HESTER   Oh, but he can give me something in return, and even does, from time to time.
COLLYER   What?
HESTER   Himself.[16]

In postwar austerity Britain, Freddie even rations his passion: 'moderation in all things – that's always been my motto'; 'I can't be a ruddy Romeo all the time'. In doing so he increases Hester's ardour, frustration and consequently her sense of shame at being so sexually dependent: 'You see I was brought up to think that in a case of this kind it's more proper for it to be the man that does the loving'.[17] But Hester denies to her husband that her feeling for Freddie can be simply defined and dismissed as lust:

Bill – in sober truth neither you nor I nor anyone else can explain what I feel for Freddie. It's all far too big and confusing to be tied up in such a neat little parcel and labelled lust. Lust isn't the whole of life – and Freddie is, you see, to me. The whole of life – and of death, too, it seems. Put a label on that if you can.[18]

Hester's hysterical plea for Freddie to stay one more night is born of desperate sexual hunger, the need for one more fix, but it also resounds with a terrifying anxiety of being alone: 'Freddie, come back. . . . Don't go. . . . Don't leave me alone tonight. . . . Not tonight. . . . Don't leave me alone tonight . . .'[19] Hester's need of Freddie and fear of isolation echoes Blanche's. Just as Mitch represents Blanche's last chance of love and happiness, Hester clings to Freddie, her 'desperate choice'. Whilst waiting for her husband to come home, like the protagonist of a Dorothy Parker story, Ann Welch confesses, 'I'm not very good at being alone'. Hester, Ann Welch and Mr Miller each sit alone in their separate bedsitting rooms in a bleak rooming-house that was once some family's home. The postwar housing shortage has created many such rootless communities, who have little in common other than an ability to pay the same cheap rent and between whom there is civility but little real warmth.

Throughout the play, Hester's love for Freddie is dismissed as 'an ordinary and rather sordid infatuation'. Those around her insist on devaluing the power of passion. Are they afraid to admit the wrenching impulse of passion, which undermines good sense? Philip Welch admits to Hester that he too, like her, has succumbed to illicit desire in the past, but had ultimately reasoned himself out of it: 'It is really the spiritual values that count in life, isn't it? I mean the physical side is really awfully unimportant – objectively thinking, don't you think?'[20] But Welch's advice means nothing to Hester, who has given up a whole life and culture to be with Freddie. She cannot think 'objectively'. Freddie is the 'whole of life' to her, despite the fact that she realizes him to be 'morally and intellectually a mile [her] inferior, and has absolutely nothing in common' with her. The discussion between Hester and her husband of their mutual society friends – artists, writers, witty raconteurs – provides a great contrast to the cheap pub-crawls that she now goes on to please Freddie. But Hester is only one part of Freddie's life. He plays golf, drinks, goes to clubs and enjoys the vacuous camaraderie of pub life, a continual pursuit of shallow entertainment to distract him from his feelings of uselessness. He was happiest as a daring flying ace dodging the dangers of 1940; consequently civilian life holds few charms for him. Freddie does love Hester in his own way, but his love is much more casual. He suffers from Forster's 'undeveloped heart', which Rattigan later identified as 'the English vice ... our refusal to admit to our emotions':

FREDDIE   My God how I hate getting tangled up in other people's emotions. It's the one thing I've tried to avoid all my life, and yet it's always happening to me.[21]

Freddie had been casually involved with a woman called Dot during the war, who had ultimately started 'messing about with [his] service revolver'.[22] When he remembers Dot, Freddie continues as if to recall another similar incident, but stops himself. He seems to be a focus for women like Dot and Hester who are initially attracted by his boyish nonchalance and once 'hooked' are driven to despair by his casual attitude towards them. Freddie would be so easy to despise if he were knowingly callous, but Rattigan's argument is beautifully balanced: Freddie can't help himself. He has managed to dispassionately reduce love to a simple mathematical equation:

FREDDIE   Take two people – A and B. A loves B – B doesn't love A, or at least not in the same way. He wants to but he can't. It's not in his nature.[22]

The result is stalemate in an emotional game which neither Freddie nor Hester can win:

FREDDIE   *(reading Hester's suicide note)* You can't help being as you are – and I can't help being as I am. The fault lies in whichever of the gods had himself a good laugh up above by arranging for the two of us to meet.[23]

Their differing expectations of each other have soured the relationship. Hester has driven Freddie to drink, which in turn makes it more difficult for him to hold down a job. Freddie, or more exactly Hester's overbearing need of him, drives Hester to attempt suicide. Rattigan observes the minutiae of the death of their relationship with painful precision.

Freddie humiliates Hester throughout the play, but she allows herself to be humiliated. When Freddie is insensitively reading out her suicide note aloud to a drinking pal, Hester hears him doing so and calmly asks for the letter back. Before he leaves for the pub, Freddie asks Miller if he can borrow a shilling for the gas meter, and cruelly tosses it on a table: 'Just in case I'm late for dinner.' They are trapped in an emotional impasse and it is Freddie who recognizes that the relationship is not only destructive but that they have become 'death to each other'. Hester's love flickers quietly even as she subserviently polishes Freddie's shoes for the interview which will lead to his leaving her for good. After Freddie's final goodbye, Hester carefully packs her lover's clothes. She stops a moment and 'buries her face in his mackintosh' attempting to recapture his smell now that the man himself has gone for good. It's a beautiful, sensual and ultimately heartbreaking image of a woman mourning the death of her love, but still clinging to the last:

COLLYER   Hester what's happened to you?
HESTER   Love, Bill, that's all.[24]

Like Laura Jesson, Hester breaks with convention and society. She rejects the morality imposed upon her by church and state as represented by her clerical father and lawyer husband. These two institutions and the two men who represent them have defined the tenor and the boundaries of Hester's life. Judgement, both legal and social, as well as the judgement of self-worth, echoes throughout the play. Hester confesses to Miller that she wants to die because she doesn't deserve to live. But Miller challenges her: 'Why should you accept the world's view of you as a weak-willed neurotic – better dead than alive? What right have they to judge? To judge you they must have the capacity to feel as you feel.'[25] Miller has been dismissed as an unsatisfactory character, merely a device to present Hester with the argument against suicide. But his function in the play is more subtle and more complex than that. Rattigan continually suggests a similarity between the two characters. Hester, once married to the law, has now set herself on the other side of it: 'attempted suicide is a crime, anyway, isn't it? People get gaoled for it, don't they?'[26] Miller has been a criminal too. It is implied that he has been struck off and imprisoned for some homosexual misdemeanour. Mrs Elton confides to Hester that 'what he did wasn't – well – the sort of thing people forgive very easily. Ordinary, normal people, I mean.'[27] Hester identifies her position with Miller's instinctively:

HESTER   I knew he'd been in trouble.
MRS ELTON   How, dear?
HESTER   Fellow-feeling I suppose.[28]

Having forfeited the status of their former lives, both Hester and Miller refuse to be addressed by their former titles. When Philip Welch refers to Hester as Lady Collyer, she corrects him: 'Do you mind not using that name?' Her identity has changed and she does not want to cling to the vestiges of her other, old self. When Hester thanks Mr Miller as 'doctor', he reminds her, 'I've asked you before not to call me that'. The sense of mutual identity between Miller and Hester increases as the play progresses. Experienced in suicide himself, Miller antici-pates Hester's second attempt by noting that she has put a rug in front of the door to prevent the gas escaping. She, in turn, recognizes a fel-low sufferer: 'How near did you come to the gas fire once?'[29] There is a certain logic, therefore, that Miller should share the benefits of his painful experiences with Hester and that he should be the one to sug-gest that she apply an existential philosophy to her situation. Frith Ban-bury remembers that the third act of the play was rewritten by Rattigan about four times in an effort to refine the rather philosophical debate between Hester and Miller about the purpose of living. Tynan believed the last act flawed because when Hester 'chooses survival, it is for all the wrong reasons'. Banbury concurs: a vague talent at painting doesn't seem enough to pull Hester through her present crisis. But Banbury has always regarded the conclusion as an existentialist one that really needed the pen of a poet to resolve satisfactorily, but 'Terry wasn't a poet'.[30] In the end Hester must accept that 'the only purpose in life is to live it'. Though she talks in the language of the Bible and religious discourse – 'when you're between any kind of devil and the deep blue sea, sometimes the deep blue sea looks very inviting'[31] – she has no feelings of sinfulness about her adultery or her attempted suicide. Despite her religious upbringing, she does not seek solace in religion or spiritual guidance before her attempt to kill herself. Hester seems to have lost her faith altogether.

Hester's journey charts her abandonment of the conventional mores that had been thrown into question by the war. She has risked the path of passion, rather than conform to the dictates of reason. Having had the door of the doll's house opened for her by the social changes of the 1940s, Hester has thrown off the shackles associated with it, but now the door closes behind her, she finds herself unsure how to cope beyond it. Divorced from her past as Lady Collyer and estranged from the lover who gave her life meaning for the first time, Hester must face herself:

MILLER   Your Freddie has left you. He's never going to come back again. Never in the world. Never.
          Hester wilts at each word as if it were a physical blow.
HESTER   I know. I know. That's what I can't face.
MILLER   Yes, you can. That word 'never'. Face that and you can face life. Get beyond hope. It's your only chance.
HESTER   What is there beyond hope?
MILLER   Life.[32]

Here, Rattigan consciously invokes Lear's cry of despair, echoing in a bleak, Godless universe: 'Never, never, never, never, never.' With neither husband nor lover to absorb her, with no children to live through or distract her, Hester must accept human isolation. The play ends as it begins with Hester at the gas fire. But now she strikes the match and lights the gas. It is a small flame of life, not necessarily hopeful, but at least a flame of possibility.

The Deep Blue Sea is a painful, uncompromising study of the fear of loneliness and the frustratingly unreliable nature of love. It explores the anxieties, particularly for women, of the immediate postwar years. Its bleak, cynical tone and ultimately existential conclusion reflect the preoccupations of European writers of the period such as Sartre, Pirandello and Genet. Blanche Dubois and Sylvia Plath's heroine in *The Bell Jar* both apprehend the reality of human loneliness and retreat into nervous breakdown: 'The silence depressed me. It wasn't the silence of silence. It was my own silence.'[33] But Hester Collyer ultimately reconciles herself to her own silence and, rejecting both madness and suicide, opts for life, 'solitary, poor, nasty, brutish, and short' though it be.

The Browning Version

> Dear me! What a lot of fuss about a little book – and a not very good little book at that.[34]

In his notorious *Face to Face* interview with the pompous gameshow panellist Gilbert Harding, John Freeman famously exposed a man emotionally crippled by a life of frustration and disappointment. Probed too far and perhaps too harshly about the death of his mother, Harding broke down on screen. Variously a teacher at private schools and crammers as well as spending a stint with the police force, Harding seems to be a very typical casualty of English emotional repression:

FREEMAN   Is there any truth in the notion I have at the back of my mind that it is this particularly deep relationship that you obviously had with your mother which has made it impossible so far for you to marry?

HARDING   Yes, I think so. You see, my sister didn't marry and I didn't marry and my mother was a widow when she was thirty and so when we came to live together we put up a sort of *cloud of sexual frustration that was enough to block out the sun* [italic added], and I've never been particularly affectionate; one of my troubles is that I don't attract affection very much and when I do I tend to repel it. I'm not an intimate or cosy person. I don't really like living in close contact with anybody. I think I'm pretty difficult to live with.

FREEMAN   Are you lonely as a result of this?

HARDING   Profoundly lonely, yes.[35]

Harding's revelation of his pain and isolation, together with his heart-breaking discomfort about homosexuality, makes his a portrait that looks all too familiar in Rattigan's gallery of awkward, bruised and lonely outsiders. Rattigan, the poet of 'middle-class vernacular', would have been proud of a phrase such as Harding's 'cloud of sexual frustration that was enough to block out the sun': such a line wouldn't sound out of place in *The Deep Blue Sea* or *The Browning Version*, the story of a 'profoundly lonely' man disappointed by himself. Echoes of *The Browning Version* resound in the transcripts of the Freeman/Harding interview, indicating just how accurately Rattigan had exposed the reality of Crocker-Harris's world and dilemma.

Fifty years after its first production in 1948, *The Browning Version* has secured itself the reputation as one of the best, if not *the* best, one-act plays of the twentieth century. It is a small masterpiece of construction and delicate stagecraft, exploring the failures, deceits and cruelties of upper-middle-class England with agonizing precision. Set in an English public school, most probably Rattigan's Harrow, the play is a painful study of reticence and humiliation. Andrew Crocker-Harris, once 'the most brilliant classical scholar we have ever had', has been with the school for eighteen years, but is still only teaching the 'soul-destroying' lower fifth, having been passed over by brighter and more ambitious masters. Though only forty, Crocker-Harris is about to retire early to teach at a 'crammer for backward boys because of a heart condition'. His is both a physical and emotional 'heart failure': his heart has almost literally failed him and his sickness is a 'sickness of the soul'. 'The Crock' is a dried up, disappointed failure. His wife Millie is a snob and adulteress, currently conducting an affair with Frank Hunter, a young science master. Crocker-Harris is refused a much-needed pension by the school governors and the headmaster adds insult to injury by asking him to give up his prerogative, as a senior master, of speaking last at the end-of-term prize-giving. The head feels that as a younger, more popular master is also leaving, he ought to be allowed to speak last to ensure the occasion ends with a climax.

After a series of smaller humiliations, Crocker-Harris is given a copy of Robert Browning's translation of Aeschylus's *Agamemnon* as a leaving present by Taplow, a boy he takes for extra lessons. It is a small gift of kindness which causes Crocker-Harris to break down. Moved by the gift, he proudly shows it to Millie. She only laughs and tells him that she had discovered Taplow doing impersonations of her husband and that he has only given the book as a cheap token of appeasement to secure his 'remove' to Hunter's science class next term. Crocker-Harris is devastated and Hunter, appalled by Millie's cruelty, decides to drop her. Hunter tries to sympathize with Crocker-Harris, but 'The Crock' bristles, revealing that he has known all along about Hunter's affair with Millie on her own admission, and adds that Hunter is not the first young master to have succumbed to her voracious sexual appetite. Hunter attempts a reconciliation with Crocker-Harris and plans to visit him at the crammer, rather than continue his fling with Millie that summer in Bradford. Slightly recovered from Millie's cruelty, Crocker-Harris telephones the headmaster and tells him that he intends to speak last at the prize-giving as is his prerogative, as 'occasionally an anti-climax can be surprisingly effective'. The play ends on an unresolved note: the Crocker-Harrises sit down together for yet another dinner of interminable silences born of years of mutual frustration and resentment.

In his review of Rattigan's *Man and Boy* (1963) in the *Financial Times*, Cuthbert Worsley made the following observation:

> The art of Terence Rattigan's theatre consists in crystallising in a bare one or two hours the character patterns that shape a personality; and his deceptively simple (because so engrossing) narrative epitomises the attitudes of a lifetime and the relationships that spring from them. The subject of his new play . . . is humiliation, which has been the subject of all Mr Rattigan's serious plays.[36]

This astute observation was never more relevant than in an examination of *The Browning Version*, *The Deep Blue Sea* and *Separate Tables*. The tone of *The Browning Version* is characterized by almost Catholic feelings of guilt, shame and embarrassment. The action of the play is a series of petty cruelties and vicious humiliations, culminating in the breaking of Crocker-Harris's heart. But despite this bleak scenario, Rattigan offers the possibility of relief in the power of love and basic human sympathy, revealed in a small act of kindness.

In his first conversation with Hunter, Taplow reveals his regard and pity for Crocker-Harris in telling how he had once laughed at one of his bad classical jokes, 'not out of sucking-up, sir, I swear, but ordinary common politeness, and feeling a bit sorry for him for having made a dud joke'.[37] Taplow feels that Crocker-Harris deliberately rejects other people's attempts to connect with him: 'He's all shrivelled up inside like a nut and he seems to hate people to like him . . . I do rather like him. I can't help it. And sometimes I think he sees it and that seems to shrivel him up even more—'[38] Crocker-Harris humiliates Taplow in front of the class for pretending to share the joke: 'I am flattered at the evident advance your latinity has made that you should so readily have understood what the rest of the form did not. . . . Come along, Taplow. Do not be so selfish as to keep a good joke to yourself. Tell the others . . .'[39] For

Taplow it is a complex humiliation. His classmates will think he's 'sucking-up' to Crocker-Harris and Crocker-Harris, whom Taplow genuinely likes, will either think the same or assume that Taplow is trying to send him up. Either way, Taplow's small attempted kindness is suffocated. Similarly, Millie Crocker-Harris humiliates herself when she asks Frank Hunter to stay with her in Bradford during the holidays, but Frank is quite apparently not keen to go:

MILLIE   I shan't see you for six weeks.
FRANK   *(lightly)* You'll survive all right.
MILLIE   Yes, I'll survive it – but not as easily as you will.
             Frank says nothing.
             I haven't much pride, have I? *(She approaches him.)* Frank, darling, I love you so much—
             He kisses her mouth rather perfunctorily, and then breaks quickly away, as if afraid someone had come in the room.[40]

Again, a recent humiliation is discussed. Frank had forgotten that the Crocker-Harrises had invited him to Lord's to watch the cricket. They could only afford grandstand seats and Frank had turned up oblivious and watched the match from a box with Carstairs, a more successful master at the school, and his wife Betty:

MILLIE   I know you're not in love with me – but haven't you ever been in love with anyone? Don't you realize what torture you inflict on someone who loves you when you do a thing like that?[41]

Millie's dependency anticipates Hester Collyer's. But even Frank's apology makes things worse. Millie had imagined that Frank would rather watch the match from the comfort of a box with a charming companion like Betty Carstairs than watch with them, but Frank simply 'clean forgot'.

MILLIE   Do you think it's any pleasanter for me to believe that you cut me because you forgot? Do you think that doesn't hurt either?[42]

Millie has previously given Frank a cigarette case: 'You haven't given it away yet, I see'. When Crocker-Harris enters, she deliberately makes Frank use it in Andrew's presence: a shared private joke between the lovers. With hindsight, knowing that Crocker-Harris is aware of the affair, the gesture is cruelly insulting as Andrew knows that Millie is digging the knife in and using Frank as an unknowing accomplice. In a direct response to the flaunting of the cigarette case, Crocker-Harris makes a return shot at Millie by mentioning Lord's, which he knows has mortified her: 'We expected you at Lord's, Hunter'. He mentions that they managed to sell the extra seat to a certain Dr Lambert and Millie sees an opportunity to hurt Frank by implying she has had somebody else to flirt with:

ANDREW   You liked him, didn't you, Millie?
MILLIE   *(looking at Frank)* Very much indeed. I thought him quite charming.

But Crocker-Harris has let Millie walk into a little trap and triumphs with a small put-down: 'A charming old gentleman'.[43]

Bruised by this exchange, when Crocker-Harris proudly shows Hunter the completed timetable he has been working on for the next term, Millie contemptuously dismisses Crocker-Harris's enthusiasm and effort:

ANDREW   Millie, this might interest you—
MILLIE   *(suddenly harsh)* You know it bores me to death—[44]

The tone of the play is characterized by these small but vicious sallies and the daily attempts of Millie and Crocker-Harris to degrade each other. Occasionally these indignities are unknowing, such as Crocker-Harris's humiliation of Taplow in class, but more often the barbs are deliberately aimed and calculated to wound. Humiliation is the fabric of Andrew Crocker-Harris's life and when the headmaster tells him of the failure of his application for a pension, he stoically accepts the judgement, despite the fact that an exception had been made to the pension rules five years earlier. Buller, a popular master, had sustained an injury playing rugby against the school, and the governors had received a large petition from boys, old boys and parents on his behalf. Not only is Buller's popularity rubbed in, but Crocker-Harris's unpopularity is emphasized:

ANDREW   I would have signed that petition myself, but through
          some oversight I was not asked—[45]

Crocker-Harris is overlooked, passed over, a non-person. When Millie
hears about the pension, she viciously challenges Andrew's status as a
husband: 'Doesn't the marriage service say something about the husband supporting the wife? ... And how do you think you're going to
do that on two hundred a year?'[46] The marriage service also mentions
mutual love and honour, but Millie seems to have forgotten that part of
the ceremony. Already humbled personally, Crocker-Harris's professional status is now further diminished when the headmaster requests
that Fletcher, a popular cricketer this time, speak last in the prize-giving
ceremony:

FROBISHER   It's extremely awkward, and I feel wretched about ask-
            ing it of you – but it's more for your own sake than for
            mine or Fletcher's that I do. After all, a climax is what
            one must work up to on these occasions.
ANDREW   Naturally, headmaster, I wouldn't wish to provide an
            anti-climax.
FROBISHER   You really mustn't take it amiss, my dear fellow. The boys
            in applauding Fletcher for several minutes, and yourself
            say – for – well, not quite so long – won't be making any
            personal demonstration between you. It will be quite
            impersonal – I assure you – quite impersonal.[47]

However, it's very personal. But after years of such humbling, Crocker-
Harris has walled up his heart against such pain and capitulates: he will
allow Fletcher to speak last and avoid an 'anti-climax'.
    After the headmaster has done his dirty work, the Crocker-Harrises
are unexpectedly visited by Mr and Mrs Gilbert. Gilbert is a young master who will be taking over Andrew's form and the young couple will be
moving into the Crocker-Harrises' home. The fact that Gilbert is only
twenty-two emphasizes just how poor Andrew's career at the school has
been. It transpires that like the Crocker-Harrises the Gilberts had first
met in the Lake District. Their presence, with their youth and enthusiasm, sharply contrasts with the jaded Crocker-Harrises. Whilst Millie
shows Mrs Gilbert the rest of the flat, Gilbert asks Andrew about the

lower fifth. For Crocker-Harris, Gilbert represents the possibility, hope and ambition he had had when he first started teaching. He had wanted to communicate his 'own joy in the great literature of the past' but had found that he failed 'nine hundred and ninety-nine times out of a thousand'. Gilbert tactlessly mentions that the headmaster had referred to Crocker-Harris as the 'Himmler of the lower fifth'. Himmler, of course, was head of the SS, the most hated leader of the Nazis other than Hitler. In 1948, just a few years after the war, such a reference would have characterized Crocker-Harris as 'the enemy'. The revelation shocks and hurts him:

ANDREW   I knew, of course, that I was not only not liked, but now positively disliked. I had realized too, that the boys – for many years now – had ceased to laugh at me. . . . Perhaps it was my illness. . . . Not a sickness of the body, but a sickness of the soul. At all events, it didn't take much discernment on my part to realize I had become an utter failure as a schoolmaster. Still, stupidly enough, I hadn't realized that I was also feared. The Himmler of the lower fifth! I suppose that will become my epitaph.[48]

This incident with Gilbert complicates the series of events which form the heart of the play: Taplow's gift, Crocker-Harris's breakdown and Millie's finest, cruellest hour.

Crocker-Harris is taking Taplow for extra Greek lessons. They are studying the *Agamemnon* of Aeschylus and Taplow is hugely enthusiastic about the ancient bloody tale of adultery and murder. Whereas Taplow interprets the spirit of the play, 'We marvel at how bold thou art that thou canst utter such a boastful speech over the bloody corpse of the husband you have slain',[49] Crocker-Harris translates very literally, as if immune to its poetry. He then reveals that in his youth, 'only a year or two older than you are now, Taplow', he had been 'so excited and moved' by the play that he made his own translation in rhyming couplets. But now the manuscript is lost 'like so many other things'. The play has now taken on a cruel meaning for Crocker-Harris. Millie plays Clytemnestra to Hunter's Aegisthus and near the end of the play Frank actually warns Crocker-Harris that Millie is 'out to kill you'. But unlike Clytemnestra's swift, brutal slaying of Agamemnon in his bath, Millie's murder of Andrew is a slow, agonizing torture of the heart.

Crocker-Harris has told Gilbert that one single success can 'atone and more than atone for all the failures in the world'. Taplow now brings a copy of Browning's version of the *Agamemnon*, in which he has written an inscription to Crocker-Harris: 'God from afar looks graciously upon a gentle master'.[50] Taplow is potentially Crocker-Harris's saviour. It is a simple gift of affection in a barren life of isolation and domestic misery. It represents the possibility that Andrew has succeeded, if only once, in communicating his love of literature to another human being and that his life as a teacher, at least, has been worthwhile. Crocker-Harris breaks down in an uncontrollable release of emotion. The release expresses the pain and anguish of the past, the humiliations and failures, as well as the joy of Taplow's gift: 'I think I would rather have had this present than almost anything I can think of'.[51] The little book restores Crocker-Harris to life again. But the resurrection is cruelly short-lived. Millie enters and tells Crocker-Harris that the gift is nothing but a cheap trick:

MILLIE	The artful little beast—
FRANK	*(urgently)* Millie—
ANDREW	Artful? Why artful?
	Millie looks at Frank who is staring meaningly at her.
	Why artful, Millie?
	Millie laughs again, quite lightly, and turns from Frank to Andrew.
MILLIE	My dear, because I came into this room this afternoon to find him giving an imitation of you to Frank here. Obviously he was scared stiff I was going to tell you, and you'd ditch his remove or something. I don't blame him for trying a few bob's worth of appeasement.

It is Millie's most devastating and calculated blow: 'Why should he be allowed his comforting little illusions? I'm not'[52]

The vital role played by the young Taplow is typical of Rattigan's drama. Much of his work revolves around the moral education of a young man at a delicate stage of adolescence. Ronnie Winslow, the Winslow boy, is the focus of a legal drama which will dominate his growth to maturity. The boy is accused of a petty crime and his family suffer much hardship and humiliation in order to see that 'right be done'. In *Cause Célèbre*, the young Tony Davenport, curious about the mystery of sex, visits a prostitute and contracts a venereal disease. At the same time,

George Wood, who is not much older than Tony, is being prosecuted for murder, an accomplice of his lover, Mrs Rattenbury, who is old enough to be his mother. In *Man and Boy*, Basil Anthony allows himself to be mistaken for his father's lover so that his father can gain the trust of a homosexual business partner. In *In Praise of Love*, the evening of the broadcast of Joey Crutwell's first TV play is the focus of the family crisis: Sebastian Crutwell is unable to attend because he has found out that his wife is terminally ill. B. A. Young recalls that when discussing *The Browning Version*, Rattigan believed that Crocker-Harris, Taplow and Millie were the main characters of the piece, which attributes a particular importance to the boy's role over Frank Hunter's. Certainly Taplow's life is changed during the course of the play. He is keen to get a 'remove' to Hunter's science class next term and must pass his Greek exam in order to do so. Hunter's world of science represents the future and is set in opposition to the study of the ancient past which Crocker-Harris teaches. Like Leo in L. P. Hartley's *The Go-Between* (1953), Taplow sees more of the adult world than he can yet understand, but he isn't sullied by the adults' behaviour as Leo is. At the end of the play, as Crocker-Harris informs Frank that he has got his remove, Taplow is the only character who gets exactly what he wants. In the moral scheme of the play, Taplow is rewarded for his act of human kindness.

The tie which binds Crocker-Harris and Taplow is their mutual enthusiasm for Greek drama. Crocker-Harris's absorption in the ancient world is an oblique suggestion of his yearning for what Goldsworthy Lowes Dickinson discreetly termed, in his 1896 essay, 'the Greek view of life'. Kenneth Dover, writing as recently as 1979, advises modern readers of the *Symposium* or *Phaedrus* that they might well find them 'in the pornography section of a bookshop'.[53] Crocker-Harris's particular aptitude for translation gives him access to such works as the *Symposium* which discussed idealized relationships between men. The social operation of paederasty in classical Athens differs from our contemporary understanding of homosexuality. Based on various ancient sources, both historical and literary, most ancient historians agree that same-sex relationships in classical Athens had a social, civic function, marking a stage towards citizenship. Relationships would be formally conducted between the *eromenos* (beloved) and the *erastes* (lover). The *eromenos* was a youth in a formative period of development, between the ages of about fourteen and eighteen (Taplow's age in *The Browning Version* and

Crocker-Harris's when he translated *Agamemnon*). The *eromenos* would have an intellectual and sexual bond with an adult male, the *erastes*. The relationship usually ended when the *eromenos* himself became an *erastes* at the time he first develops a beard. The *erastes* usually continued heterosexual relationships with women and was most often married. Relationships between men of the same age are not unheard of in ancient sources, but seem to have been less common. Same-sex relationships are closely bound with education in classical Athens and the assumption of an active role in the practice of democracy. This relationship of tutelage is one that was adopted and encouraged in the public-school system, both officially in the 'fagging' system, where a younger boy would serve and carry for an older boy, and less publicly in a rather different sort of service in the dormitory. The relationship of the *eromenos* and the *erastes* of ancient Greek culture haunted the trials of Oscar Wilde:

> There is nothing unnatural about it. It is intellectual, and it repeatedly exists between an elder and a younger man, when the elder has intellect, and the younger man has all the joy, hope and glamour of life before him.[54]

Surely Wilde's words must have echoed in Rattigan's mind as he constructed the delicate, moving relationship between Taplow and Crocker-Harris. Cyril Connolly observes in *Enemies of Promise* how integral Neoplatonism was to the culture of public schools, ironically based in their teaching of the classics:

> For there was no doubt that homosexuality formed an ingredient in this ancient wisdom. It was the forbidden tree around which our little Eden dizzily revolved. In a teaching conscious and somewhat decadently conscious of visual beauty, its presence in the classics was taken for granted; it was implicit in Plato's humour and aesthetic. Yet Eton, like all public schools, had no solution for sex. ... The Eton attitude was in line with the wishes of most parents, for the dilemma is inherent in all education, lurking in the playing-fields and vinegarscented cloisters of our seats of learning as, in the preaching of the careful Pater, beckon the practices of Wilde.[55]

Crocker-Harris had led a typical career, leaving public school for

Oxford and returning as a junior master. Despite his misgivings, he had married, as was expected of him. But the marriage is a sham. Crocker-Harris is trapped by his desire to be accepted by the school, by the boys and by society. In a revival of the play at the Greenwich Theatre in 1993, when Crocker-Harris (Clive Merrison) broke down, Millie (Diana Hardcastle) appeared as a vision in his mind in a Lake District setting. Such a directorial liberty is a simplistic visual imposition, avoiding the complexity of Crocker-Harris's dilemma and the subtlety of Rattigan's art in discussing it. Crocker-Harris isn't simply regretting the fact that his marriage to Millie has gone sour. He is regretting his life. The reasons for Crocker-Harris's breakdown become clearer as the play goes on, as we accumulate more evidence about his life. Like many heterosexual marriages in the plays I have discussed from this period, the Crocker-Harrises don't have the luxury of making up for the disappointments in their own relationship by fulfilling themselves with children in the next generation; they are locked together alone. Crocker-Harris doesn't have sex with Millie, so she has been forced to seek sexual solace elsewhere. He hasn't left her, because he accepts that he is partly responsible for his wife's bitterness. According to Geoffrey Wansell, Rattigan referred to Millie Crocker-Harris as 'an unmitigated bitch'. But Rattigan's examination of the Crocker-Harrises' situation is much more even-handed than he gives himself credit for:

ANDREW   Two kinds of love. Hers and mine. Worlds apart, as I know now, though when I married her I didn't think they were incompatible. In those days I hadn't thought that her kind of love – the love she requires and which I was unable to give her – was so important that its absence would drive out the other kind of love – the kind of love that I require and which I thought, in my folly, was by far the greater part of love.[56]

Having understood the ideal love relationship as adumbrated in the *Symposium*, Crocker-Harris realizes that it wasn't fair of him to marry Millie, suspecting as he did that he could never be a proper husband to her. His position at the school, surrounded by young men whose affection he craves, is both a permanent temptation and a cruel penance. Consequently, as protection from temptation and from any affection that the boys, like Taplow, might show him he has adopted a 'mask of pedantry and ruthless discipline'. Corin Redgrave, in his moving memoir of his father (who played Crocker-Harris in the 1951 film version of the play), says that he can never watch Redgrave/Crocker-Harris's breakdown without recalling a night in 1967 when Redgrave 'came out' to his son as bisexual. Like Gilbert Harding and Crocker-Harris, Michael Redgrave was a casualty of his time, his class and the country he lived in. Crocker-Harris has attempted to suppress a sexuality which he can neither understand nor come to terms with. In doing so, he has withered spiritually, spurred on by the daily cruelties of his frustrated and unhappy wife:

MILLIE   You can't hurt Andrew. He's dead.
FRANK   Why do you hate him so much, Millie?
MILLIE   Because he keeps me from you.
FRANK   That isn't true.
MILLIE   Because he's not a man at all.[57]

When Hunter warns Crocker-Harris that his wife is out to kill him, he replies that she has already succeeded, 'long ago'. His 'hysteria' over Taplow's present was simply 'the muscular twitchings of a corpse'. As classicists, Rattigan and Crocker-Harris would have been aware that the root of the word 'hysteria' is the Greek word for 'womb' (*hystera*), hence the Victorian definition of hysteria as a female malady. Crocker-Harris's breakdown is not 'masculine'; it is the crisis of a married homosexual. Taplow tells Frank Hunter that he thinks Crocker-Harris doesn't want people to like him. He actually doesn't want men (like Hunter) or more particularly boys (like Taplow) to like him, as such friendships painfully remind him of his own difference. At the end of the play, once the deceits have been exposed, Hunter rejects Millie in favour of Crocker-Harris. Crocker-Harris doesn't want Hunter to visit him at his crammer, but Hunter insists. Millie can't believe it:

MILLIE   He's coming to Bradford. He's not going to you.
ANDREW   The likeliest contingency is that he's not going to either of us. Shall we have dinner?
MILLIE   He's coming to Bradford.
ANDREW   I expect so. Oh, by the way, I'm not.[58]

Millie feels that she has to compete with Andrew over Frank, rather in the way that the siblings Kath and Ed compete for the attentions of Orton's Mr Sloane. But Crocker-Harris doesn't crow over the fact that Hunter has chosen to visit him; partly because he can't believe that Frank is actively seeking his friendship and partly because he suspects that Frank *might* possibly keep his word and visit him, thereby snubbing Millie.

Michael Redgrave gave one of the finest screen performances of his career in the 1951 film, which also starred Jean Kent as Millie and Nigel Patrick as Frank Hunter. Rattigan himself wrote the screenplay and opened out the action to include the paraphernalia of school life, laboratories, assemblies, cricket matches and prize-givings. Rattigan actually has Taplow discover Crocker-Harris's own translation of *Agamemnon* and stealthily pocket it to read. At the end of the film, Crocker-Harris is allowed to speak last at the speech day and apologizes to the school for his failure to teach them properly. After a hesitant moment, the boys applaud his honesty and Crocker-Harris becomes something of a hero. When the speeches have ended, Taplow approaches Crocker-Harris with the manuscript he has stolen and tells him that he thinks it's rather good and that he ought to finish it. Like Hester and her paintings or the hopeful lighting of the match at the gas fire, Rattigan gives his screen Crock a reason, a small reason, to carry on living.

The manuscript which appeared in Rattigan's screenplay almost found its way into a 1976 revival of the play at the King's Head Theatre in Islington. Rattigan was worried that the play had dated and that it really needed an interval. He had considered rewriting parts of it and wanted to add a first-act curtain with Crocker-Harris asking Millie if she has located his translation of the *Agamemnon*. Millie admits that she has burned it. Such a revised ending is a great homage to Ibsen's *Hedda Gabler* and certainly emphasizes the importance of the translation to Crocker-Harris; as for Hedda the text is a surrogate child. It would also have made Millie an absolutely unmitigated, irredeemable cow. Thanks to the persuasion of the director, Stewart Trotter, Rattigan's proposed changes were never utilized.

Like the small but resounding triumph of the Major in *Separate Tables*, Crocker-Harris's final speech on the phone to the headmaster is a moment of enormous human dignity which sends a shiver down the spine and lights a spark in the heart:

In *The Browning Version* there is not a single sentence that in itself would raise the emotional level of a railway time-table ... and when at the end Mr Portman utters into the telephone these apparently unexciting words, 'I am of the opinion that occasionally an anti-climax can be surprisingly effective,' [the audience's] heart responds as to the sound of a trumpet. It is not, Mr Rattigan reminds us, the intrinsic quality of the words that matter, but the amount and nature of the emotion they can be made to convey.[59]

Separate Tables

No man is an island, entire of itself.
John Donne, *Devotions*

Rattigan had been a friend of John Gielgud ever since the actor directed the OUDS production of *Romeo and Juliet* in 1932 which Rattigan utilized in *First Episode*. Rattigan had then become a regular visitor at Gielgud's home near Henley-on-Thames. At the time, Gielgud lived with John Perry, who was later to become adviser to Binkie Beaumont, the most important West End producer from the 1940s to the 1960s. Gielgud and Perry played hosts at parties for their circle of theatrical friends, which included many gay men. Not yet twenty-one, Rattigan was introduced to a social world where attitudes to sexuality were liberal and relaxed. In the late 1940s, Rattigan had tried to persuade Gielgud to create the role of Crocker-Harris in *The Browning Version*, but after an initial enthusiasm Gielgud went cold on the idea. When he ultimately withdrew from the project, he sent Rattigan a letter in the hope that 'I may create a part for you one day not too far off'.[60] Ironically, Gielgud was to become the inspiration for a part which he was never actually to play, Major Pollock in *Separate Tables*.

In the autumn of 1953 Gielgud was arrested for homosexual importuning in a public lavatory in Chelsea. The police had been observing the actor's activities for some time. When first arrested, he had claimed that he was a clerk, in an attempt to avoid any scandalous publicity. Unfortunately, Gielgud was recognized at the police station. Consequently, the press gallery was much busier than usual at Gielgud's hearing in the magistrates' court the next day. He was fined £10 and advised by the magistrate to consult a doctor. Gielgud became anxious that his arrest might harm the business for his forthcoming play, N. C. Hunter's *A Day by the Sea*, of which he was both star and director. The play was due to open in Liverpool the next week. At the same time the Hollywood film version of *Julius Caesar* was about to be released, with Marlon Brando starring as Brutus and Gielgud as the treacherous Cassius. The *Daily Express* then picked up the story and emblazoned it across their pages, for the case provided great fuel for the paranoiac homophobia of the early 1950s that was fanned by the enthusiastic tabloids. Gielgud's reputation and career seemed to be in the balance. But despite fears that some public demonstration against him might occur in Liverpool, with the support of the producer, Binkie Beaumont, and his co-star, Sybil Thorndike, Gielgud braved the first-night audience and the perform-ance continued as if nothing untoward had occurred. Some years later, Rattigan recalled how moved he was by Gielgud's courage and the Liver-pool audience's quiet tolerance of Gielgud's misdemeanour:

> He had enough courage to go on and the audience had enough grace and sympathy to accept him purely as an actor. Everyone reacted with dignity rather than hysteria, as might have been expected. The accep-tance by these very ordinary people of something about which they had little understanding was very moving.[61]

Gielgud's dilemma and the response of the 'very ordinary' audience in Liverpool inspired in Rattigan a new work, a double-bill of plays examining human isolation and culminating in a plea for tolerance and the revelation of common humanity at the heart of good, conven-tional people. Though ostensibly two self-contained pieces, the two plays are closely related thematically, with the supporting characters appearing in both plays. The performers who play Anne Shankland and John Malcolm in the first play take on the roles of Sibyl Railton-Bell and Major Pollock in the second, implying a close relationship between the apparently diverse dilemmas of the four protagonists.

Table by the Window

> We are all so afraid, we are all so alone, we all so need from the outside the assurance of our own worthiness to exist.
> Ford Madox Ford[62]

The Beauregard Private Hotel is situated near Bournemouth and popu-
lated by transients, sometimes seasonal visitors, but mostly by long-
term residents. The privacy of the hotel hides lives of great loneliness
beneath a superficial veneer of politeness and the daily courtesies which
take the place of genuine social communication and emotional warmth.
Forster's depiction of the disappointingly English hotel in *A Room with a
View* (1908) begins in the dining-room where the dinner-time chatter of
the English residents is formal and polite; as usual they are disparaging
about the food: 'This meat has surely been used for soup.' *Separate Tables*
depicts the same sort of society and similar preoccupations almost half a
century on:

MR FOWLER   What about the cold pie?

DOREEN   I shouldn't have that if I were you. I saw what went into
it. If I were you, I'd have the tongue——[63]

But this is 1954, two world wars after Forster's portrayal of English
gentility abroad. Rattigan examines a society that in many ways hasn't
changed, but with a consciousness that he is portraying the passing of
a dying breed. Most of the permanent guests are elderly, anxious about
making ends meet whilst clinging to the niceties of respectability.
Each of the residents attempts to avoid their sense of loneliness and
isolation by distracting themselves with trivial obsessions. The spinster Miss Meacham seeks solace in horse-racing and spiritualism. Lady
Matheson, the distressed gentlewoman stretching an ever-dwindling
pension, distracts herself with the wireless in *Table by the Window*, but
eighteen months later in *Table Number Seven*, the Beauregard has
acquired a television set which now defines the structure of her day.
Mr Fowler, the retired schoolmaster, keeps making arrangements for
old boys to stay, but is always disappointed as they never arrive: 'I'm
beginning to doubt the very existence of Mr Fowler's famous young
painter friend.'[64] The odious dragon, Mrs Railton-Bell, occupies herself with petty gossip and an obsessive fussing about her spinster
daughter, Sibyl. Miss Cooper, the manager of the hotel, avoids con-
fronting her own solitariness by throwing herself into salving the isolation of her residents: 'I hate any of my guests to feel lonely.
Loneliness is a terrible thing...'[65] The young medical student, Charles
Stratton, buries himself in textbooks. Jean Tanner is his fiancée and

fellow-student in the first play and seems to represent the new genera-tion: 'Most people aren't as sensible as we are. They get married and are miserable when it goes wrong. Thank Heavens that can't happen to us. We're too integrated.'[66] Eighteen months later, however, Jean has mar-ried Charles and has a young, demanding baby who distracts her from the tensions and frustrations of their recent marriage.

Table by the Window sets up the themes which bind the two plays together and prepares us for Major Pollock's scandalous attempts at human contact in the second play, *Table Number Seven*. Rattigan sets up the milieu of awkward, emotionally repressed individuals in the first play so that in the second he can challenge their humanity when it is revealed that one of their number is taking his distractions too far. Just as the characters in *The Deep Blue Sea* make up a haphazard and tempor-ary community but remain isolated in their bedsitting rooms, each of the residents of the Beauregard Private Hotel is trapped in his or her own isolation. Their separate tables in the dining-room are the labels of their loneliness: each individual *is* an island, separated from fellow men by an ingrained cultural reticence and politeness. Nobody shares a table, each eats alone, sometimes discussing the weather or a wireless programme across the unfathomable gulf of the good-quality but well-worn Axminster carpet. The focus of *Table by the Window* is an estranged couple, Anne Shankland and John Malcolm. Like the other residents, these too have sought distraction from their loneliness, he in alcoholic binges and she in prescription drugs. In *Table by the Window*, Rattigan develops his examination of cosmic human isolation which he had initiated in *The Deep Blue Sea*. Anne Shankland looks as if she is heading for the same antidote to loneliness that Hester had tried, the oblivion of gas:

MISS MEACHAM [Anne Shankland]'s not an 'alone' type.

MISS COOPER Is any type an 'alone' type, Miss Meacham?

MISS MEACHAM Oh yes, they're rare, of course, but *you* are for one, I'd say.

MISS COOPER Am I?

MISS MEACHAM Oh, I'm not saying you won't fall in love one day, and get married, or something silly like that. I'm only saying that if you don't you'll be all right. You're self-sufficient.

MISS COOPER	I'm glad you think so, Miss Meacham . . .
MISS MEACHAM	Well – I don't suppose you are glad, really. Probably you haven't had to face up to it yet. I faced up to it very early on – long before I was an old wreck – while I was still young and pretty and had money and position and could choose from quite a few. *(reminiscently)* Quite a few. Well, I didn't choose any of them, and I've never regretted it – not for an instant. People have always scared me a bit you see. They're so complicated. I suppose that's why I prefer the dead ones. Any trouble from them and you switch them off like a television set.
	She rises.
	No, what I've always said is – being alone, that's the real blessed state – if you've the character for it. Not Mrs Whats-her-name from Mayfair, though. I could tell that at a glance. A couple of weeks and she'd have her head in the gas oven.[67]

Anne's despair is akin to Hester's and her relationship just as destructive. Anne and Malcolm, like Hester and Freddie, are death to each other. Miss Cooper tells Malcolm, 'When you're together you slash each other to pieces, and when you're apart you slash yourselves to pieces.'[68] Whilst retaining the core relationship of *The Deep Blue Sea*, Rattigan deliberately opts for the alternative ending, in which the warring couple stay together. In his notes for a new play originally entitled *Table by the Door*, Rattigan consciously wanted to reverse Hester's situation. What would happen if Freddie did stay with her, despite the fact that they each know that the relationship will fail?: 'Reverse of DBS. Better for an evil affinity to torture each other than to be tortured alone.'[69] 'Reverse of DBS' is actually another examination of the 'two types of love' that Millie and Crocker-Harris fail to reconcile in *The Browning Version*, but in *Table by the Window* it is the woman who can't or won't sexually engage in the relationship.

When younger, John Malcolm had been a promising and enthusiastic Labour MP, but his career had soured since he was imprisoned for violently attacking Anne when they were still married. He is now reduced to writing articles for a socialist magazine under a pseudonym and spending his earnings on drink. Since her divorce from Malcolm, Anne Shankland has got remarried to a man who 'doesn't really like women'; coincidentally she now turns up at the Beauregard claiming that she hadn't known that Malcolm was staying there. Anne is a neurotic model just turned forty. She is obsessed with ageing and anxious about her future without the youth and beauty she has previously relied on both professionally and emotionally. Her marriage to Malcolm had been 'a kind of war', between his desire and her frigidity. Anne is 'carved in ice', terrified of sex, like the spinster Sybil Railton-Bell, who cannot even bring herself to say the s-word. In her efforts to avoid sex, Anne had claimed that she didn't want to have any children, for, as Malcolm recriminates, 'a famous model mustn't gamble her figure merely for posterity.' Children, in fact, might well have solved her current anxieties about her future loneliness and fading career, providing her with companionship and purpose. Ironically, Anne had remarried a man as equally cold as she. Rattigan hints that it was a 'marriage of convenience'and that her husband might have been gay. As Anne has experienced both extremes of sexual hunger and impotence in her two husbands, Malcolm cynically asks her what sort of man makes the ideal husband: 'One who loves you too little – or one who loves you too much?' Malcolm's marriage to Anne had been a failure to reconcile their opposite temperaments – his too keen, hers too cold: a torturous partnership made in hell:

> What enjoyment would there have been for you in using your weapons on [a polite, weak] husband? But to turn them on a genuine, live roaring savage from the slums of Hull, to make him grovel at the vague and distant promise of delights that were his anyway by right, or goad him to such a frenzy of drink and rage by a locked door that he'd kick it in and hit you with his fist so hard that you'd knock yourself unconscious against a wall – that must really have been fun.[70]

Though her arrival at the Beauregard seems like a coincidence, Anne has deliberately sought Malcolm out in order to attempt a reconciliation, not out of love but out of fear of being left on her own:

ANNE   What a life. I can just see myself in a few years' time at one of those separate tables—

JOHN   Is there no one on the horizon?

ANNE   No one that I'd want. And time is slipping. God, it goes so fast, doesn't it?[71]

As she had planned, Anne manages to rekindle Malcolm's desire for her again and then quite brazenly and uncharacteristically suggests that he spend the night with her. She invites him up to her 'very isolated room'. For Malcolm, she offers the fulfilment of his greatest fantasy: consensual, enthusiastic sex with the woman he has always loved and desired. But the dream is shattered when Malcolm discovers that he has been set up and that their reunion, which had seemed to be the blessing of benign fate, is merely another of Anne's manipulative deceits. He is appalled that even now she could not have been honest with him, but must have yet another conquest: 'unconditional surrender ... and if you could do it by lying and cheating then so much better. It makes the greater triumph.'[72] Anne claims that her actions were prompted by her wish to cling to a little pride, rather than humiliate herself by begging him to come back to her. In a cruel scene that resonates with those in *Lady Frederick* and *A Streetcar Named Desire*, Malcolm pulls Anne close to him and explores the signs of ageing in her face. For the anxious, narcissistic Anne, as for Blanche, this is torture:

JOHN   Yes, I can see the make-up now, all right. Yes, Anne, I can see little lines there that weren't there before and it won't be very long now before this face will begin to decay and then there'll be nothing left to drive a man to—
        He has slipped his hands on to her throat.
ANNE   *(quietly)* Why don't you?
        He stands looking at her for a moment and then pushes her violently away.[73]

When Anne realizes that her plan has backfired she submits to being throttled by John rather than rely on her own nerve to switch on the gas. The physical love which she had steeled herself to submit to has ironically ended in the physical violence that had characterized their past relationship. The next day both Anne and John decide to leave the Beauregard to prevent any further confrontation. John had been having a relationship with the hotel manageress, Miss Cooper, but both of them realize that she couldn't hope to compete with Anne for his affections. John feels that he and Anne will never be able to reconcile their different views of love and that neither could ever be satisfied – he sexually, she emotionally – in a renewed relationship: 'our two needs for each other are like two chemicals that are harmless by themselves, but when brought together in a test-tube can make an explosive as deadly as dynamite'.[74] Despite this mutual realization that the relationship will inevitably fail, Anne and John decide to risk a life together, if only to distract themselves from their sense of alienation. She will replace his drink and he her drugs: different distractions, but just as addictive and just as destructive. Anne ultimately admits to her own cowardice, acknowledging that she would rather be unhappy with John than unhappy alone:

> There are worse deaths, aren't there? *(She looks around the room at the empty tables.)* Slower and more painful and more frightening. So frightening, John. So frightening. *(She lowers her head as once more the tears come.)* I'm an awful coward you see. I never have been able to face up to anything alone – the blitzes in the war, being ill, having operations, all that. And now I can't even face – just getting old.[75]

They talk across the dining-room from their separate tables and as she weeps, John goes to join her. The waitress brings in his cup of tea and asks whether the pair will share a table from now on? Though they do not have much hope together, John will join Anne at her table to mark the start of their doomed reconciliation. But like Elyot and Amanda, whatever happens, perhaps their inner sense of solitariness, their need of human comfort and their fear will result in endless attempts to reconcile themselves to each other.

Table Number Seven

> *The Children's Hour* is not about lesbianism, it's about the power of lies to destroy people's lives.
>   William Wyler, 1962

> *The Sergeant* is not about homosexuality, it's about loneliness.
>   Rod Steiger, 1968

> *Windows* is not about homosexuality, it's about insanity.
>   Gordon Willis, 1979

Staircase is not about homosexuality, it's about loneliness.
  Rex Harrison, 1971

It was the first film in which a man said 'I love you' to another man. I wrote that scene in. I said, 'There's no point in half-measures. We either make a film about queers, or we don't.'
  Dirk Bogarde on *Victim*[76]

Table Number Seven takes place eighteen months after *Table by the Window*. It is now summer and there are a few seasonally dictated changes to the environment as well as the guest book. Anne Shankland and John Malcolm have left for London to continue their unstable relationship. Jean Tanner has given up medical school to marry Charles Stratton and they now have a young baby. The Beauregard has acquired a television set which makes for a new shared interest for Lady Matheson and Mr Fowler. Sibyl Railton-Bell who had been away visiting in *Table by the Window* has now returned to the clutches of her mother. Major Pollock is back at the Beauregard after a stay away in London. He and Sibyl have evolved a gentle, understanding relationship which enables her to go for walks in company and escape for a while from her overbearing mother. But the Major is a fraud. He has adopted the persona of the typical retired English major, equipped with army slang, public-school humour and fictitious tales of successful campaigns; he is actually only a council-school-educated second lieutenant.

The Major's double life also hides his aberrant sexual behaviour. In the published version of the play, he is arrested and charged for 'insulting behaviour', molesting women in a Bournemouth cinema. The case is reported in a local newspaper and on reading it, Mrs Railton-Bell insists on a residents' meeting. At the meeting, the Major is tried in absentia and each of the guests, some more reluctantly than others, agree that Miss Cooper should ask the Major to leave before dinner. Sibyl becomes hysterical about the Major's deceits and behaviour. Only Charles Stratton, in a 'minority of one', defends the Major's sexual idiosyncrasies:

my dislike of the Major's offence is emotional and not logical. My lack of understanding of it is probably a shortcoming in me. The Major presumably understands my form of lovemaking. I should therefore understand his. But I don't. So I am plainly in a state of prejudice against him, and must be very wary of any moral judgements I may pass in the matter.[77]

Stratton's defence of the Major's misdemeanour and his logical appeal to tolerance and basic 'Christian ethics' is the clearest signal that there is more to the Major's offence than meets the eye. Having discussed the pain of loneliness in all the characters' stories in *Table by the Window*, as well as the uneasy marriage of sexual obsession and frigidity in the story of Anne Shankland and John Malcolm, Rattigan intended his *coup de théâtre* in *Table Number Seven* to focus all the dilemmas of the first play onto a single character, a bogus homosexual Major. After the successful London production of the plays, it was arranged that the original cast would open the play in New York. With no Lord Chamberlain to contend with in America, Rattigan saw the opportunity to slightly rewrite the second play and present *Separate Tables* as he had first envisaged it. He believed that in England he had had to collude with the audience:

> I had in fact appealed over the head of the Lord Chamberlain to the sensibilities and particular awareness of an English audience. I was in fact saying to them, 'Look, Ladies and Gentlemen, the Lord Chamberlain has forced me into an evasion, but you and I will foil him. Everybody in the play is going to behave as if there were no evasion at all and as if the more important and serious theme were still the issue.'[78]

Rattigan was worried that an American audience, unused to censorship and the evasiveness that British dramatists had had, of necessity, to resort to, would not interpret the Major's offence as the symbol he had intended it, but as a 'literal fact'. And after all, *Tea and Sympathy*, a controversial drama of homosexuality and repression in an American boys' school, had been one of the great successes of the 1953 Broadway season. Rattigan consulted many of his friends and colleagues about his proposal to change the Major's sexuality and many of them, such as the Oliviers, Alec Guinness and Margaret Leighton, were very enthusiastic. Even the director of the play was keen to instigate Rattigan's changes. In 1956 Rattigan wrote with great enthusiasm to Bob Whitehead, the American producer who was to produce the plays on Broadway:

The play as I had originally conceived it concerned the effect on a collection of highly conventional people of the discovery that one of their number was a sexual deviant, and that deviation I had naturally imagined as the one most likely to be outside the sphere of their sympathetic understanding; the one which the Major would be most ashamed at their finding out and the one for which the whole of the character was originally conceived: obviously homosexuality.[79]

Rattigan then lists a catalogue of the extreme reactions of the other long-term residents at the Beauregard to the revelation of the Major's sexual offence. He concludes that the extremity of the reactions (SIBYL It made me sick! It made me sick! It made me sick! It made me sick!) are indicative that the Major's offence is a homosexual one. Rattigan stresses the 'otherness' of the Major from the rest of the guests: his behaviour is alien to their polite English values. In the course of the play, they are forced to engage not only with the issue of sex (tricky enough for the English) but with a sexuality that is anathema to them, and criminal. Yet, ultimately, the shared humanity of the other guests inspires in them a tolerance of the Major's difference: 'though a *different* being from the others and in fact an "outsider", he is still a *human* being that makes the last scene moving without being sentimental'.[80]

Contrary to Rattigan's expectations, Whitehead was appalled by his intentions to make the Major homosexual. He argued that by doing so, Rattigan would narrow the play's agenda, so that rather than having a play about 'man's inhumanity to man' it would be reduced to a work ' "about homosexuality", which of course, it isn't'.[81] Of course. Of course Rattigan wasn't capable of writing a play about the toleration of homosexuality which was also 'about man's inhumanity to man'. Of course a play which discussed such a narrow issue could not speak of universal isolation. And of course the box office had nothing to do with it. But Whitehead's was not the only objection Rattigan had to field. Eric Portman, who had so successfully created the role of Crocker-Harris in *The Browning Version*, was homosexual. Portman had created the roles of John Malcolm and Major Pollock opposite Margaret Leighton's portrayal of Anne Shankland and Sibyl Railton-Bell. His own inherent reticence about his homosexuality, which he believed to be a very private matter, made him very uneasy about appearing as an unambiguously homosexual character when the play transferred to Broadway.

Whitehead prevailed and Rattigan's amendment to the text was suppressed. As Geoffrey Wansell observes, if Rattigan had persevered and insisted that the amendment be integrated into the Broadway production, his reputation, which suffered so severely in the late 1950s and 1960s with so many accusations of 'playing safe', might well have been transformed 'overnight'. And in Peter Hall's 1994 revival with Peter Bowles and Patricia Hodge, Rattigan's intended amendments were not utilized, despite playing in a West End littered with explicitly gay plays. If we are still haunted by the ghost of that 'hopeless lowbrow' Aunt Edna, with whom does the fault lie? The audience? The producers? The actors? The critics? Even now, are we reluctant to accept that the apparently safe, reliable Rattigan, the chronicler of sturdy, mid-century Britain, actually promotes and has always promoted a gently subversive, if 'well-made', agenda? Whoever is at fault, it's surely not Rattigan.

An explicitly homosexual Major certainly alters the tone of both of the plays that make up *Separate Tables*. His relationship of fellow-feeling with Sibyl Railton-Bell clearly becomes much more complex. After the Major's exposure he admits to Sibyl that he has 'always been scared to death of women' and that his adoption of a grand military past might make some woman like him but 'I'm made in a certain way, and I can't change it. It has to be in the dark, you see, and strangers . . .'. Rattigan was adamant that the audience should not believe that Sibyl and the Major could ever get together at the end of the play, rather, like Hester and Mr Miller in *The Deep Blue Sea*, they should be united in friendship by fellow-feeling. Initially Sibyl is appalled that the Major thinks they share any characteristics: 'He says we're both scared of life and people and sex. There – I've said the word. He says I hate *saying* it even, and he's right, I do. What's the matter with me? There must be something the matter with me.'[82] The Major's revelations about himself inspire an examination of her own identity: 'I'm a freak, aren't I?' Rattigan isn't necessarily implying that Sibyl is a lesbian, but he certainly presents her as sexually repressed. As he intended the audience to read the Major's offence as a cipher, then perhaps Sibyl is also an allegorical figure: the suffocated homosexual mother's boy whose fear of his sexuality is so great that he cauterizes the very notion of sex from his being. As homosexual figures, Sibyl and the Major represent the options in a culture where sex between men is criminalized: Sibyl withdraws from sex altogether and the Major, who chooses an active sex life, must operate against the law and 'in the dark' with strangers. Such a reading also binds the two plays more tightly together thematically. For Anne and John in *Table by the Window* also represent the repressed/sexually active dichotomy. The fact that the two main characters in each play are played by the same actor also seems to 'homosexualize' *Table by the Window*. At the end of the play John Malcolm believes that their relationship is doomed to failure. If the couple's relationship is intended to be interpreted 'over the head of the Lord Chamberlain', like other elements of the play, perhaps their uneasiness is inspired as much by the fact that it is illegal as by their personal incompatibility.

The two plays end as they began, in the dining-room. The Major walks in to take his place at his isolated table. Then slowly, each of the other residents, apart of course from Mrs Railton-Bell, makes some trivial piece of conversation. One by one they desert Mrs Railton-Bell's punitive attitude until she is frozen out of the dining-room. She demands that Sibyl accompany her into the lounge. There is a moment of silence and then, very quietly, Sibyl refuses: 'No, Mummy. I'm going to stay in the dining room and finish my dinner.'[83] It is a seemingly insignificant moment. But like Crocker-Harris's telephone call, it is a moment of genuine triumph. Through the Major's suffering, Sibyl has discovered herself, the freedom of the individual. She now includes the Major in a visit to look at the moon: 'We must all go and look at it afterwards'. That simple 'we' is a welcoming invitation of compassion and simple humanity.

Peter Hall believes that Rattigan, as well as Coward, was handicapped by his inability to discuss his own dilemmas in his work. But surely, their careful evolution of strategies which enabled them to give voice to their own feelings largely accounts for their success in speaking with a universal voice. Rattigan's amended scene to *Table Number Seven* expresses the fear and guilt of gay men living in this period as well as the cheap attempts by the police to arrest harmless, ordinary men. Mrs Railton-Bell represents the type of opinionated bigot who learns her shallow morality from the tabloid press. And in Lady Matheson, we have the typical ostrich-like English character who would rather not confront issues that she knows to go on: 'do we really want to hear this?' But though 'flustered to the core of her being', Lady Matheson's comments on the Major's offence, whilst expressing her reprehension and disappointment, are also coloured with genuine human sympathy ('Oh dear. Oh dear. Oh dear.'):

MRS RAILTON-BELL	No, no. Ex-officer bound over.
LADY MATHESON	*(brightly)* Oh yes. *(reading)* Ex-officer bound over. One a.m. arrest on Esplanade. . . . *(looking up)* On Esplanade? Oh dear, do we really want to hear this?
MRS RAILTON-BELL	*(grimly)* Yes, we do. Go on.
LADY MATHESON	*(reading resignedly)* On Thursday last, before the Bournemouth magistrates, David Angus Pollock, 55, giving his address – *(she starts violently)* – as the Beauregard Hotel, Morgan Crescent. *(in a feverish whisper)* Major Pollock? Oh!
MRS RAILTON-BELL	Go on.
LADY MATHESON	*(reading)* Morgan Crescent – pleaded guilty to a charge of persistently importuning – *(Her voice sinks to a horrified murmur.)* – male persons – *(She stops, unable to go on. At length.)* Oh no. Oh no. He must have been drinking.
MRS RAILTON-BELL	He's a teetotaller.
LADY MATHESON	Perhaps just that one night.
MRS RAILTON-BELL	No. Read on.
LADY MATHESON	A Mr William Osborne, 38, of 4, Studland Row, giving evidence, said that at about eleven fifteen p.m. on July the eighteenth Pollock had approached him on the Esplanade, and asked him for a cigarette, which he accepted. A few words were exchanged, following which Pollock made a certain suggestion. He (Mr Osborne) walked away and issued a complaint to the first policeman he saw. Under cross-examination by L. P. Crowther, the defendant's counsel, Mr Osborne admitted that he has twice given evidence in Bournemouth in similar cases, but refused to admit that he had acted as 'a stooge' for the police. Counsel then observed that it was indeed a remarkable coincidence. Inspector Franklin, giving evidence, said that following Mr Osborne's complaint, a watch was kept on Pollock for roughly an hour. During this time he was seen to

approach no less than four persons, on each occasion with an unlighted cigarette in his mouth. There was quite a heavy drizzle that night and the Inspector noted that on at least two occasions the cigarette would not light, and Pollock had had to throw it away. None of them, he admitted, had seemed particularly disturbed or shocked by what was said to them by the defendant, but of course this was not unusual in cases of this kind. At one a.m. Pollock was arrested and, after being charged and cautioned, stated, 'You have made a terrible mistake. You have the wrong man. I was only walking home and wanted a light for my cigarette, I am a Colonel in the Scots Guards.' Later he made a statement. A petrol lighter, in perfect working order, was found in his pocket. Mr Crowther, in his plea for the defendant, stated that his client had had a momentary aberration. He was extremely sorry and ashamed of himself and would undertake never to behave in so stupid and improper a manner in the future. He asked that his client's blameless record be taken into account. He had enlisted in the army in 1925 and in 1939 was granted a commission as a second lieutenant in the Royal Army Service Corps. During the war he had held a responsible position in charge of an Army Supply Depot in the Orkney Islands, and had been discharged in 1946 with the rank of full lieutenant. Pollock was not called. The Chairman of the Bench, giving judgement, said: 'You have behaved disgustingly, but because this appears to be your first offence we propose to deal leniently with you.' The defendant was bound over for twelve months.

She lowers the paper, disturbed and flustered to the core of her being.

Oh dear. Oh dear. Oh dear.[84]

Epilogue

Goodbye to all that

England has always been disinclined to accept human nature.
E. M. Foster[1]

I *am* England and England is me. We have a love-hate relationship
with each other. It's everything I stand for.
Noël Coward[2]

I fell wildly in love with *Entertaining Mr Sloane* . . . Vivien [Leigh] saw it
as a funny, rather camp play. I saw style . . . I saw Congreve in it. I saw
Wilde. To me, in some ways, it was better than Wilde because it had
more bite. I was delighted by Orton's feeling for words. Albee and
Coward have a certain kind of verbal felicity that usually isn't meant
to express character. They are still in a naturalistic tradition. Joe had
something richer.
Terence Rattigan[3]

In the last act of *Who's Afraid of Virginia Woolf?*, Edward Albee has the
drunken Martha refer to Tennessee Williams's original title for *A Streetcar Named Desire*, 'The Poker Night'. Shortly afterwards, George turns up
on the doorstep with a bunch of snapdragons and quotes the Mexican
flower-seller who so terrifies Blanche with her refrain, 'Flores para los
muertos'. Obliquely, but very consciously, Albee connects the world of
George and Martha to the world of Blanche. Surely this is more than a
simple homage? Is it a clue for the audience of how to read the play? It's
certainly an indication of a shared agenda possibly (probably?) defined
by the two authors' gay sensibilities. Albee, like Williams, explores the
'blonde-eyed, blue-haired' 'One-hundred per-cent American' culture
which characterized perceptions of normality, morality and success in

the mid twentieth century. It's the sort of wholesomely dull America that Dorothy wants to escape from in *The Wizard of Oz*. But ultimately Dorothy returns home to it. I've always found it rather unsettling that the land of Oz is a technicolor dream, full of adventure and even risk, but the farm back in Kansas is a bleak world of monochrome. Black and white, one thing or the other. This is a world where dreams are dismissed and the possibility of difference is barely whispered.

The vicious and violent world of Albee and Williams seems to be the antithesis of Rattigan and Coward's work in the same period. Here is a more genteel world of drawing-rooms and cocktails, railway stations and public schools, where individuals drink tea and talk about the weather as they attempt to evade embarrassment and disguise their fractured emotions. Wilde, Maugham, Coward and Rattigan dissect this English world, whilst at the same time contributing to the mythology of it which we understand today. These writers have defined our perception of twentieth century Englishness: Coward's dressing-gowns, cigarettes and cocktails are as emblematic as Wilde's tea-time ritual and Rattigan's terse, clipped dialogue. In *The Deep Blue Sea*, when Freddie is leaving Hester for good and her world seems on the point of collapse, she asks him, 'Had any food?' In extreme pain, these English characters cauterize their emotional responses, in contrast to the self-dramatizing arias of Blanche and Martha. Within this cautious, repressive culture, gay writers throughout the twentieth century have found a convenient world of allusion and metaphor to express their own dilemmas as gay men. Like gay men, Laura Jesson and Hester Collyer are defined by this world and feel an integral part of it, yet at the same time they struggle gently to relieve themselves of its conventions.

In *Dirty Dancing* (1987, dir. Emile Ardolino), Baby Houseman (Jennifer Grey) remembers the last summer of her youth, which with hindsight she relates to the ending of a cultural era, for this is 1963, 'the summer before the Beatles'. The 1960s saw a series of social and cultural changes in Britain which initiated a re-vision of ourselves. Attitudes to gender and sexuality were reassessed and the laws which had limped behind social changes were ultimately revised, though still hampered by the prewar prejudices of the legislators. In 1967 the Sexual Offences Act decriminalized private sexual activity between men over twenty-one. This, together with the Abortion Act of 1967 and the wider availability and use of the contraceptive pill, challenged the principle that sex should be primarily motivated by a will to procreate. After continuous pressure from within the theatre the Lord Chamberlain's powers of censorship were finally abolished in 1968.

The new voices in the new theatre of the 1960s claimed the stage for a young, energetic working class whose work was characterized by a defiant sexual frankness. The world of Coward and Rattigan seemed to be an uncomfortable, easily ridiculed memory. But though their world and the one we have inherited today are so different in so many ways, it is the resonances of these plays which seem so surprising now. Their great success is in articulating the anxieties of difference, of the will to fit in, to be ordinary; and of a corresponding desire to be extraordinary, to be different, to be individual. It is this tension that has enabled these works to transcend the trappings of their period, which had been much of their original attraction for my grandmother in the 1940s and 1950s, and to resonate emotionally for me today.

Just when he seemed least in sympathy with the changing times, the establishment icon Terence Rattigan recognized the promise of his own earlier self in the work of a young iconoclast who appeared to be diametrically opposed to Rattigan and his style of theatre. Rattigan was instrumental in propelling this young writer's controversial play ('absolutely filthy') into the West End. The play was *Entertaining Mr Sloane* (1964) and the author, Joe Orton. Rattigan and Orton, soul mates? Twenty years ago, my parents and their contemporaries would have laughed at the very idea. But the echoes and unexpected similarities of works by gay writers throughout the past century are as sharp as their differences. In the same way that *Who's Afraid of Virginia Woolf?* is a reinvention of (and homage to) *Private Lives* thirty years later, doesn't Kevin Elyot's *My Night with Reg* (1994) share some sort of debt to *Blithe Spirit*? Two very different and yet so similar explorations of the grief of two generations, half a century apart, each of which is attempting to reconcile itself to an early acquaintance with death.

Plays about gay men or by gay men aren't news any more, and we probably won't ever have to return to the subterfuge of the writers discussed in this book. But it was a subterfuge which suited their purpose and the times they lived in. Rattigan's attempts to deal directly with homosexual characters like Lawrence of Arabia in *Ross* or Alexander the Great in *Adventure Story* didn't really work, because his reticence about their sexual motivations leaves an inexplicable vacuum at the centre of the two plays.

Rattigan's most successful characters, like Hester Collyer and Alma Rattenbury, are clearly driven by their sexuality. In avoiding the discussion of Lawrence and Alexander's sexuality, Rattigan deprived himself of one of his favourite themes. Similarly, Coward's *A Song at Twilight* is a rather dry plea for tolerance at the expense of character. Plots and political posturing were never Coward's strong points, and some of his most successful works, such as *Private Lives* and *Hay Fever*, are almost plotless examinations of his characters' idiosyncrasies. The direct discussion of homosexuality didn't suit Coward or Rattigan even when they were free to do so at the end of their careers. Ironically, freedom hindered these men who had refined the art of emotional reticence and oblique dialogue. Plays about gay men or by gay men *aren't* news any more and perhaps, as the American playwright and activist George Whitemore records, homosexuality in itself isn't a 'theme to write about . . . *love* is a theme'.[4] Removed from the stalls as they are, and presumably squeezed into the gods somewhere, I think Oscar, Willie, Noël and Terry might well agree with that.

Chronology of Key Events

1854   Oscar Wilde born in Dublin on 16 October.

1874   Somerset Maugham born on 25 January.

1880   Publication of *Vera*.

1882   Death of Maugham's mother.

1883   Wilde writes *The Duchess of Padua*. Production of *Vera* in New York.

1884   Wilde marries Constance Lloyd. Death of Maugham's father.

1885   Cyril Wilde born.

1886   Vyvyan Wilde born.

1887   Wilde becomes editor of *Woman's World*.

1891   Production of *The Duchess of Padua* (retitled *Guido Ferranti*) in New York. Wilde writes *Salomé*. Publication of Wilde's *Intentions* (comprising *The Truth of Masks*, *The Critic as Artist*, *Pen, Pencil and Poison* and *The Decay of Living*) and *The Picture of Dorian Gray*. Wilde meets Lord Alfred Douglas (Bosie).

1892   Wilde writes *A Woman of No Importance*. Production of *Lady Windermere's Fan* at St James's theatre.

1893   Wilde writes *An Ideal Husband*. Production of *A Woman of No Importance* at the Haymarket.

1894   Wilde writes *The Importance of Being Earnest*.

1895   Productions of *An Ideal Husband* at the Haymarket and *The Importance of Being Earnest* at St James's Theatre. Wilde's first trial opens on 26 April. After jury fail to agree on a verdict, a second trial begins on 20 May. On 25 May Wilde is convicted and sentenced to two years' hard labour. Wilde is declared bankrupt.

1896   Production of *Salomé* in Paris.

1897   Wilde writes *De Profundis* and *The Ballad of Reading Gaol*. Released from prison on 19 May.

1898   Wilde moves to Paris. Constance Wilde dies in April. Publication of *The Ballad of Reading Gaol*.

1899	Noël Coward born in Teddington on 16 December. Maugham writes *The Explorer*.
1900	Wilde dies on 30 November.
1903	Maugham writes *Lady Frederick*.
1904	Maugham writes *Mrs Dot*.
1905	Publication of *De Profundis*. Maugham writes *Jack Straw*.
1907	Production of *Lady Frederick* at the Royal Court.
1908	Production of *Mrs Dot* at the Comedy, *Jack Straw* at the Vaudeville and *The Explorer* at the Lyric. Maugham writes *Penelope*.
1909	Production of *Penelope* and *Smith* at the Comedy.
1911	Terence Rattigan born on 10 June.
1913	Maugham writes *The Land of Promise*.
1914	Production of *The Land of Promise* at the Duke of York's.
1915	Maugham writes *Our Betters* and *Of Human Bondage*.
1916	Maugham marries Syrie Wellcome.
1918	Coward writes *The Rat Trap*.
1919	Production of Maugham's *Home and Beauty* at the Playhouse. Maugham writes *The Circle* and *The Moon and Sixpence*.
1921	Production of *The Circle* at the Haymarket.
1923	Coward writes *The Vortex*. Production of *Our Betters* at the Globe.
1924	Production of *The Vortex* at the Everyman. Coward writes *Hay Fever* and *Easy Virtue*.
1925	Production of *Hay Fever* at the Ambassador's. Maugham writes *The Painted Veil*.
1926	Production of *Easy Virtue* at the Duke of York's and *The Rat Trap* at the Everyman. Maugham writes *The Letter* and *The Constant Wife*.
1927	Production of *The Constant Wife* at the Strand and *The Letter* at the Playhouse. Maugham and Syrie divorce.
1929	Production of Coward's *Bitter Sweet* at His Majesty's. Coward writes *Private Lives*.
1930	Production of *Private Lives* at the Phoenix.
1932	Production of Maugham's *For Services Rendered* at the Globe. Film version of Maugham's *Rain*. Coward writes *Cavalcade* (also a film version) and *Design for Living*. Production of Coward's *Words and Music* at the Adelphi.
1933	Production of Maugham's *Sheppey* at the Wyndham's. Maugham publicly retires from the theatre.

1934   Film version of *The Painted Veil*. Rattigan writes *First Episode*.

1936   Coward writes *Tonight at 8.30*. Productions of Rattigan's *French Without Tears* at the Criterion and Coward's *The Astonished Heart* and *Still Life* at the Phoenix. Release of *The Secret Agent* (a film version of Maugham's *Ashenden* stories).

1939   Film version of *French Without Tears*. Coward writes *Present Laughter*. Production of *Design for Living* at the Haymarket.

1940   Film version of *The Letter*. Production of Rattigan's *Follow My Leader* at the Apollo.

1941   Production of *Blithe Spirit* at the Piccadilly.

1942   Coward writes and stars in the film *In Which We Serve*.

1943   Production of *Present Laughter* at the Haymarket.

1944   Coward writes and produces the film *This Happy Breed*.

1945   Film version of *Blithe Spirit*. *Still Life* filmed as *Brief Encounter*.

1946   Production of Rattigan's *The Winslow Boy* at the Lyric. Film version of *The Razor's Edge*.

1947   Coward writes *Long Island Sound* (unproduced).

1948   Production of Rattigan's *The Browning Version* at the Phoenix. Release of *Quartet*, a film version of four Maugham short stories.

1949   Film version of *The Astonished Heart*. Production of Rattigan's *Adventure Story* at St James's theatre.

1950   Production of Rattigan's *Who Is Sylvia?* at the Criterion.

1951   Film version of Rattigan's *The Browning Version*.

1952   Production of Coward's *Quadrille* at the Phoenix and Rattigan's *The Deep Blue Sea* at the Duchess. Release of *Meet Me Tonight* (film version of three of Coward's plays).

1954   Production of Rattigan's *Separate Tables* at St James's theatre.

1955   Maugham writes *Up at the Villa*. Death of Syrie Maugham.

1958   Production of Rattigan's *Variation on a Theme* at the Globe.

1960   Coward writes *Pomp and Circumstance*.

1962   Maugham publishes his memoirs, *Looking Back*.

1963   Production of Rattigan's *Man and Boy* at the Queen's. Rattigan writes the screenplay for *The VIPs*.

1964   Rattigan writes the screenplay for *The Yellow Rolls-Royce*. Coward's *Hay Fever* revived by the National Theatre.

1965   Maugham dies on 16 December. Coward writes *A Song at Twilight*.

1966   Production of *A Song at Twilight* at the Queen's.

1968   Coward stars in *Boom!*, a film version of Tennessee Williams's play *The Milk Train Doesn't Stop Here Any More*.

1969   Coward stars in *The Italian Job*.

1970   Coward receives a knighthood.

1973   Rattigan writes *In Praise of Love*. Coward dies in Jamaica on 26 March.

1977   Rattigan writes *Cause Célèbre*. Rattigan dies on 30 November.

Notes

Introduction

1. 'Cemetry Gates', Morrissey, from *The Queen Is Dead* by The Smiths (1986).
2. Andy Medhurst, 'That special thrill: *Brief Encounter*, homosexuality and authorship', *Screen*, **32** (Summer 1991), 197–208.
3. Frances Partridge, *Everything to Lose: Diaries 1945–1960* (London: Gollancz, 1985), p. 145.
4. *Ibid.*, p. 18.
5. *Design for Living*, Noël Coward, in *Plays: Three* (London: Methuen, 1987), p. 21.
6. Noël Coward, 'Introduction' to *Three Plays*, with the author's reply to his critics (London: Ernest Benn, 1925), p. v. Coward defends the protagonists of his critically reviled plays *The Vortex* ('crazed with dope') and *Fallen Angels* ('suburban sluts') as well as his earlier play *The Rat Trap*. He discusses contemporary 'Sex Plays' and the censor:

   The censorship as an institution is merely a figure-head for all those worthy British qualities most detrimental to the progress of true art, hypocrisy, sex-repression, lack of education, religious mania, respectability, and above all moral cowardice. It may be that, having as a nation achieved so much by physical courage, we have grown up in the belief that that is all that matters, which anyhow supplies a reason for our rather paltry progress in art as compared with other countries. The truth of the matter is that morally we allow ourselves to be governed too much by "fear"; fear of giving ourselves away, fear of what other people may think, fear of exposing real emotions of any sort, and a very definite fear of seeing ourselves as we really are. This being so, it is possible to realise how very necessary a Censor is to the general peace of mind – one more protecting arm of security, one more fortification built up in order to shut out unpleasant truths, but it must be painfully uncomfortable for the old Buffer. (*ibid.*, pp. xi–xii)

7. Quoted in Geoffrey Wansell, *Terence Rattigan* (London: Fourth Estate, 1995), p. 273.
8. I'm aware that words like 'gay' and 'queer' would have very different meanings for Oscar, Willie, Terry and Noël at different points in their lives. Though 'gay' had gained its current usage – certainly in the theatre – in the 1950s, I doubt that any of these writers would have felt very comfortable with the label. They would probably have been much happier with 'queer'. Generally I've been arbitrary in the use of the terms gay and homosexual, with the knowledge that 'homosexual' is as ahistorical in discussing Wilde as 'gay' is in discussing same-sex male culture in the 1920s and 1930s.

9. See Nicholas de Jongh, *Not in Front of the Audience* (London: Routledge, 1992) and the Methuen series of Gay Plays, all edited by the playwright, Michael Wilcox: *Gay Plays: Volume One* (1984); *Gay Plays: Volume Two* (1985); *Gay Plays: Volume Three* (1988); *Gay Plays: Volume Four* (1990). Mordaunt Shairp, *The Green Bay Tree* (1933) appears in *Gay Plays: Volume One*; Philip King, *Serious Charge*, in *Plays of the Year 11* (London: Elek, 1955); and Keith Winter, *The Rats of Norway*, in *Six Plays* (London: Heinemann, 1934).

10. Rodney Ackland's *Absolute Hell* was presented at the National Theatre in 1995, directed by Antony Page. An earlier version of the play, entitled *The Pink Room*, was produced in 1951 at the Lyric Hammersmith, directed by Frith Banbury. Ackland himself, according to Banbury, was a 'genuine bi-sexual' and in both his life and in his writing challenged the moral climate of his times. At the time of writing a new production of his 1936 play *After October* (revised by Ackland before his death) is opening at Chichester Festival Theatre. The reassessment of his work continues.

11. Neil Bartlett and Nicholas Bloomfield, *Night after Night*, Preface (London: Methuen, 1993), p. 3.

12. Experimentation with theatrical forms was much more common in European and American Theatre, e.g. Pirandello, Cocteau, Elmer Rice, Eugene O'Neill. I suppose the closest British drama came to such 'experimental' theatre before the 1960s was in J. B. Priestley's 'Time' and prophetic plays such as *I Have Been Here Before* (1937), *Time and the Conways* (1937), *An Inspector Calls* (1946) and *They Came to a City* (1943).

13. Quoted from Samuel Butler's *The Way of All Flesh* in Colin Dale, *Queer People* (c. 1940), unlicensed and unperformed. Lord Chamberlain's unlicensed play collection, British Library. MS, Act II, p. 20.

14. See Alan Sinfield, 'Closet Dramas: homosexual representation and class in postwar British theater', *Genders*, **9** (1990), pp. 112–31.

15. Boze Haywood, *Conversations with My Elders* (London: Gay Men's Press, 1986), p. 75.

16. Alan Sinfield, *The Wilde Century* (London: Cassell, 1994), p. 12.

17. Nancy Mitford, *The Pursuit of Love* (1945), in *The Nancy Mitford Omnibus* (London: Hamish Hamilton, 1956), pp. 10–11.

18. See Jeffrey Weeks, *Sex, Politics and Society* (London: Longman, 1989). See also Jeffrey Weeks, *Coming Out: Homosexual Politics in Britain from the 19th Century to the Present* (London: Quartet, 1977).

19. The career of Fanny and Stella/Boulton and Park is imaginatively re-told by Neil Bartlett in *Who Was That Man? A Present for Mr Oscar Wilde* (London: Serpent's Tail, 1988). See also William Roughhead, *Bad Companions* (Edinburgh: W. Green & Son, 1931).

20. From Rev. J. M. Wilson, 'Morality in public schools', *Journal of Education*, November 1881. Quoted in Jeffrey Weeks, *Coming Out*, p. 18. The great expansion of public schools from the 1850s to the 1870s had produced, according to Wilson, a 'rich crop of sexual scandals'.

21. Cate Haste, *Rules of Desire: Sex in Britain World War One to the Present* (London: Chatto and Windus, 1992), p. 85.

22. Maxwell Fyfe also famously rejected pleas for leniency in the ('Let him have it!') Craig and Bentley murder case of 1954. Despite the strength of public opinion in his favour, Bentley was executed.

23. Graham Payn and Sheridan Morley (eds), *The Noël Coward Diaries* (London: Weidenfeld & Nicolson, 1982), 10 November 1955, p. 291.

24. 'Somerset Maugham makes a very odd request', *Daily Mail*, 12 November 1957, p. 12.

25. *The Noël Coward Diaries*, 13 February 1966, p. 624.

26. E. M. Forster, Diary, 16 June 1911. Quoted in *The Life to Come and Other Stories*, introduction by Oliver Stallybrass (London: Penguin, 1984), p. 16.

27. *Ibid.*, 31 December 1964.

28. Clement Scott (1892), quoted in John Johnston, *The Lord Chamberlain's Blue Pencil* (London: Hodder & Stoughton, 1990), p. 16.

29. Lord Chamberlain's correspondence concerning *The Children's Hour*.

30. W. Somerset Maugham, *For Services Rendered*, in *Collected Plays*, Vol. III (London: Heinemann, 1955), p. 181.

31. The gay canonization of Blanche is as much to do with Vivien Leigh's adoption of the role on stage and screen. The hinterland that Leigh brought to the role complicated her performance as well as our reception of it. Here was the woman who in the war years had played the feistiest of southern belles, Scarlett O'Hara, and now presented the faded, damaged Blanche. From *Gone with the Wind* to *A Streetcar Named Desire*, Vivien Leigh embodied the decline of the South and of a particular image of America.

32. Tennessee Williams, *A Streetcar Named Desire* (London: Penguin, 1987), pp. 203–4.

33. Winston Leyland (ed.), *Gay Sunshine Interviews*, Vol. I (San Francisco: Gay Sunshine Press, 1984), p. 322. In the same interview with George Whitmore recorded in 1976, Williams also states

     I can get just as much satisfaction, if not more, writing about love between a perfectly normal man and a perfectly normal woman, as . . . well, I never tried really, there's never been any reason for me to write a play about a love affair between two men unless you can interpret that between Skipper and Brick in *Cat [on a Hot Tin Roof]* as a love affair, and it's legitimately interpretable that way.

34. Quoted in Raymond Williams, *Drama from Ibsen to Eliot* (London: Chatto & Windus, 1952), p. 41.

35. *Licenced Victualler's Mirror*, 17 March 1891.

36. Henrik Ibsen, *Notes for a Modern Tragedy*, quoted in *Plays: Two* (London: Methuen, 1988), p. 13.

Chapter one

1. Merlin Holland, Introduction to *Complete Works of Oscar Wilde* (London: Harper-Collins, 1994), p. 1.

2. *Ibid.*

3. *Ibid.*

4. Oscar Wilde, *The Importance of Being Earnest*, in *Complete Works of Oscar Wilde* (hereafter *CW*), p. 409.

5. *Ibid.*, *An Ideal Husband*, p. 537.

6. This famous line appears in dramatizations of Mrs Henry Wood's hugely popular novel of 1861, but it doesn't actually feature in the novel itself.

7.	Wilde, 'De Profundis', in Rupert Hart-Davis (ed.), Selected Letters (Oxford: Oxford University Press, 1979), p. 195.
8.	Quoted in Mary M. Lago and Karl Beckson (eds), Max and Will. Max Beerbohm and William Rothenstein: Their Friendship and Letters (London: John Murray, 1975), p. 18.
9.	Daily Telegraph 22 February 1892, quoted by Richard Ellman, Oscar Wilde (London: Hamish Hamilton, 1987), p. 348. According to Ellman, this review has been attributed to Wilde's brother, Willie.
10.	Wilde, 'The Critic as Artist I', Plays, Prose Writings and Poems (London: Dent, 1975), p. 49.
11.	W. B. Yeats, Autobiographies (London: Macmillan, 1987), p. 130.
12.	Wilde, 'Critic as Artist I', Plays, Prose Writings and Poems, p. 49.
13.	Charles Marowitz, 'A play postcript', Plays and Players (London), October 1971, p. 73.
14.	Sinfield, The Wilde Century, p. 71.
15.	Charles Baudelaire, 'Le Dandy', in La Peinture de la Vie Moderne, quoted in Arthur Ganz, 'The meaning of The Importance of Being Earnest', Modern Drama, 7 (1963), pp. 42–52.
16.	Wilde, 'De Profundis', Selected Letters, p. 195.
17.	Wilde, Selected Letters, to Wemyss Reid, 5 September 1887, note on p. 67.
18.	Arthur Fish, 'Memories of Oscar Wilde', Cassells Weekly, 2 May 1893, quoted in E. H. Mikhail, Oscar Wilde: Interviews and Recollections (London: Macmillan, 1975), p. 152.
19.	Wilde, Duchess of Padua, Act III, CW, p. 641.
20.	Ibid., p. 629.
21.	Wilde, An Ideal Husband, Act IV, CW, p. 579.
22.	Ibid., Act II, p. 552.
23.	Ibid., Act IV, p. 579.
24.	Wilde, Duchess of Padua, Act III, CW, p. 649.
25.	Wilde, A Woman of No Importance, Act III, CW, p. 493.
26.	Wilde, The Importance of Being Earnest, Act I, CW, p. 366.
27.	Wilde, An Ideal Husband, Act II, CW, p. 552.
28.	Wilde, Duchess of Padua, Act III, CW, p. 641.
29.	Tennessee Williams, A Streetcar Named Desire, Scene IV (London: Penguin, 1987), p. 163.
30.	Quoted in Richard Ellman, Oscar Wilde, p. 548.
31.	Declan Kiberd, 'Introduction to the Poems', CW, p. 743.
32.	Wilde, 'De Profundis', Selected Letters, p. 174.
33.	Wilde, Lady Windermere's Fan, Act I, CW, p. 422.
34.	Ibid., p. 429.
35.	Ibid., p. 438.
36.	Ibid., p. 461.
37.	Ibsen, Notes for a Modern Tragedy, quoted in Plays: Two (London: Methuen, 1988), p. 13.
38.	Wilde, Lady Windermere's Fan, Act III, CW, p. 445.
39.	Wilde, An Ideal Husband, Act II, CW, p. 552.
40.	Royal General Theatrical Fund report of speech by Wilde, 26 May 1892, George Alexander in Chair (New York Public Library: Berg Collection).
41.	Wilde, Lady Windermere's Fan, Act I, p. 430 (emphasis in original).
42.	Ibsen, A Doll's House, Act III (London: Methuen, 1988), p. 101.
43.	Wilde, Lady Windermere's Fan, Act II, CW, p. 439.

44. *Ibid.*, pp. 447–8.
45. *Ibid.*, p. 459.
46. *Ibid.*, Act IV, p. 463.
47. *Ibid.*, Act I, p. 431.
48. Edward Carpenter, *Defence of Criminals* (1889). Quoted in Jeffrey Weeks, *Coming Out* (London: Quartet, 1977), p. 68.
49. Vyvyan Holland, *Son of Oscar Wilde* (London: Rupert Hart-Davis, 1954), p. 11.
50. Wilde, *A Woman of No Importance*, Act III, *CW*, p. 503.
51. *Ibid.*, Act IV, p. 509.
52. *Ibid.*, Act IV, p. 508.
53. Wilde, *Lady Windermere's Fan*, Act IV, *CW*, p. 460.
54. Wilde, *A Woman of No Importance*, *CW*, p. 508.
55. W. B. Yeats, *Autobiographies* (London: Macmillan, 1987), p. 289.
56. Wilde, *A Woman of No Importance*, Act III, *CW*, p. 492.
57. *Ibid.*, p. 502.
58. H. Montgomery Hyde, *The Trials of Oscar Wilde* (London: William Hodge, 1948), p. 236.
59. Wilde, *A Woman of No Importance*, Act III, *CW*, p. 494.
60. *Ibid.*, Act II, p. 489.
61. Michael Holroyd, *Lytton Strachey: The Unknown Years* (London: 1967), p. 319.
62. Wilde, *A Woman of No Importance*, Act II, *CW*, p. 483.
63. *Ibid.*
64. *Ibid.*, p. 484.
65. *Ibid.*, Act IV, p. 504.
66. *Ibid.*
67. *Ibid.*, p. 510.
68. *Ibid.*, p. 508.
69. *Ibid.*, p. 510.
70. *Ibid.*, p. 509.
71. Wilde, 'De Profundis', *Selected Letters*, p. 207.
72. Wilde, *Pen, Pencil and Poison*, reprinted in Richard Ellman (ed.), *The Artist as Critic* (London: W. H. Allen, 1970), p. 323.
73. Wilde on the critical response to *An Ideal Husband*, in *The Sketch*, 9 January 1895.
74. Wilde, *An Ideal Husband*, Act III, *CW*, p. 561.
75. *Ibid.*, Act I, pp. 534–5.
76. *Ibid.*, Act II, p. 552.
77. *Ibid.*, Act I, pp. 520–1.
78. *Ibid.*, Act II, p. 537.
79. *Ibid.*, Act II, p. 552.
80. *Ibid.*, Act I, p. 534.
81. *Ibid.*, Act II, p. 536.
82. Wilde, *The Decay of Lying*, in *Complete Works*.
83. The *Echo*, quoted in Holland, *Son of Oscar Wilde*, p. 268.

Chapter Two

Originally published by Heinemann in 1931 in six volumes, the same eighteen of Maugham's collected plays were re-printed in three volumes in 1952. As the original typesetting and pagination was adhered to in the 1952 edition, page references can seem confusing. As this is the edition I have primarily referred to, see below for clarification.

Volume I	*Lady Frederick*	pp. 1–89
	Mrs Dot	pp. 91–184
	Jack Straw	pp. 185–271
	Penelope	pp. 1–110
	Smith	pp. 111–212
	The Land of Promise	pp. 213–310
Volume II	*Our Betters*	pp. 1–118
	The Unattainable	pp. 119–224
	Home and Beauty	pp. 225–324
	The Circle	pp. 1–90
	The Constant Wife	pp. 91–198
	The Bread-winner	pp. 199–296
Volume III	*Caesar's Wife*	pp. 1–98
	East of Suez	pp. 99–219
	The Sacred Flame	pp. 221–319
	The Unknown	pp. 1–89
	For Services Rendered	pp. 91–181
	Sheppey	pp. 183–304

1. W. H. Auden, *Forewords and Afterwords* (New York: Random House, 1973), pp. 307–8.
2. W. Somerset Maugham, *The Painted Veil* (London: Pan, 1978), p. 67 (first published by Heinemann, 1925).
3. E. M. Forster, *Aspects of the Novel* (London: Pelican, 1964), p. 33.
4. Quoted in Frederic Raphael, *Somerset Maugham and His World* (London: Thames & Hudson, 1978), p. 11.
5. Robin Maugham, *Somerset and All the Maughams* (London: Penguin, 1975), p. 240.
6. Harold Acton, *Memoirs of an Aesthete* (London: Methuen, 1948), p. 188.
7. Wilson Menard, *The Two Worlds of Somerset Maugham* (Los Angeles: Sherborne Press, 1965), p. 169.
8. Quoted by Robert Calder, *The Life of Somerset Maugham* (London: Heinemann, 1989), p. 29, from Leslie Rees, 'Remembrance of things past: A meeting with Somerset Maugham', *Meanjin Quarterly* (Summer 1967), p. 493.
9. Oscar Wilde, *A Woman of No Importance*, Act III, *CW*, p. 494.
10. Maugham, *Collected Plays*, Vol. I (London: Heinemann, 1952), Preface, p. xv.
11. Maugham, *Lady Frederick*, in *Collected Plays*, Vol. I, p. 8.
12. *Ibid.*, p. 9.
13. *Ibid.*, p. 89.
14. *Ibid.*, p. 73.
15. *Ibid.*, p. 77.
16. *Ibid.*, p. 42.
17. *Ibid.*, p. 28.
18. *Ibid.*, p. 29.
19. Maugham, *Our Betters*, in *Collected Plays*, Vol. II, p. 12.
20. *Ibid.*, pp. 36–7.
21. Oscar Wilde, *Lady Windermere's Fan*, in *Collected Works*, p. 433.
22. *Ibid.*, pp. 440–1.

23. Maugham, *Our Betters*, p. 28.
24. *Ibid.*, pp. 17–18.
25. *Ibid.*, p. 81.
26. *Ibid.*, p. 78.
27. *Ibid.*, p. 97.
28. *Ibid.*, p. 67.
29. *Ibid.*, p. 85.
30. *Ibid.*, p. 53.
31. *Ibid.*, p. 111.
32. *Ibid.*, p. 113.
33. Maugham, *Home and Beauty*, in *Collected Plays*, Vol. II, p. 235.
34. *Ibid.*, p. 291.
35. Anthony Curtis, *The Pattern of Maugham* (London: Hamish Hamilton/Quality Book Club, 1974), p. 116.
36. Maugham, *The Circle*, in *Collected Plays*, Vol. II, p. 37.
37. *Ibid.*, p. 50.
38. *Ibid.*, p. 51.
39. *Ibid.*, p. 19.
40. *Ibid.*, p. 47.
41. *Ibid.*, p. 55.
42. *Ibid.*, p. 57.
43. *Ibid.*, p. 70.
44. *Ibid.*, pp. 17–18.
45. *Ibid.*, pp. 73–4.
46. *Ibid.*, p. 78.
47. *Ibid.*, p. 87.
48. Wilde, Letter to George Alexander, August 1894, reprinted in Rupert Hart-Davis (ed.), *Selected Letters* (Oxford: Oxford University Press, 1979), pp. 118–20.
49. Maugham, *The Constant Wife*, in *Collected Plays*, Vol. II, p. 100.
50. *Ibid.*, p. 101.
51. *Ibid.*, p. 157.
52. *Ibid.*, p. 180.
53. Somerset Maugham, *Up at the Villa* (London: Heinemann, 1941), pp. 33–4.
54. Maugham, *The Letter*, in *Best Mystery and Suspense Plays of the Modern Theatre*, Stanley Richards (ed.) (New York: Avon Books, 1979), p. 291.
55. *Ibid.*, p. 289.
56. *Ibid.*, p. 293.
57. *Ibid.*, p. 297.
58. *Ibid.*, p. 311.
59. Leslie's story of the rape is told in pp. 281–88.
60. *Ibid.*, p. 342. In the published version of the play, Maugham includes two versions of the ending. The original one has Leslie repeat the same tale she recounted at the beginning, this time telling the truth. In the first production this was replaced by a 'flash-back' showing Leslie arguing with and then killing Hammond. Maugham thought 'it would bore the audience to listen to two long narratives in one play. I have a notion that an author may prudently take a risk to avoid tediousness.'
61. *Ibid.*, p. 342.
62. *Ibid.*, p. 343.

Chapter three

1. Graham Payn (with Barry Day), *My Life with Noël Coward* (London: Applause, 1994), p. 278.
2. Edward Albee, article in *New York Times*, quoted in *Evening Standard* (London), undated cutting.
3. Oscar Wilde in Richard Ellman (ed.), *The Artist as Critic* (London: W. H. Allen, 1970), p. 192.
4. Kenneth Tynan, 'A tribute to Mr Coward (1953)', in *A View of the English Stage 1944–65* (London: Methuen, 1984), p. 137.
5. Noël Coward, *The Rat Trap*, in *Play Parade*, Vol. III (London: Heinemann, 1950), p. 370.
6. Graham Payn, *My Life with Noël Coward*, p. 297.
7. *Blithe Spirit* (1945), director, David Lean; screenplay by Anthony Havelock-Allan, David Lean and Ronald Neame from Coward's play.
8. Noël Coward, *Present Laughter*, in *Plays: Four* (London: Methuen, 1983), p. 182.
9. Payn, *My Life with Noël Coward*, p. 209.
10. Coward, *Present Laughter*, p. 236.
11. *Ibid.*, p. 242.
12. *Ibid.*, p. 174.
13. *Ibid.*, p. 222.
14. *Ibid.*, p. 224.
15. Noël Coward, *A Song at Twilight*, in *Plays: Five* (London: Methuen, 1983), p. 371.
16. Coward, *Present Laughter*, p. 233.
17. *Ibid.*, p. 231.
18. *Ibid.*, p. 234.
19. Philip Hoare, *Noël Coward: A Biography* (London: Sinclair-Stevenson, 1995), p. 509.
20. Payn, *My Life with Noël Coward*, p. 138.
21. *Ibid.*, p. 139.
22. Coward, *A Song at Twilight*, p. 409.
23. *Ibid.*, p. 406.
24. *Ibid.*, p. 418.
25. *Ibid.*, p. 424.
26. Cecil Beaton, *Self-portrait with Friends*, edited by Richard Buckle (London: Weidenfeld & Nicolson, 1979), pp. 11–12.
27. Payn, *My Life with Noël Coward*, p. 238.
28. Alan Sinfield, 'Private lives/public theatre: Noël Coward and the politics of homosexual representation', *Representations*, **36** (Fall 1991), pp. 43–63.
29. Robert Graves and Alan Hodge, *The Long Weekend* (London: Faber, 1940), p. 12.
30. Cecil Beaton, *The Glass of Fashion* (London: Cassell, 1954), p. 153 (reprinted 1989).
31. Noël Coward, *Bitter Sweet*, in *Plays: Two* (London: Methuen, 1979), p. 171.
32. Noël Coward, *The Lyrics of Noël Coward* (New York: Tusk/Overlook, 1983).
33. Payn, *My Life With Noël Coward*, p. 4.
34. Sinfield, 'Private lives/public theatre'.
35. John Osborne, *The Entertainer* (London: Faber & Faber, 1957), p. 60.
36. Noël Coward, *Private Lives*, in *Plays: Two* (London: Methuen, 1985), p. 16.
37. *Ibid.*, pp. 33–4.
38. Coward, *The Rat Trap*, p. 395.

39. *Ibid.*, p. 401.
40. Coward, *Private Lives*, p. 7.
41. *Ibid.*, p. 8.
42. Noël Coward, Introduction, *Plays:Two*, p. xiv.
43. Coward, *Private Lives*, p. 15.
44. *Ibid.*, p. 7.
45. *Ibid.*, p. 73.
46. *Ibid.*, p. 64.
47. Cecil Beaton, *The Glass of Fashion* (London: Cassell, 1954), pp. 153–4.
48. Coward, *Private Lives*, p. 17.
49. *Ibid.*, pp. 42–3.
50. Coward, *The Rat Trap*, p. 433.
51. Coward, *Private Lives*, p. 43.
52. *Ibid.*, p. 46.
53. Noël Coward, *Present Indicative: The Autobiography of Noël Coward* (London: Methuen, 1986), p. 229.
54. Coward, *Private Lives*, p. 50.
55. E. M. Forster, *A Passage to India* (London: Arnold, 1971), p. 157.
56. Coward, *Private Lives*, p. 57.
57. T.S. Eliot, 'Sweeney Agonistes', in *Collected Poems and Plays* (London: Faber & Faber, 1969), p. 122.
58. Coward, *Private Lives*, p. 35.
59. *Ibid.*, p. 16.
60. *Ibid.*
61. *Ibid.*, p. 56.
62. Daphne du Maurier, Stage version of *Rebecca* (London: Samuel French, 1939), p. 37.
63. Hoare, *Noël Coward*, p. 321.
64. Noël Coward, *Blithe Spirit*, in *Plays Four*, p. 24.
65. *Ibid.*, p. 9.
66. *Ibid.*, p. 48.
67. Jean-Paul Sartre, *Huis Clos*, translated by Stuart Gilbert as *In Camera*, in *Three European Plays* (London: Penguin, 1965), p. 191.

Chapter Four

1. Shakespeare, *Antony and Cleopatra*, Act I, Scene v, l. 73.
2. Somerset Maugham, Preface to *Collected Plays, Vol. II* (London: Heinemann, 1952), p. xii.
3. Geoffrey Wansell, *Terence Rattigan: A Biography* (London: Fourth Estate, 1995), p. 30.
4. *Ibid.*
5. Cyril Connolly, *Enemies of Promise* (London: Penguin, 1979), p. 271.
6. Terence Rattigan, *Cause Célèbre* (London: Samuel French, 1978), p. 15.
7. Wansell, *Terence Rattigan*, p. 43.
8. Terence Greenidge, *Degenerate Oxford?* (London: Chapman and Hall, 1930), pp. 90–1. I am indebted to Alan Sinfield's work for bringing this strange but fascinating little volume to my attention.

9. *Ibid.*, pp. 94–5.
10. Michael Darlow and Gillian Hodson, *Terence Rattigan: The Man and His Work* (London: Quartet Books, 1979), p. 56.
11. Wansell, *Terence Rattigan*, p. 72.
12. *Ibid.*, p. 60.
13. Wayne Koestenbaum, *Double Talk: The Erotics of Male Literary Collaboration* (New York: Routledge, 1989), p. 3.
14. Unpublished manuscript of *First Episode* by Terence Rattigan and Philip Heimann. Courtesy of Michael Imison. The version I worked from is mostly an original typescript with Rattigan's deletions and additions. Some missing pages have been re-typed and I refer to these as MS II. All other references are to the original typescript. Act I, p. 21.
15. *Ibid.*, Act II, p. 3.
16. *Ibid.*, Act I, p. 41.
17. *Ibid.*, Act II, scene I, p. 11.
18. *Ibid.*, Act III, scene I, p. 3 (deleted in manuscript).
19. *Ibid.*, Act I, scene I, p. 34 (deleted in manuscript).
20. *Ibid.*, Act II, scene II, p. 33.
21. *Ibid.*, Act III, scene II, p. 12 (MS II).
22. *Ibid.*, Act III, scene II, pp. 13–14 (MS II).
23. *Ibid.*, Act III, scene II, p. 14 (MS II).
24. *Ibid.*, Act III, scene II, p. 9 (MS II).
25. E. M. Forster, 'Notes on the English character', in *Abinger Harvest* (London: Arnold, 1936), pp. 4–5.
26. Terence Rattigan, *French without Tears*, in *Plays: One* (London: Methuen, 1984), pp. 3–4.
27. *Ibid.*, pp. 57–8.
28. *Ibid.*, pp. 19–20.
29. *Ibid.*, p. 56.
30. *Ibid.*, p. 24.
31. Production at the Palace Theatre Watford, Autumn 1995. Director, Tim Luscombe, designer, James Merifield.
32. Rattigan, *French without Tears*, p. 45.
33. *Ibid.*, pp. 13–14.
34. *Ibid.*, p. 33.
35. Terence Rattigan, *Who Is Sylvia?* (London: Hamish Hamilton, 1951), pp. 84–5.
36. Rattigan, *French without Tears*, p. 57.
37. *Ibid.*, p. 61.
38. *Ibid.*, pp. 33–4.
39. *Ibid.*, p. 50.
40. *Ibid.*, p. 54.
41. *Ibid.*, pp. 79–80.
42. Terence Rattigan, *French without Tears*, edited by Dan Rebellato (London: Nick Hern Books, 1995), Introduction, p. xxiii.
43. Quoted in Wansell, *Terence Rattigan*, p. 82.

Chapter five

1. Noël Coward, *Fallen Angels*, in *Plays: One* (London: Methuen, 1985), p. 195.
2. Noël Coward, *Brief Encounter*, in Roger Manvell (ed.), *Three British Screen Plays* (London: Methuen, 1950), p. 47.
3. Graham Payn and Sheridan Morley (eds), *The Noël Coward Diaries* (London: Weidenfeld & Nicolson, 1982), 12 September 1952, p. 199.
4. Coward, *Brief Encounter*, pp. 81–2.
5. Richard Dyer, *Brief Encounter*, BFI Film Classics (London: BFI, 1993), p. 11.
6. Andy Medhurst, 'That special thrill: homosexuality and authorship', *Screen*, 3(2), 1991, p. 204.
7. Attributed to David Lean, *Daily Express*, 3 November 1968.
8. Graham Payn, *My Life with Noël Coward* (London: Applause, 1994), p. 324.
9. Kenneth Branagh (director and screenplay), *In The Bleak Midwinter* (1995).
10. C. A. Lejeune, *The Listener*, 29 November 1945.
11. Quoted in Kate Fleming, *Celia Johnson, a Biography* (London: Weidenfeld & Nicolson, 1991), p. 137.
12. Dyer, *Brief Encounter*.
13. Alison Light, *Forever England; Femininity, Literature and Conservatism between the Wars* (London: Routledge, 1991).
14. Dyer, *Brief Encounter*, p. 67.
15. *Theater Arts* (October 1946), p. 596. Quoted in Antonia Lant, *Blackout; Reinventing Women for Wartime British Cinema* (Princeton: Princeton University Press, 1991), p. 169.
16. Fleming, *Celia Johnson*, p. 139.
17. Coward, *Brief Encounter*, p. 47.
18. Lant, *Blackout*, p. 169.
19. See *Brief Encounter*, p. 68.
20. *Ibid.*, p. 38.
21. *Ibid.*, p. 70.
22. *Ibid.*, pp. 71–2.
23. *Ibid.*, p. 81.
24. Noël Coward, *Still Life*, in *Plays: Three* (London: Methuen, 1983), pp. 358–9.
25. Philip Larkin, 'Home Is So Sad', in *The Whitsun Weddings* (London: Faber, 1984), p. 17.
26. Coward, *Still Life*, p. 345.
27. Coward, *Brief Encounter*, p. 20.
28. Noël Coward, *Pomp and Circumstance* (London: Heinemann, 1960), p. 276. 'Owing to a number of unforeseen circumstances the huge cloudy symbols of Eloise's high romance have dwindled considerably.'
29. Compare:

   > When I have fears that I may cease to be
   > Before my pen has glean'd my teeming brain,
   > Before high-piled books, in charact'ry,
   > Hold like rich garners the full-ripen'd grain;
   > When I behold upon the night's starr'd face,
   > Huge cloudy symbols of a high romance,
   > And think that I may never live to trace
   > Their shadows, with the magic hand of chance;

And when I feel, fair creature of an hour!
That I shall never look upon thee more,
Never have relish in the faery power
Of unreflecting love! – then on the shore
Of the wide world I stand alone, and think
Till love and fame to nothingness do sink.

> Keats, 'Postuma I', *Poetical Works* (London: Macmillan, 1896), p. 253.

When I have fears, as Keats had fears,
Of the moment I'll cease to be
I console myself with vanished years,
Remembered laughter, remembered tears,
And the peace of the changing sea.

When I feel sad, as Keats felt sad,
That my life is so nearly done
It gives me comfort to dwell upon
Remembered friends who are dead and gone
And the jokes we had and the fun.

How happy they are I cannot know,
But happy I am who loved them so.

> Noël Coward, quoted in Graham Payn (with Barry Day), *My Life with Noël Coward* (London: Applause, 1994), p. 209.

30. Coward, *Still Life*, pp. 347–8.
31. Coward, *Brief Encounter*, p. 53.
32. Coward, *Still Life*, p. 359.
33. *Ibid.*, p. 357.
34. Noël Coward, *The Astonished Heart* (screenplay). These scenes were transcribed by the author from the screen, though a shooting copy of the screenplay is available in the BFI Library.
35. Terence Rattigan, *In Praise of Love*, in *Plays: Two* (London: Methuen, 1985), p. 247.
36. Quoted in Sheridan Morley, *A Talent to Amuse* (London: Heinemann, 1970), p. 264.

Chapter six

1. Graham Payn and Sheridan Morley (eds), *The Noël Coward Diaries* (London: Weidenfeld and Nicolson, 1982), entry for 20 January 1957, p. 346.
2. John Goodwin (ed.), *Peter Hall's Diaries – The Story of a Dramatic Battle* (London: Hamish Hamilton, 1983), p. 456 (entry for 4 August 1979).
3. Quoted in Trevor Royle, *The Last Days of the Raj* (London: Michael Joseph, 1989), p. 5.
4. Geoffrey Wansell, *Terence Rattigan: A Biography* (London: Fourth Estate, 1995), p. 270.
5. B. A. Young, *The Rattigan Version* (London: Hamish Hamilton, 1986), p. 127.
6. Michael Darlow and Gillian Hodson, *Terence Rattigan, the Man and His Work* (London: Quartet, 1979), p. 223.
7. Sylvia Plath, *The Bell Jar* (London: Faber & Faber, 1963), p. 87.
8. Wansell, *Terence Rattigan*, p. 219.

9. Young, *The Rattigan Version*, p. 91.
10. Quoted in Wansell, *Terence Rattigan*, p. 218.
11. Epigraph to Tennessee Williams, *A Streetcar Named Desire*. From Hart Crane, *The Broken Tower* (Newcastle: Bloodaxe, 1984), p. 173 (first published 1932).
12. Rattigan, *The Deep Blue Sea*, in *Plays: Two* (London: Methuen, 1985), p. 3.
13. *Ibid.*, p. 64.
14. Wansell, *Terence Rattigan*, p. 217.
15. Rattigan, *The Deep Blue Sea*, p. 29.
16. *Ibid.*, pp. 23–4.
17. *Ibid.*, p. 23.
18. *Ibid.*, p. 46.
19. *Ibid.*, p. 54.
20. *Ibid.*, p. 67.
21. *Ibid.*, p. 38.
22. *Ibid.*, p. 39.
23. *Ibid.*, p. 36.
24. *Ibid.*, p. 45.
25. *Ibid.*, p. 73.
26. *Ibid.*, p. 8.
27. *Ibid.*, p. 59.
28. *Ibid.*, p. 58.
29. *Ibid.*, p. 60.
30. Frith Banbury in conversation with the author, autumn 1996.
31. Rattigan, *The Deep Blue Sea*, p. 18.
32. *Ibid.*, pp. 71–2.
33. Plath, *The Bell Jar*, p. 20.
34. Terence Rattigan, *The Browning Version*, in *Plays: One* (London: Methuen, 1981), p. 218.
35. *Face to Face with John Freeman* (London: BBC Books, 1989), pp. 112–22.
36. Quoted in Wansell, *Terence Rattigan*, pp. 339–40.
37. Rattigan, *The Browning Version*, p. 185.
38. *Ibid.*, p. 185.
39. *Ibid.*, p. 186.
40. *Ibid.*, p. 188.
41. *Ibid.*, p. 190.
42. *Ibid.*, p. 191.
43. *Ibid.*, p. 192.
44. *Ibid.*, p. 193.
45. *Ibid.*, p. 199.
46. *Ibid.*, p. 204.
47. *Ibid.*, p. 202.
48. *Ibid.*, pp. 207–8.
49. *Ibid.*, p. 195.
50. *Ibid.*, p. 212.
51. *Ibid.*, pp. 213–14.
52. *Ibid.*, p. 214.
53. K. J. Dover, *Greek Homosexuality* (London: Duckworth, 1979), p. 13.
54. H. Montgomery Hyde, *The Trials of Oscar Wilde* (London: William Hodge, 1948), p. 236.

55. Cyril Connolly, *Enemies of Promise* (London: Penguin, 1979), p. 234.
56. Rattigan, *The Browning Version*, pp. 220–1.
57. *Ibid.*, p. 216.
58. *Ibid.*, p. 223.
59. Undated review by Harold Hobson, *The Sunday Times*, quoted in Young, p. 79.
60. Wansell, *Terence Rattigan*, p. 168.
61. *Ibid.*, p. 257.
62. Ford Madox Ford, *The Good Soldier* (London: Penguin, 1982), p. 109.
63. Terence Rattigan, *Separate Tables*, in *Plays: Two* (London: Methuen, 1985), p. 81.
64. *Ibid.*, p. 86.
65. *Ibid.*, pp. 91–2.
66. *Ibid.*, p. 95.
67. *Ibid*, pp. 118–19.
68. *Ibid*, p. 121.
69. Wansell, *Terence Rattigan*, p. 250.
70. Rattigan, *Separate Tables*, p. 107.
71. *Ibid.*, p. 111.
72. *Ibid.*, p. 115.
73. *Ibid.*
74. *Ibid.*, p. 126.
75. *Ibid.*, pp. 126–7.
76. All quotations from Vito Russo, *The Celluloid Closet, Homosexuality in the Movies* (New York: Harper and Row, 1981), p. 147.
77. Rattigan, *Separate Tables*, p. 147.
78. Wansell, *Terence Rattigan*, p. 273.
79. Quoted in *ibid.*, p. 252.
80. *Ibid.*, p. 275.
81. Quoted in *ibid.*, p. 276.
82. Rattigan, *Separate Tables*, p. 159.
83. *Ibid.*, p. 168.
84. Quoted in Wansell, *Terence Rattigan*, p. 277.

Epilogue

1. E. M. Forster, *Maurice* (London: Penguin, 1975), p. 185.
2. Noël Coward, quoted in Philip Hoare, *Noël Coward: A Biography* (London: Sinclair-Stevenson, 1995), p. 491.
3. Quoted in John Lahr, *Prick Up Your Ears* (London: Penguin, 1987), p. 203.
4. Tennessee Williams interviewed by George Whitmore, in Winston Leyland (ed.), *Gay Sunshine Interviews*, Vol I (San Francisco: Gay Sunshine Press), p. 318.

Index